ECONOMIC INSTITUTIONS IN A DYNAMIC SOCIETY

Economic Institutions in a Dynamic Society: Search for a New Frontier

Proceedings of a Conference held by the International Economic Association in Tokyo, Japan

Edited by
Takashi Shiraishi

and

Shigeto Tsuru

St. Martin's Press   New York

First published in the United States of America in 1989

Printed in Hong Kong

ISBN 0–312–03088–6

Library of Congress Cataloging-in-Publication Data
Economic institutions in a dynamic society: search for a new frontier:
proceedings of a conference held by the International Economic
Association in Tokyo, Japan/edited by Takashi Shiraishi and
Shigeto Tsuru.
p. cm.
Includes index.
ISBN 0–312–03088–6
1. Institutional economics—Congresses. 2. Corporations–
–Congresses. 3. Corporations, Japanese—Congresses.
4. International business enterprises—Congresses. 5. International
business enterprises—Japan—Congresses. I. Shiraishi, Takashi,
1921– . II Tsuru, Shigeto, 1912– . III. International
Economic Association.
HB99.5.E23   1989
338.7′4′0952—dc19
                                                    88–36750
                                                        CIP

Contents

PART V   REVIEWS AND CONCLUSIONS

The International Economic Association

A non-profit organisation with purely scientific aims, the International Economic Association (IEA) was founded in 1950. It is in fact a federation of national economic associations and presently includes fifty-eight such professional organisations from all parts of the world. Its basic purpose is the development of economics as an intellectual discipline. Its approach recognises a diversity of problems, systems and values in the world and also takes note of methodological diversities.

The IEA has, since its creation, tried to fulfil that purpose by promoting mutual understanding of economists from the West and the East, as well as from the North and the South, through the organisation of scientific meetings and common research programmes, and by means of publications on problems of current importance. During its thirty-seven years of existence, it has organised seventy-nine round-table conferences for specialists on topics ranging from fundamental theories to methods and tools of analysis and major problems of the present-day world. Eight triennal World Congresses have also been held, which have regularly attracted the participation of a great many economists from all over the world. The proceedings of all these meetings are published by Macmillan.

The Association is governed by a Council, composed of representatives of all member associations, and by a fifteen-member Executive Committee which is elected by the Council. The present Executive Committee (1986–89) is composed as follows:

President: Professor Amartya Sen, India
Vice-President: Professor Béla Csikós-Nagy, Hungary
Treasurer: Professor Luis Angel Rojo, Spain
Past President: Professor Kenneth J. Arrow, USA

Other Members: Professor Edmar Lisboa Bacha, Brazil
                    Professor Ragnar Bentzel, Sweden
                    Professor Oleg T. Bogomolov, USSR
                    Professor Silvio Borner, Switzerland
                    Professor P. R. Brahmananda, India
                    Professor Phyllis Deane, United Kingdom

Professor Luo Yuanzheng, China
Professor Edmond Malinvaud, France
Professor Luigi Pasinetti, Italy
Professor Don Patinkin, Israel
Professor Takashi Shiraishi, Japan

Adviser: Professor Tigran S. Khachaturov, USSR

Secretary-General: Professor Jean-Paul Fitoussi, France

General Editor: Mr Michael Kaser, United Kingdom

Advisor to General Editor: Professor Sir Austin Robinson,
United Kingdom

Conference Editor: Dr Patricia M. Hillebrandt, United Kingdom

The Association has also been fortunate in having secured the following outstanding economists to serve as President:

Gottfried Haberler (1950–53), Howard S. Ellis (1953–56), Erik Lindahl (1956–59), E. A. G. Robinson (1959–62), G. Ugo Papi (1962–65), Paul A. Samuelson (1965–68), Erik Lundberg (1968–71), Fritz Machlup (1971–74), Edmond Malinvaud (1974–77), Shigeto Tsuru (1977–80), Victor L. Urquidi (1980–83), Kenneth J. Arrow (1983–86)

The activities of the Association are mainly funded from the subscriptions of members and grants from a number of organisations, including continuing support from UNESCO.

Acknowledgements

The International Economic Association Conference on Economic Institutions in a Dynamic Society: Search for a New Frontier, held in Tokyo from 15 to 17 September 1987, was hosted by the Union of National Economic Associations in Japan and supported by the Japan Science Council. In addition, a number of institutions, companies, associations and individuals lent their support for the conference. The International Economic Association wishes to thank them all for helping to make the conference a success, and in particular the Union of National Economic Associations in Japan for its organisation of the conference and for its hospitality, which together ensured that the discussions within and outside the conference room were both fruitful and congenial.

The International Economic Association expresses its thanks to the International Social Science Council under whose auspices the publications programme is carried out and to UNESCO for its financial support.*

* Grant 1986–1987/DG/7.6.2/SUB.16(SHS)

x

List of Contributors and Participants

Professor Masahiko Aoki, Department of Economics, Stanford University, California, USA and University of Kyoto, Japan

Professor Ragnar Bentzel, Economics Department, Uppsala University, Sweden

Academician Oleg T. Bogomolov, Institute for the Socialist World Economic System of the Academy of Sciences of the USSR

Professor Silvio Borner, Basel Centre for Economics and Business Administration, University of Basel, Switzerland

Dr Jenny Corbett, Nissan Institute of Japanese Studies, University of Oxford, UK

Mr Greg J. Crough, Geography Department, University of Sydney, Australia

Professor Béla Csikós-Nagy, Hungarian Economic Association, Budapest, Hungary

Professor Phyllis Deane, Faculty of Economics and Politics, University of Cambridge, UK

Professor Giovanni Dosi, Science Policy Research Unit, University of Sussex, UK

Professor Jean-Paul Fitoussi, Institut d'Etudes Politiques, Paris, France

Professor Yataro Fujii, Faculty of Business and Commerce, Keio University, Tokyo, Japan

Dr Patricia Hillebrandt, University of Reading, UK

Professor Leonid Hurwicz, Department of Economics, University of Minnesota, Minneapolis, USA

Professor Jun Ikegami, Faculty of Economics, Kyoto University, Japan

Professor Ken'ichi Imai, Faculty of Commerce, Hitotsubashi University, Japan

Professor Masayuki Iwata, Faculty of Law and Economics, Chiba University, Japan

Professor Tadao Kagono, Faculty of Business Management, Kobe University, Japan

Mr Michael Kaser, St Antony's College, Oxford, UK

Professor John A. Kay, London Business School, UK

Academician Tigran Khachaturov, Academy of Sciences of the USSR, Moscow, USSR

Professor Siro Lombardini, Economics Department, Universitá Cattolica del Sacro Cuore, Milan, Italy

Professor Luo Yuanzheng, Beijing College of Economics, China

Professor Edmond Malinvaud, Ecole Pratique des Hautes Etudes, France

Professor Tasuku Noguchi, Keio University, Japan

Professor Mikiro Otsuki, Faculty of Economics, Tohoku University, Japan

Professor Józef Pajestka, Academy of Sciences of Poland

Professor H. Polemarchakis, Center of Planning and Economic Research, Athens, Greece

Professor Nathan Rosenberg, Department of Economics, Stanford

Professor Andrew Schotter, New York University USA

Professor Amartya Sen, Harvard University, USA

Professor Takashi Shiraishi, Keio University, Japan

Professor Norio Tamaki (Convenor of the Conference), Secretary General of the Union of the National Economic Associations of Japan, Keio University, Japan

Professor Moriaki Tsuchiya, Faculty of Economics, University of Tokyo, Japan

Professor Shigeto Tsuru, Faculty of International Affairs, Meiji Gakuin University, Yokohama, Japan

Professor Masu Uekusa, Faculty of Economics, University of Tokyo, Japan

Professor Hirofumi Uzawa, Faculty of Economics, University of Tokyo, Japan

Professor Edward L. Wheelwright, Department of Geography, University of Sydney, Australia

There were a number of other economists from Japan at the conference. In particular, the Union of National Economic Associations in Japan was well represented by members of the Executive Committee and others. A number of Councillors of the Japan Science Council also attended.

RAPPORTEUR

Dr Jenny Corbett, Nissan Institute of Japanese Studies, University of Oxford, UK

Abbreviations and Acronyms

AFL	American Federation of Labour
AT & T	American Telephone and Telegraph
BT	British Telecom
CAN	City Area Network
CATV	Cable television
CCITT	Consultative Committee for Telegraph and Communications (Japan)
CIO	Congress of Industrial Organisations (USA)
CSS	Computer System Software
DRC	Designated research centre
EEC	European Economic Community
EM	Electronic mails
FAX	Facsimiles
FDC	Fully-distributed costs
FTC	Fair Trade Commission (Japan)
GATT	General Agreement on Tariffs and Trade
GNP	Gross national product
IBM	International Business Machines
IC	Integrated circuits
IMF	International Monetary Fund
INTAP	Interoperability Technology Association for Information Processing
ISDN	Integrated services by digital networks
ISO	International Standards Organisation
JAL	Japan Airlines
JISA	Japan Information Service Industry Association
JNR	Japanese National Railways
KDD	Kokusai Densin Denwar Co.
LAN	Local Area Network
MAN	Metropolitan Area Network
MITI	Ministry of International Trade and Industry (Japan)
MPT	Ministry of Posts and Telecommunications (Japan)
NCC	New common carriers
NEDO	National Economic Development Office (UK)
NIEO	New International Economic Order
NSF	National Science Foundation

NTT	Nippon Telegraph and Telephone
OECD	Organisation for Economic Co-operation and Development
OFGAS	Office of Gas Supply (UK)
OFTEL	Office of Telecommunications (UK)
OPEC	Organisation of Petroleum Exporting Countries
OSI	Open systems for interconnection
POS	Point of sales data control
POSI	Promotion Conference for Open Systems Interconnection
R & D	Research and development
RITE	Research Institution of Telecommunications and Economics (Japan)
RPI	Retail price index
SDR	Special Drawing Rights
SNA	Standard Network Architecture
SPRU	Science Policy Research Unit (Sussex, UK)
TIL	Telecommunications Industry Law (Japan)
TNC	Transnational corporation
TSB	Trustee Savings Bank (UK)
TTNet	Tokyo Telecommunications Network
TTX	Teletext
UNEAJ	Union of National Economic Associations in Japan
VAN	Value-added network
VCR	Video-cassette recorder
VRS	Video Response System
VTX	Videotex
WAN	Wide Area Network

Introduction

Shigeto Tsuru
and
Takashi Shiraishi

Under the title 'Institutions in A New Dynamic Society – Search For A New Frontier', the Tokyo Round Table Conference of The International Economic Association was successfully held from 15 to 17 September 1987 at the beautiful Keio Plaza Hotel. The Conference was hosted by the Union of National Economic Associations in Japan (UNEAJ) and supported by the Japan Science Council.

With the careful arrangements invested over many days and weeks by the Organisation Committee of the Conference, as well as the Secretariat of UNEAJ, the three days' programme was full of excitement both academic and practical. We certainly appreciate those efforts given to the Conference by the participants playing many different roles, like an orchestra playing a symphony.

The first movement of our symphony was given by a searching Keynote Address 'Economics of Institution or Institutional Economics' by Shigeto Tsuru, which virtually ruled much of the discussions which followed, as we can see in the Reviews so brilliantly given by Michael Kaser and Tigran Khachaturov at the very end of the Conference. Of the introductory remarks by the President Amartya Sen gave more flavour and insights into the subject. Since Tsuru's address will be read in full text, let us be content with the quotation at the conclusion of his address from the latest book by Galbraith:

> The separation of economics from politics and political motivation is a sterile thing. It is also a cover for the reality of economic power and motivation. And it is a prime source of misjudgement and error in economic policy. No volume on the history of economics can conclude without the hope that the subject will be reunited with politics to form again the larger discipline of political economy.

Session I, chaired by Phyllis Deane, had the title 'Market and Institutions: Roles of Multinationals and Transnationals' and this is reported in Part I. The two invited papers were 'Market and Institutions' by Siro Lombardini, discussed by Andrew Schotter, and 'The Changing Pacific Rim Economy: with special reference to Japanese Transnational Corporations', by Edward L. Wheelwright and Greg J. Crough, discussed by Moriaki Tsuchiya.

These papers represent two polar stances on the subject, one purely theoretical and the other totally empirical. Leaving the contents and evaluations to the text in the following pages, however, we can say that they gave a good start to the Conference, showing the aims and tentative conclusion of the various lines of argument, and also giving satisfaction to both the theorists and those inclined to a more or less practical approach. We also appreciate that the comments given were very constructive and suggestive in paving the way for the following sessions. The contents were neatly summarised in the Closing Remarks on the session by Professor Deane presented in Part V of this volume.

'Economic Theories and Institutions: Economic System, Planning and Transition' was the title for Session II chaired by Hirofumi Uzawa and covered in Part II of this volume. This session has given us another excellent example of the productive division of labour by the pure theorist and those in the field of political economy. Sharing a common background, Leonid Hurwicz's paper, 'Mechanisms and Institutions', discussed by Mikiro Otsuki, concentrated, of course, on the purely theoretical aspects of the subject. On the other hand, Józef Pajestka has elaborated the empirical developments in his paper, 'Institutional Change for the Future: Socialist Experience and New Horizons', discussed by Masayuki Iwata. In the Closing Remarks reported in Part V, the Chairman, a rare person contributing to both economic theory and political economy, contributed an able discussion to bridge the two poles.

Ken'ichi Imai chaired Session III with the title 'Technological Change and Institutions: Development of Information Technologies' (corresponding to Part III) with two invited papers. The first paper written jointly by Nathan Rosenberg and Masahiko Aoki dealt with the now popular subject of Japanese firms, 'The Japanese Firm as an Innovative Institution', discussed by Giovanni Dosi. The second contribution was given by Masu Uekusa under the title, 'The Effect of Innovations in Information Technology on Corporate and

Industrial Organisation in Japan', with a discussion by Tadao Kagono.

As you can imagine, these subjects are the most difficult and up-to-date. Fortunately, however, the Chairman, Imai himself, is ranked as one of the top persons in that field, and gave leadership with many helpful suggestions, along with the contributions of the other participants from the floor. His summary in the Closing Remarks, presented in Part V, gives us the lively flavour of the discussion.

Session IV, chaired by Edmond Malinvaud, with the title, 'Incentives for Changing Society and Institutional Development: Significance of Privatisation', had only one paper. However, John A. Kay's paper, 'The State and the Market: The UK. Experience of Privatisation', discussed by Yataro Fujii and Jun Ikegami contains many insights and suggestions explored through experiences in the United Kingdom, and criticised interests at various levels including business and governments in Japan. Edmond Malinvaud's Closing Remarks in Part V of this volume well covered these important fields of reference.

There is no need to emphasise the greatness and importance of the general reviews given by Tigran Khachaturov and Michael Kaser. They are not the summaries nor evaluations of the discussions given in the Conference. They are genuine contributions given from very high levels of human understanding. We shall be most happy to be able to read them again in this volume, since the time given to them at the Conference was too brief to get a full understanding of their scope and depth. We have no hesitation to give our sincere salute to this, the concluding movement of our symphony given by them.

1 Keynote Address: Economics of Institutions or Institutional Economics

Shigeto Tsuru
MEIJI GAKUIN UNIVERSITY, YOKOHAMA

The major theme of this Tokyo Round Table Conference is: 'Economic Institutions in a Dynamic Society: Search for a New Frontier'. Specific aspects of this broad subject-matter will be dealt with in the four subsequent sessions. Therefore I may be permitted to focus on a somewat general issue related to the major theme of our conference, incidentally recalling the most outstanding contributions to our discipline by Gunnar Myrdal who departed from us just four months ago. I think it is only proper to pay tribute to him on this occasion by highlighting, in particular, his concern with institutional economics. Please note that I make a distinction between 'economics of institutions' and 'institutional economics' as I shall presently explain.

1 NATURE AND ORIGINS OF INSTITUTIONAL ECONOMICS

Many of you, I am certain, must have read with keen interest Professor Matthews's Presidential Address to the Royal Economic Society of Great Britain, delivered in April 1986 and entitled: 'The Economics of Institutions and the Sources of Growth' (Matthews, 1986). This address, probably, serves as an admirably suitable 'Keynote Speech' for this conference – actually far better than my faltering attempt which follows. There is a genuine reason for me to say this. Our conference's title 'Economic Institutions in a Dynamic Society' appears to imply that the term 'institutions' is a subset within a society, just as Professor Matthews defines them in terms of 'system of

1

property rights', '*conventions* or economic behaviour', 'types of *contract* in use' and 'the character of *authority*'. He does say that 'institutions *do* matter'; but when he speaks of 'institutional change', he is not thinking of a type of *evolution of socioeconomic systems* (or of the mode of production, in Marxian terminology). Such was the concern, according to him, of what he calls 'the so-called institutional school in America, including Veblen'. His critique of this school is summarised succinctly in a phrase: 'they had little impact, largely because their doctrines were too ill-defined: rather like "structuralists" in our own times, they agreed that there was something seriously wrong with neoclassical economics, but that was about the only clear message'.

There seems to be a general agreement among mainstream economists with Professor Samuelson's dictum: '40 years ago Institutionalism seemed to wither away as an effective counterforce in economics'.[1] Professor Kenneth Boulding, too, who has certainly broadened the vista of our discipline into sociological and even natural-scientific dimensions, had an occasion to describe institutional economics as an 'interlude nevertheless which ended for all practical purposes in the 1930s (Boulding, 1957, p. 1).

I do not agree with such an interpretation. Even Schumpeter, who has never been classified as an 'institutional economist', had a kind of insight typically stated in a dictum:

> The capitalist process not only destroys its own institutional framework but it also creates the conditions for another ... The outcome of the process is not simply a void that could be filled by whatever might happen to turn up; things and souls are transformed in such a way as to become increasingly amenable to the socialist form of life. With every peg from under the capitalist structure vanishes an impossibility of the socialist plan. (Schumpeter, 1947, p. 162)

Here is expressed a point of view which economists of institutionalist orientation, from Karl Marx to Veblen to Myrdal, have shared, and from which each in his own way developed his theory of societal evolution.

In other words there are contrasting views in dealing with institutions in economics: one which postulates objective laws of socioeconomic development, such as how capitalism evolved and may give place to a different system of socioeconomic organisation, and another which is typically represented by Professor Matthews's approach where the concept of institutions is grasped as 'sets of rights and obligations affecting people in their economic lives' (Matthews, 1986). I suspect that among the participants of this conference there is no unanimity on this matter. But I myself side with the former view and shall pursue the doctrinal development of this approach, giving more emphasis on the present-day institutionalists, and at the end speculating on the future of institutional economics.

Let me begin with a quotation from Allan Gruchy who rather recently characterised 'institutionalists' as those who 'inquired into problems such as the impact of technological change on the structure and functioning of the economic system, the power relations among economic interest groups, the logic of the process of industrialisation, and the determination of national goals and priorities' (Gruchy, 1977, p. 11).

If this is the proper definition of 'institutionalism', I would say that the best hope for the revitalising of economic science today lies in pursuing our inquiry in the direction Gruchy suggests; in particular, in focusing upon 'the impact of technological change on the structure and functioning of the economic system' – which, incidentally, is none other than what Marx had in mind when he spoke of a dialectic relation of productive powers and the mode of production. Myrdal, too, included Marx among institutional economists (Myrdal, 1976, p. 85), but today I prefer to stay clear of Marx, mainly on the ground I suggested a moment ago, namely, that I should like to concentrate on more recent protagonists.

In summarising the chronological tree of institutional economists, Allan Gruchy wrote:

Although there has been some overlapping of generations of institutionalists, one can discern three well-defined periods in the development of institutional economic thought. The first period is associated with Thorstein Veblen's work, which was done in the years 1890–1925. The second period includes institutionalists such as Wesley C. Mitchell, John R. Commons, and John M. Clark who came after Veblen and worked during the years 1925–39. The third or current period is that of the present-day institutionalists such as John K. Galbraith, Clarence E. Ayres, and Gunnar Myrdal whose contributions to institutional economics have been made primarily since 1939. (Gruchy, 1977, p. 11)

One can immediately see in this group of economists mentioned here that there is nothing like sectarian homogeneity which usually characterises a particular school of economists. This is perhaps because institutional economists, all of them, emphasise open models in their methodological approach – models which do not exclude any fresh orientation in different directions.

Besides, Veblen, from whom the institutional school is said to have started, was in many ways an eccentric man. Although he displayed flashes of insight which opened the minds of his colleagues and students to new ways of thinking on sundry matters of our society, it was difficult to obtain a systematic picture of his doctrine from his lectures or conversations. Temperamentally he was not eager to have himself understood. Further more, Veblen, during his academic life, moved from one place to another, and did not have the chance of planting roots, so to speak, in the academic soil conducive to cultivating a coterie of his disciples. As Galbraith wrote: 'he was always regarded as an ideal man for some other institution ... all [the institutions] were glad to see him go; it is now the pride of all that he was there' (Galbraith, 1977, p. 60).

Take the case of Wesley Mitchell, who both subjectively and objectively was one of the closest disciples of Veblen. It has been acknowledged that 'Veblen's influence on him was profound' (Mills, 1952, p. 109), and

> Mitchell appears to have been jarred out of whatever predilections he may have held for classical or neoclassical economic theory by Veblen's essays near the turn of the century. He was impressed by the view that economics must approach its problems from the evolutionary point of view, and by the idea that the key to an adequate understanding of the working of the economic system must rest upon an understanding of the human habits of thought and institutions which direct economic activity. (Homan, 1952, pp. 161–2).

But it must be admitted that although Mitchell

> delighted in Veblen's play of ideas, and upsetting of revealed orthodoxies, he departed from Veblen's type of study, or at least went beyond it, in so far as Veblen was content to stand orthodoxy on its head, and to offer brilliant heretical insights, without undergoing the labor of systematic verification, and especially of measurement. These last were Mitchell's intellectual passion. (Clark, 1952, p. 142).

And probably Homan was right in saying that

> it is not a little curious that the most eminent of our economic workmen in the field of minute analysis of statistical data should be so

heavily indebted to an impressionistic cosmic philosopher like Veblen, who heroically distorts facts and shows no evidence of commerce with figure. (Homan, 1952, p. 192)

But again, Milton Friedman may also be right in saying that

I am inclined to believe that Mitchell's conception of the business cycle as a self-generating process is ultimately traceable to the influence of Thorstein Veblen, less, however, through Veblen's cycle theory than through *his emphasis on the importance of studying the evolution of institutions and his conception of economic history as a process of 'cumulative change' in which one phase of historical development can be understood only in terms of the conditions out of which it grew and itself becomes the source of further change.* (Friedman, 1952, p. 256)

One can see from these accounts how even the most direct successor of Veblen is related only in a limited fashion to the mentor's teachings. Other economists who are classified as institutionalists are also unique in their own ways; but there are still certain common characteristics which, if loosely, bind them together. What then are the elements which ally them in the same camp? We may summarise them under four headings as follows:

(1) The emphasis on the *open-system* character of production and consumption, thus a broader view of the scope of economics.
(2) An interest in the *evolutionary* course along which the industrial economies are moving, with emphasis on the dynamic process of *technological change* and *circular cumulative causation*.
(3) Awareness of a growing need for guidance that can be supplied only through some form of overall social management or *planning*.
(4) Recognition that economics has to become a *normative* science, positively formulating social goals and objectives.

2 MAJOR CONTRIBUTIONS TO MODERN INSTITUTIONALISM

For the purpose of illustrating modern institutionalism in the above sense, we may draw upon the examples of Gunnar Myrdal (1898–1987), J. K. Galbraith (1908–) and K. Wilhelm Kapp (1910–76). All three of them echoed the warning that the conventional mainstream economics was no longer able to meet the requirements for an effective tool of analysis for the problems confronted by modern society. Myrdal spoke, in the American Economic Association meeting of December 1971, that 'economic science is in a serious crisis, in my view very much more revolutionary for our research approaches than was the Keynesian revolution three decades ago' (Myrdal, 1972, p. 461). Galbraith referred to the situation as the 'disconcerting obsolescence in the profession of economics', which was due to the fact that 'economics becomes progressively more inadequate as a basis for social judgment and as a guide to public policy' (Galbraith, 1967, pp. 407–8). Kapp, too, made the similar point by describing the traditional doctrine as a case of 'conceptual freeze' and predicted that 'it is not unlikely that this freeze will be broken in the calculable future under the impact of new facts, new evidence of environmental disruption, new catastrophes and an increasing public opposition to the deterioration of the physical and social environment' (Kapp, 1976, p. 105).

This last point that Kapp made was repeatedly emphasised by Myrdal as he said: 'a crisis and the ensuing alteration of research approaches are not simply an autonomous development of our science but are mostly caused by the external forces of change in the society we are studying and living in as participants' (Myrdal, 1972, p. 456). As a matter of fact Myrdal confesses that when he

> first came to America at the very end of the 1920's ... , the 'wind of the future' was insitutional economics ... At that time I was utterly critical of this new orientation of economics. I was in the 'theoretical' stage of my personal development as an economist. I even had something to do with the initiation of the Econometric Society, which was planned as a defense organization against the institutionalists. (Myrdal, 1972, p. 457)

However, as Myrdal came to be involved in social equality problems in Sweden, especially after a Labour government came into power in 1932, he found that this type of problem could not be handled scientifically except by broadening the approach to all human relations. And when subsequently (in 1938) he accepted responsibility for a study of race relations in America, he found himself writing a book about the entire American civilisation. He wrote:

> From then on more definitely I came to see that in reality there are no economic, sociological, psychological problems, but just problems and they are all mixed and composite. In research the only

permissible demarcation is between relevant and irrelevant conditions. The problems are regularly also political and have moreover to be seen in historical perspective. (Myrdal, 1977, p. 106)

In other words, again in his own words, 'Through the type of problems I came to deal with, I became an institutional economist after having been in my early youth one of the most ardent "theoretical" economists' (Myrdal, 1972, p. 459). And he now argues that 'we are going to see a rapid development of economic science in the institutional direction and that much which is how hailed as most sophisticated theory will in hindsight be seen to have been a temporary aberration into superficiality and irrelevance' (Myrdal, 1972, p. 459). Institutional economics is destined to be winning ground at the expense of conventional economics, according to Myrdal, not only because of the strength of its logic, but also 'because a broader approach will be needed for dealing in an effective way with the practical and political problems that are now towering and threatening to overwhelm us' (Myrdal, 1977, p. 112).

2.1 Gunnar Myrdal

Myrdal had established himself as a first-rate economist already by the beginning of the 1930s through the publication of *The Political Element in the Development of Economic Theory*.[2] There are two other publications by him during the period up until 1932, when he considered himself a 'theorist'. One, *The Problem of Price Formation* (available in Swedish only), was published in 1927; and the other, *Monetary Equilibrium* (for which both German and English translations exist) came out in 1931.

As stated earlier, Myrdal moved gradually toward institutional economics after 1932, and by the time he write 'preface to the English Edition' of *The Political Element* book in 1953, he identified in his own words the basic weakness of his earlier work as follows:

Throughout the book there lurks the idea that when all metaphysical elements are radically cut away, a healthy body of positive economic theory will remain, which is altogether independent of valuations. Political conclusions can then be inferred simply by adding to the objective scientific knowledge of the facts a chosen set of value premises.

This implicit belief in the existence of a body of scientific knowledge acquired independently of all valuations is, as I now see it, naive empiricism ... Valuations are necessarily involved already at the stage when we observe facts and carry on theoretical analysis, and not only at the stage when we draw political inferences from facts and valuations.

I have therefore arrived at the belief in the necessity of working always, from the beginning to the end, with explicit value premises. (Myrdal, 1953, pp. vii–viii)

Now that Myrdal came to be convinced that economics had to be a 'moral science' and could not shirk the issue of valuations, he had to answer the question of what comes first in the bill of particulars demanding the attention of economists. He had no hesitation in replying to this query by highlighting the importance of the *equality* issue. He spoke when he addressed the American Economic Association meeting in 1971:

A basic deficiency in the writings of economists in the establishment school is their playing down of the equality issue ... In regard to the study of development in underdeveloped countries, we are now in a period of transition ... The new approach will be institutional, focusing on the equality issue and taking into due account social and economic stratification, the political forces anchored in these institutions and in peoples' attitudes, and the productivity consequences when levels of living are extremely low. (Myrdal, 1972, p. 460)

Appropriately enough, Myrdal developed this idea more extensively in the subsequent years, culminating in his Nobel Memorial Lecture (17 March 1975) after he received the Nobel Economics Prize in December 1974. This lecture was entitled: 'The Equality Issue in World Development', and it gave an admirable summary of his basic view as an institutional economist, in particular as regards what should be done to cope with the aggravating inequality in the international scene. He cited in this lecture the problems of population explosion and of depletion of non-renewable resources, along with the food crisis, as factors which are involved in circular causation with cumulative effects – a typical institutional approach, one may say. And he formulated his prescription for developing countries as follows:

What they do need is fundamental changes in the conditions under which they are living and working. The important thing is that these changes regularly imply both greater equality and increased productivity at the same time. The two purposes are inextricably joined, much more, in fact, than in developed countries. To these imperatively needed radical changes belong, first, land reform, but also a fundamental redirection of education and health work. (Myrdal, 1977, p. 19)

2.2 J. Kenneth Galbraith

There is little question that J. K. Galbraith qualifies as a modern institutional economist. He himself wrote:

Veblen was perhaps dangerously attractive to someone of my background ... Veblen's scholarship was an eruption against all who, in consequence of wealth, occupation, ethnic origin or elegance of manner, made invidious claim (a Veblen phrase) to superior worldly position. I knew the mood. (Galbraith, 1981, p. 30)

However, Galbraith was of the opinion that

Veblen was not a constructive figure; no alternative economics system and no penetrating reforms are associated with his name. There was danger here. Veblen was a skeptic and an enemy of pretense. Those who drank too deeply could be in doubt about everything and everybody; they could believe that all effort at reform was humbug. I've thought to resist this tendency. (Galbraith, 1981, p. 30)

And indeed, he did. As Arthur Schlesinger, Jr, wrote,

What is salient from the viewpoint of political economy is the skill with which Galbraith brought institutionalism to bear on public policy. A political leader could steep himself in Veblen, Patten, Commons, Mitchell, Ayres and other notable institutionalists without gaining much enlightenment about specific policy decisions; what to do with the budget, interest rates, exchange convertibility, tariff and so on ... Galbraith [on the other hand] was especially qualified to unite institutionalism with dynamic equilibrium analysis; to marry, so to speak, Veblen and Keynes. The result was an institutionalist model that could deliver policy choices. (Schlesinger, 1984, pp. 10–11)

Of the four characteristic strands of institutionalism mentioned earlier, Galbraith shares all of them, though in differing fullness. Before he launched upon his famed trilogy (*The Affluent Society*, 1955; *The New Industrial State*, 1967; *Economics and the Public Purpose*, 1973), he proposed the concept of 'countervailing power' in his analysis of American capitalism (Galbraith, 1952) – the concept which clearly goes beyond the closed-system character of neoclassical economics. The concept of 'dependence effect' is also an example of the open-system character of consumption where the consumers' sovereignty is circumscribed by the aggressive policies of suppliers.

Then on the role which technology plays in the evolutionary process of modern economies, Galbraith made a telling point that 'the enemy of the market is not ideology but the engineer (Galbraith, 1967, p. 32), and he developed the theme of the imperatives of technology under six headings as follows:

First.   An increasing span of time separates the beginning from the completion of any task ... The more thoroughgoing the application of technology – in common or at least frequent language, the more sophisticated the production process – the farther back the application of knowledge will be carried. The longer, accordingly, will the time between the initiation and completion of the task ...

Second.   There is an increase in the capital that is committed to production aside from that occasioned by increased output. The increased time, and therewith the increased investment in goods in process costs money. So does the knowledge which is applied to the various elements of the task ...

Third.   With increasing technology the commitment of time and money tends to be made ever more inflexibly to the performance of a particular task. That task must be precisely defined before it is divided and subdivided into its component parts ...

Fourth.   Technology requires specialized manpower. This will be evident. Organized knowledge can be brought to bear, not surprisingly, only by those who possess it ...

Fifth.   The inevitable counterpart of specialization is organization. This is what brings the work of specialists to a coherent result ... So complex, indeed, will be the job of organizing specialists that there will be specialists on organization ...

Sixth.   From the time and capital that must be committed, the inflexibility of this commitment, the needs of large organization and the problems of market performance under conditions of advanced technology, comes the necessity for planning. (Galbraith, 1967, pp. 13–16)

Thus we are led to the third characteristic strand of institutionalism, i.e., the problem of planning, not only as an inevitable concomitant of technological progress for modern business firms on the forefront, but also for economy as a whole. On this latter point, another of typical Galbraithian terminology came into vogue, i.e., 'social imbalance'. According to his own words:

> The line which divides our area of wealth from our area of poverty is roughly that which devides privately produced and marketed goods and services from publicly rendered services. Our wealth in the first is not only in startling contrast with the meagerness of the latter but our wealth in privately produced goods is, to a marked degree, the cause of crisis in the supply of public services. For we have failed to see the importance, indeed the urgent need, of maintaining a balance between the two. (Galbraith, 1955, p. 195)

Thus the undeniable condition of 'social imbalance', recognition of which comes from Galbraith's institutionalist inference that market mechanism by itself does not 'deliver the goods', so to speak, which the normative criterion of social goals and objectives demands. This, incidentally, is the fourth strand of institutional economics mentioned earlier. Galbraith's concern with this aspect led him to *The Nature of Mass Poverty* (Galbraith, 1979), in which he developed the theme of 'the equilibrium of poverty', evoking an explanatory tool of circular causation – a methodology common with Myrdal.

2.3 K. Wilhelm Kapp

Let us, then, turn to Kapp, whose conversion to institutional economics was quite early. Already in his doctoral dissertation (Kapp, 1936), which he wrote in his formative years as an economist, Kapp pointed out the importance of *how we posed* the question of cost. Traditional economic theory posed the question of 'what is the cost of public policy', but Kapp held that the question we should pose was: 'what is the social cost attendant to the situation where government leaves the economy in the condition of laissez-faire?' He carried on his research with keen awareness of the importance of this problem of social cost and produced his *opus*, *The Social Costs of Private Enterprise* (1950), which was later revised with a new title of *The Social Cost of Business Enterprise* (1963).

Thus it was natural for him to be concerned with the problem of environmental spill-over effects. It is well known that Pigou popularised the concept of externalities, arguing for government action in correcting for undesirable external effects. Kapp deals with the similar problem, but he objects to the use of such terms as 'externalities' on the ground that such a term implies the *closed-system* character of the economy. Pollution of air, for example, may be 'external' to business enterprises, but should be considered, according to Kapp, 'internal' to the economy as a whole and should be dealt with as such. In other words, Kapp shares, with other institutional economists, the methodological precept of the *open-system* character of the economy.[3] He was more conscious of this need than either Myrdal or Galbraith, since his major concern throughout his life was the fight against environmental disruption.

It was again natural for him to emphasise the *normative* character of economic science – the fourth of the institutionalist strands mentioned earlier. As he wrote:

> As soon as the open character of economic systems is fully realised the formulation of social goals and objectives and the problem of collective choices can no longer be avoided. Such objectives and choices with respect to the maintenance of dynamic states of ecological and economic balance essential for the maintenance and improvement of the conditions of social and individual existence (quality of life) must become the point of departure for a normative science of economics. (Kapp, 1976, p. 101)

In more concrete terms,

> what is required is to overcome the essentially dualistic conceptual- isation of economy and environment in order to give our analysis the necessary empirical content. Determination of basic needs and requirements of health and survival, of environmental norms and maximum tolerable levels of contamination; environmental-impact studies of alternative technologies in specific localities rather than linear physical flow models are some of the empirical and quantitative problems that call for exploration and analysis; social science will have to come to terms with the key problem of the open-system character of the economy – the fact, namely, that production derives material inputs from the physical and decisive impulses from the social system which, in turn, may be disrupted and disorganised by the emission of residual wastes up to a point where social reproduction itself may be threatened. (Kapp, 1976, p. 98)

At almost every one of the international conferences where environmental disruption was discussed, Kapp was an indispensable participant, and when the International Social Science Council organised a symposium of social scientists to discuss that problem in Tokyo in 1970, preliminary to the Stockholm Conference on Human Environment of 1972, Kapp played a leading role in drafting the 'Tokyo Resolution' in which it was stated:

> Above all, it is important that we urge the adoption in law of the principle that every person is entitled by right to the environment free of elements which infringe human health and well-being and the nature's endowment, including its beauty, which shall be the heritage of the present to the future generations. (Tsuru, 1970, pp. 319–20)

Kapp kept on concentrating his energy on this environmental issue until he died prematurely by heart attack while attending the Inter-University Center Conference on environmental problems in Dubrovnik, Yugoslavia, in April 1976.

3 THE FUTURE FOR INSTITUTIONAL ECONOMICS

Is there a future for institutional economics? Myrdal was confident that there is, as he wrote:

> I foresee that within the next ten or twenty years the now fashionable highly abstract analysis of conventional economists will lose out. Though its logical basis is weak – it is founded on utterly unrealistic, poorly scrutinised, and rarely even explicitly stated assumptions – its decline will be mainly an outcome of the tremendous changes which, with crushing weight, are falling upon us. (Myrdal, 1976, p. 86)

3.1 Need for Empirical Studies

Firstly, in contrast to the somewhat imperious attitude of abstract economic theorist typified by John Eatwell's remark to the effect that 'if the world is not like the model, so much the worse for the world' (Kuttner, 1985, p. 76), *institutional economists set store, above all, on the empirical studies of the subject matter – our society in its manifold aspects – which undergoes evolutionary changes in the course of historical development*. In a sense, most typical in this respect was Wesley Mitchell, about whom A. B. Wolfe wrote:

> Mitchell's Veblenian institutionalism seems to boil down to substantially this: that men in the mass, at any given time and in any given culture-complex, behave in certain standardized ways,

according to uniform but not simple patterns: these patterns undergo an evolutionary drift which can be roughly measured by the statistical device of time series and which with adequate empirical analysis is amenable to some degree of rational control and direction. (Wolfe, 1952, p. 212)

It is somewhat of surprise to read in the works of Schumpeter – that admirer of 'elegance' in theoretical constructs – the following statement which appears to side with the institutionalist approach:

What distinguishes the 'scientific' economist from all the other people who think, talk, and write about economic topics is a command of techniques that we class under three heads: history, statistics, and 'theory'. The three together make up what we shall call economic analysis.

Of these fundamental fields, economic history – which issues into and includes present-day facts – is by far the most important. I wish to state right now that if, starting my work in economics afresh, I were told that I could study only one of these three but could have my choice, it would be economic history that I should choose. And this on three grounds. First, the subject matter of economics is essentially a unique process in historic time. Nobody can hope to understand the economic phenomena of any, including the present, epoch who has not an adequate command of historical *facts* and an adequate amount of historical *sense* or of what may be described as *historical experience*. Second, the historical report cannot be purely economic but must inevitably reflect also 'institutional' facts that are not purely economic: therefore it affords the best method for understanding how economic and non-economic facts *are* related to one another and how the various social sciences *should* be related to one another. Third, it is, I believe, the fact that most of the fundamental errors currently committed in economic analysis are due to lack of historical experience more often than to any other shortcoming of the economist's equipment. (Schumpeter, 1954, pp. 12–13, italics as in original)

3.2 Normative Viewpoint Essential

Secondly, I consider that *the normative strand of institutional economics will become more and more important – not only in the formulation of economic policies, but also in the scrutiny needed on the analytical concepts we use in economics*. One such concept is 'gross national product'. On this, Myrdal wrote:

> Our politicians, of all political parties, stick to the inept concept of 'growth' which is embodied in the gross national product or one of its derivatives. We economists, by not having scrutinized more intensively that even statistically rather spurious concept, and by ourselves commonly utilizing 'growth' in that sense uncritically as a main value premise in our discussions of practical economic policy, have unfortunately contributed to restricting the mental horizon of politicians and of the common people. (Myrdal, 1977, p. 15)

The economists' habit of equating the growth of GNP with that of economic welfare used to be firmly enough grounded. There was a time, for one thing, when mass unemployment was a direct cause of severe suffering for millions of people, and any measure that expanded effective demand, even including the nonsensical digging and refilling of holes in the ground, was regarded as a positive step towards increasing welfare, so long as it brought about a net increase in employment. In fact, the close association of growth in GNP with that of economic welfare, in the minds of economists, developed in the period immediately following the Great Depression, thanks largely to the Keynesian revolution in economic thinking.

But aside from this short-run policy orientation of the GNP concept, there is a longer-range association, which could be predicated, between the size of GNP and the magnitude of economic welfare provided certain assumptions could be justified. The assumptions are of the type inherent in a mature exchange economy where practically all the economic goods are priced in the market. They are (1) that external effects, either positive or negative, are insignificant, (2) that the condition of consumer sovereignty obtains, and (3) that the failure of the reward system, for whatever reason, is insignificant.

True, even in the heyday of competitive capitalism these three assumptions could not be fully justified. Negative external effects were often serious enough. But in the era when even the minimum requirements for the health of the workers were ignored in the interest of industrial prosperity, environmental disamenities were probably of secondary consideration. The doctrine of consumer sovereignty, too, one may say, was never more than a complacent rationalisation by economists. In an address to manuacturers, John Ruskin perorated, more than one hundred years ago:

You must remember always that your business, as manufacturers, is to *form the market* as much as to supply it [...] But whatever happens to you, this at least, is certain, that the whole of your life will have been spent in corrupting public taste and encouraging public extravagance. Every preference you have won by gaudiness must have been based on the purchaser's vanity; every demand you have created by novelty has fostered in the consumer a habit of discontent; and when you retire into inactive life, you may, as a subject of consolation for your declining years, reflect that precisely according to the extent of your past operations, your life has been successful in retarding the arts, tarnishing the virtues, and confusing the manners of your country. (Ruskin, 1859, pp. 109–10, italics added)

Ruskin was no doubt a sensitive soul; but here is an insight – that 'manufacturers form the market' – which could not easily be refuted, even in the days of laissez-faire market economy. As for the third assumption, it may be enough to make reference to the discriminating bias, due to inheritance, which gave a head-start to a select group of men, enabling them to capture a share in the national pie independently of their own efforts.

In spite of these deviations, however, we may say that, in the heyday of competitive capitalism, the presumption of a close association between magnitude of GNP and that of economic welfare was relatively free of seriously misleading connotations. But today matters are different in advanced capitalist societies. Not only is it true that technological progress has heightened the possibility of negative external effects of gigantic proportions, but at the same time the preference scale of consumers is gradually evolving in such a way that amenity rights of all kinds, not susceptible to quantification, are acquiring greater importance than before.

As for the presumption of consumer sovereignty, Ruskin's indictment would surprise no one today. Galbraith, in particular, made a similar point forcibly, and in a more matter-of-fact way, by contrasting the 'accepted sequence' of the unidirectional flow of instruction from consumer to market to producer with the 'revised sequence' where 'the producing firm reaches forward to control its markets and on beyond to manage the market behaviour and shape the social attitude of those, ostensibly, that it serves (Galbraith, 1967, p. 212). As regards the third assumption concerning the reward system, however, one could point to an improvement of a kind in recent decades on the grounds that inheritance and gift taxes are severer today in most capitalist countries than before and, in addition, opportunity for higher education and training are undeniably greater now than in the last century. The principle of equal pay for equal work is also becoming a reality.

On the whole, however, the close association which once we could assume between magnitude of GNP and that of economic welfare has become tenuous in advanced capitalist countries as the impact of technological progress upon productive relations renders the old assumptions increasingly untenable. Here again is the reason why the institutionalist orientation is destined to gain greater importance.

3.3 Mixed Economy as a New Mode of Production

There is a *third* theme which I should like to take up as supporting my belief that the institutional type of approach is needed to handle the problems which are characteristically arising in the modern development of our socioeconomic system – *the development which we may designate as that of mixed economy as a mode of production*. I use the term 'mode of production' in the Marxian sense, that is to say, a definable stage of productive relations as conditioned by productive powers.

Half a century has gone by since the Rooseveltian New Deal days when governmental interventions in various aspects of the economy were introduced as necessary curative measures to cope with the near breakdown of the system. These interventions had an ameliorative role to play in an economy which had fully matured as a capitalist system. It was then that the term 'mixed economy' came into vogue. And it seems that the mixed economy pattern of society is here to stay. Paul Samuelson goes as far as to say that 'with some exaggeration, John Kenneth Galbraith and Jan Tinbergen can point to a convergence, all over the globe, to a single modern industrial state – not capitalism, not socialism, but *a mixed economy*' (Samuelson, 1980, pp. 817–18).

I also feel that we may now justifiably refer to the mixed economy as a *mode of production* sufficiently distinguishable from a classical type of capitalism, the reason being that I can at least point to the following significant departures of the present-day mixed economy from our erstwhile image of a capitalist society:

1. We no longer have untrammelled play of market mechanism. The extent to which governmental planning and controls are exercised

has become fairly broad with all kinds of legislative acts enabling administrative agencies to guide the economy as in the manner of a rudder for a sail-boat. Lester Thurow has even suggested that 'we do need the national equivalent of corporate investment committee to re-direct investment flows from our "sunset" industries to our "sunrise" industries' (Thurow, 1980, p. 95).

2. Possibly more important than the first point is the changing role of profits in the capitalist system. In the heyday of capitalism profits constituted a source of, as well as an index of contribution to, economic growth under that system. They do constitute, even now, an important source of investment funds which are *sine qua non* for economic growth. What is in doubt now is whether they can still be regarded unequivocally as 'an index of contribution to economic growth'. It is generally agreed that under imperfect competition it pays people to limit the supply to their factors somewhat and that a positive profit can be earned as the return to a contrived or artificial scarcity.

   There is a more important point than this in the age of what Galbraith calls 'the industrial state'. In the classical model of capitalism most economists would agree, profits were *temporary* excess return to innovators or entrepreneurs, thus an index of contribution to economic growth. They were temporary because they were in due course of time competed out by rivals and imitators. But of course, as one source of innovational profits was disappearing, another was being born; and economic progress continued with profits accruing to successive, successful innovators as a reward. In the latest stage of capitalism, however, giant corporations with oligopolistic power are capable or perpetuating excess returns to themselves through oligopolistic price maintenance and various other devices such as privatising particular innovations as well-guarded know-how. In other words, in such cases profits have become an index of the degree of success in *not* making others share the progress in productivity which, in the nature of things should redound to the benefit of all. I may be exaggerating this trend slightly; but I do not think we can deny that there has been an increasing tendency in this direction in the post-Second World War period.

3. Another major category among factor incomes – that is, the wage rate – has also been undergoing qualitative transformation. Let me quote a passage from a document published in 1958 by the AFL/CIO:

Automation in its largest sense means, in effect, the *end* of measurement of work – With automation, you can't measure output of a single man; you now have to measure simply equipment utilization. If that is generalized as a kind of concept – there is no longer, for example, any reason at all to pay a man by the piece or pay him by the hour. (AFL/CIO, 1958, p. 8)

4. Closely related to the above is an unmistakable trend among advanced capitalist countries towards a welfare-state type of society where the precept of 'To each according to his (or her) needs!' is being put into practice. Income redistribution schemes are quite widespread now.

Furthermore, it is being increasingly recognized that the-quality-of-life question encompasses spheres of activities which cannot easily be translated into market calculations, such as, for example, the conservation of nature, the maintenance of clean air and water, the abatement of noise, etc. To the extent we attach positive values to these matters, to that extent we have to make these somehow commensurate with market-determined values and to decide on what to do in a particular situation. The decision required is somewhat similar to a decision as regards whether we should expand our kitchen at the sacrifice of our garden within the limited area of our premises.

5. One other point cannot be missed at this juncture in the area of our international economic relations, that is, an increasingly important role being played by multinational corporations.

One piece of statistics may suffice to impress upon us how important they have become. According to *The World Directory of Multinational Enterprise*, edited by Stopford *et al.* (1980), aggregate sales values of multinational corporations of US origin, numbering 216, amounted to 979 billion (US) dollars in 1978, of which the values produced by their subsidiary companies abroad, amounting to 320 billion dollars, were actually more than twice (22.7 per cent) the total value of US exports in that year. We are coming to an age in which such expressions as exports and imports are becoming less and less significant and the entire world has become closely integrated, as if even to nullify what was once regarded as inalienable sovereignty of the state.

Now I have enumerated five points which could be considered as major departures from the classical model of the capitalist mode of production. I believe that they are sufficiently of qualitative significance that we may identify them as characterising a new mode of production for which some such term as 'sociocapitalism' might be applied.

4   THE ROLE OF TECHNOLOGY AND ITS IMPLICATIONS

One overriding factor throughout the consideration I have given is the role of technology. Galbraith wrote, as I quoted earlier, that

> the enemy of the market is not ideology but the engineer ... It is advanced technology and the specialization of men and process that this requires and the resulting commitment of time and capital. These make the market work badly when the need is for greatly enhanced reliability – when planning is essential. (Galbraith, 1967, pp. 32–3)

It is again the dictate of modern technology which almost forces giant corporations to extend the duration of their monopoly and thus to try to perpetuate their excess returns. There has even been a proposal called 'investment patent' by Mr William Kingston of Trinity College, Dublin, according to which a firm investing in a new product will be given a type of patent that would remain in force and be given public protection until the aggregate profits reached a prescribed multiple of the investment.

The impact of the latest technological progress on wage-labour is patent enough, as has been explained earlier. But there is another point that can be mentioned in this connection, i.e., a broad institutional implication of the robotic revolution and the age of automation. For one thing, robots do have the potential of replacing blue-collar workers who belong to unions with white-collar workers (e.g. programmers of robots) who may not typically belong to unions. In other words, technology may turn out to be an enemy of blue-collar unions.

Multinational corporations, too, are coeval with the latest technological progress.

There are even some people who are beginning to suspect that democracy and technology may not be compatible. Richard Sclove has written in a recent issue of *The Bulletin of the Atomic Scientists*:

> A central dilemma of our time arises from the need to reconcile democratic processes and values with the complexity introduced into human societies by modern technology. How can we keep technocratic elites from subverting the traditional political functions

of ordinary citizens and their representatives? One answer is so simple –or so threatening – that it is hardly mentioned: Throw the experts out. That, in a polite and restricted sense, is what I propose. (Schlove, 1982, p. 44)

This suggestion, I might say, is in the spirit of the erstwhile Luddite movement; and it will not do. What is required of us is to accommodate the modern technological progress into our evolving institutional setting. This is a kind of task which human societies, willy-nilly, always face in the historic past. It is a challenge which the present-day mixed economies face, and I believe that the institutional economics, with the four characteristic strands I mentioned earlier, will have to come to the stage more and more to answer that challenge we face.

Notes

1. See Samuelson (1980, p. 790). In the 12th edition of this textbook, co-authored with William Nordhaus (1985), the reference to institutionalism itself was omitted.
2. The original Swedish edition came out in 1930, with the German edition in 1932, and the English translation in 1953. A new Swedish edition appeared in 1972 with a lengthy special preface by the author.
3. Compare in particular Kapp (1961).

References

AFL/CIO (1958) *Automation and Technological Change* (Washington, DC: AFL/CIO).

Boulding, K. E. (1957) 'A New Look at Institutionalism', *American Economic Review*, vol. 47, May, p. 1.

Clark, J. M. (1952) 'Memorial Address', in Burns, A. F. (ed.), *Wesley Clair Mitchell – The Economic Scientist* (New York: National Bureau of Economic Research).

Friedman, M. (1952) 'The Economic Theorist', in Burns, A. F. (ed.), *Wesley Clair Mitchell – The Economic Scientist* (New York: National Bureau of Economic Research).

Galbraith, J. K. (1952) *American Capitalism: The Concept of Countervailing Power* (Boston, Mass.: Houghton Mifflin).

Galbraith, J. K. (1955) *The Affluent Society* (Boston, Mass.: Houghton Mifflin).

Galbraith, J. K. (1967) *The New Industrial State* (Boston, Mass.: Houghton Mifflin).

Galbraith, J. K. (1973) *Economics and the Public Purpose* (Boston, Mass.: Houghton Mifflin).

Galbraith, J. K. (1977) *The Age of Uncertainty* (London: British Broadcasting Corporation).

Galbraith, J. K. (1979) *The Nature of Mass Poverty* (Cambridge, Mass.: Harvard University Press).

Galbraith, J. K. (1981) *Life in Our Times* (Boston, Mass.: Houghton Mifflin).

Gruchy, A. G. (1977) 'Institutional Economics: Its Development and Prospects' in Steppacher, R. Zogg-Walz, B. and Hatzfeldt, H. *Economics in Institutional Perspective: Memorial Essays in Honor of K. William Kapp* (Lexington, Mass.: D. C. Heath).

Homan, P. T. (1952) 'Place in Contemporary Thought', in Burns, A. F. (ed.), *Wesley Clair Mitchell – The Economic Scientist* (New York: National Bureau of Economic Research).

Kapp, K. W. (1936) *Planwirtschaft und Aussenhandel* (Doctoral Dissertation) (Geneva: Geory et Cie SA).

Kapp, K. W. (1950) *The Social Costs of Private Enterprise* (Cambridge, Mass.: Harvard University Press) revised in 1963 with the title *The Social Cost of Business Enterprise*.

Kapp, K. W. (1961) *Towards a Science of Man in Society* (The Hague: Nizlioff).

Kapp, K. W. (1976) 'The Open-System Character of the Economy and its Implications', in Dopfer, K. (ed.), *Economics in the Future* (London: Macmillan).

Kuttner, R. (1985) 'The Poverty of Economics', *The Atlantic Monthly*, February, p. 76.

Matthews, R.C.O. (1986) 'The Economics of Institutions and the Sources of Growth', *Economic Journal*, vol. 96, December, pp. 903–18.

Mills, F. C. (1952) 'A Professional Sketch' in Burns, A. F. (ed.), *Wesley Clair Mitchell – The Economic Scientist* (New York: National Bureau of Economic Research).

Myrdal, G. (1953) *The Political Element in the Development of Economic Theory*, trans. Streeten, P. (London: Routledge & Kegan Paul).

Myrdal, G. (1972) 'Response to Introduction', *American Economic Review*, vol. 62, May, pp. 456–62.

Myrdal, G. (1976) 'The Meaning and Validity of Institutional Economics' in Dopfer, K. (ed.), *Economics in the Future* (London: Macmillan Press).

Myrdal, G. (1977) 'Institutional Economics', a lecture given at the University of Wisconsin, 15 December 1977, reprinted in Myrdal (1979).

Myrdal, G. (1979) *Essays and Lectures after 1975* (Kyoto: Keibunsha).

Ruskin, J. (1859) Lecture delivered at Bradford in March 1859. See Ruskin, J., *The Two Paths* (London: Smith & Elder).

Samuelson, P. A. (1980) *Economics*, 11th edn (New York: McGraw Hill).

Samuleson, P. A. and Nordhaus, W. (1985) *Economics*, 12th edn (New York : McGraw Hill).

Schlesinger, A. Jr (1984) 'The Political Galbraith', in *The Journal of Post-Keynesian Economics*, vol. 7, no. 1, Fall, pp. 7–17.

Schumpeter, J. A. (1947) *Capitalism, Socialism and Democracy* 2nd edn (New York: Harper & Bros.).

Schumpeter, J. A. (1954) in Boody, E. (ed.), *History of Economic Analysis* (New York: Oxford University Press; London: Allen & Unwin).

Sclove, R. (1982) *The Bulletin of the Atomic Societies*, May.

Stopford, J. M., Dunning, J. H. and Haverich, K. O. (1980) *The World Directory of Multinational Enterprises* (London: Macmillan).

Thurow, L. (1980) *The Zero-Sum Society* (New York: Basic Books).

Tsuru, S. (1970) (ed.) *Proceedings of International Symposium on Environmental Disruption: A Challenge to Social Scientists* (Tokyo).

Wolfe, A.B. (1952) 'Views on the Scope and Method of Economics', in Burns, A. F. (ed.), *Wesley Clair Mitchell – The Economic Scientist* (New York: National Bureau of Economic Research) pp. 207–34.

Part I

Market and Institutions: Role of Multinationals and Transnationals

2 Market and Institutions

Siro Lombardini
UNIVERSITY OF TURIN

This paper is divided into four parts. In Section 1 some meanings of the term 'market' are discussed, with special emphasis on the sociocultural meaning of market, namely on the market cultural attitude that results from self-interest as it is perceived and operates in certain specific cultural contexts. We are then led, in Section 2, to an analysis of the role of institutions in shaping the economic system and in assuring its structural stability. This is followed by a consideration of the shortcomings of some of the approaches by which economists analyse the strategies of firms that have to take into account, not only the behaviour of their rivals, but also that of government, parliament and social groups. In Section 3 we examine how the market affects the working of institutions, more specifically of the political system. We show that it is not possible to partition the social system into economic and institutional-political systems. In Section 4 we face some theoretical problems concerning the link between market and institutions and try to visualise the conditions for a workable state with efficiency and justice.

1 MARKET

1.1 Various Meanings of Market

The concept of market has different meanings which play different roles in economic theory:

1. By referring to an economy where goods are produced by private firms and consumed by families who can freely purchase the commodities they need, 'market' (competitive market) is conceived as a mechanism that makes possible the most efficient allocation of resources for the satisfaction of individuals' needs through simultaneous optimising behaviour by the various agents.

27

2. In less abstract analyses of the working of a free economy, 'market' means a set of procedures by which information is provided by sellers to purchasers and by purchasers to sellers and actions (and reactions) are decided by the various agents.[1]

3. 'Market' in popular usage is usually linked with specific sites. Some of the roles of the market are, in some way, associated with its spatial dimension.

4. By 'market' we can describe a *cultural attitude* of various agents. Such a meaning is implied when we talk about market-oriented economic activities.

5. We talk about 'markets' (or industries, or economic sectors) when we isolate sets of economic transactions (activities) for which we can obtain empirical data.

The meanings of markets that raise interesting theoretical and methodological problems are the second and the fourth. We shall dwell a little upon the fourth.

1.2 The Market Cultural Attitude

It is difficult to conceive of, let alone find, communities where there is no exchange of commodities. There are communities (Trobriand for instance) where exchanges of commodities (*kula*) are made on the basis of the principle of reciprocity (see Bohannan and Dalton, 1962). In primitive societies goods are produced and distributed according to social rules and customs. These societies are often multicentred economies made up of independent spheres characterised by different rules of transaction. Only in *peripheral markets*, are goods exchanged according to an imperfect market principle.[2]

Usually peripheral markets provide purchasing power to acquire some special commodities such as bicycles or to pay taxes. The introduction of money in primitive communities makes it difficult to maintain the partition of the economy into separate spheres of transaction. When it does not play the mere role of *numéraire*, money is usually associated with the emergence of the *merchant*: the market principle becomes his criterion of rational behaviour. It is because of this evolution that 'market' comes to mean a specific cultural attitude towards society. Smith is convinced that the market attitude is a natural one. According to him there is an essential link between self-interest and the propensity to trade (Smith, 1776). Yet, as Parsons (1940) has remarked, the content of self-interest cannot be considered as constant and independent of social institutions.

The market cultural attitude stems both from the self-interest motivation and from appropriate institutions. It assumes two forms: first the *merchant* attitude (*business* in Max Weber's sense) and second the *producer* attitude (*industry* in Weber's sense). Such a distinction reminds us of that between financial capital and real capital: it is reflected in the different roles that, according to Keynes, are played by rentiers and entrepreneurs in the economic process.

In the process of economic growth the two forms of market cultural attitude become interwoven, as outlined by Schumpeter. Credit can free innovation from the need for previous accumulation of capital. Speculation may help the reorganisation of the productive system. Yet the two forms of the market cultural attitude correspond to two different motivations.

In capitalistic modern economies almost all goods produced are exchanged through the market that represents the arena for the entrepreneurs. We shall speak of *market economy* when we refer to this kind of economic system. The way to introduce market mechanism to improve allocation of resources, and to foster innovations in the socialist economies, has become an important issue, especially after the reforms announced by Gorbachev (Lombardini, 1986).

1.3 Market and Self-interest

After Smith, economists have been inclined to identify self-interest with economic motivation, and economic motivation with market cultural attitude.

If by self-interest we mean personal motivation for action, then to say that an action is motivated by self-interest is to say that it is consciously conceived and decided. Self-interest is then absent only when a social action is undertaken as routine behaviour imposed by social customs.

If, on the other extreme, by self-interest we mean the identification of ultimate goals with individuals' needs, then we cannot say that all actions consciously conceived and decided are motivated by self-interest. Even economic activities cannot be fully explained by referring to the self-interest of individuals making their decisions in the market.

In fact, when we talk of self-interest as a connotation of economic activity, we must distinguish the individual's psychological attitude from his actual choices that depend, to a large extent, on constraints imposed on him and on the information available to him.

Some of the constraints are the result of decisions that are not taken in the markets (such as political decisions that affect the economy). Such decisions, taken according to majority rule, can be accepted by the dissenters, not only because the decisions are enforced by the state, but also because all individuals agree that a set of decisions is required, essentially for two reasons. The first is to assure coherence among the activities of individuals, who may pursue their own interest only up to the point where it does not clash with institutional features of the system that are thought to be essential at the time. The second is to make it possible for society to pursue goals that cannot be completely identified with the interests of specific classes. Since a large number of individuals identify themselves with society pursuing such goals, we cannot say that self-interest is the only motivation for social activities.

The individual's actual choices depend on the set of information available to him, and this is determined, to a large extent, by the features of both the economic and the sociocultural system. Economists assume that this set of data is large enough, and is structured in such a way (production functions, ordered preference fields), as to make sense of the theory of optimising behaviour. Such an assumption ignores the impact of the sociocultural system both in the production and utilisation of information. It is sufficient to stress how in given sectors (such as agriculture), and in given economies (or the less developed countries), a change in technique cannot occur without changes in some institutional and cultural features of the economy.

In the market economy only certain sets of information are made available, whereas, for the market to perform its role efficiently, other sets of information (such as the information about the plans of the innovative entrepreneur) have to be kept secret. The considerations above are sufficient to justify the statement that self-interest cannot be defined independently from the sociocultural system; nor can we determine its role in shaping the market mechanism without considering the interrelationships between sociocultural and economic systems.

2 INSTITUTIONS AND THE ECONOMIC SYSTEM

2.1 The Role of Institutions

Both for individual behaviour, and for social decisions leading to a structurally stable economic system, certain sets of social institutions are required. There is no doubt that the sociocultural system exerts influences on economic activity which contribute to the maintenance of some structural features of the economic system. This can be easily realised when we consider primitive economies, but it is also true in modern economies. We can distinguish two extreme situations. In the first (traditional communities), the influence of the sociocultural system is such as to ensure the structural stability of the system. In the second (bourgeois societies), the interrelations between sociocultural and economic systems are such that structural stability is not assured.

The second type is characterised by individuals searching for power essentially provided by money. Their activities are essentially destabilising activities. In fact, money has more far-reaching implications than has been supposed. It makes it possible to change the level and the nature of economic activities turning them into speculative activities.

Such a consideration is scarcely noticed by neoclassical economists. In fact, the role of institutions has been defined in the context of equilibrium theory. The 'equilibrium philosophy' can be traced back to the philosophical orientations of the Enlightment Age (see Lombardini, 1985) that have also influenced sociological analyses (as can be noticed also by considering Spencer's thought (Spencer, 1867)).

Spencer's conception of the social mechanism assuring structural stability brings to mind Smith's opinion on the role of the sympathy sentiment. Underneath we find a particular conception of the economic system. The fundamental activities are production activities. Exchange serves for production. All agents in all markets are powerless or can be kept without power by proper institutional arrangements and government behaviour (suffice to recall the antitrust laws).

Such an ideal state, required to conceive an equilibrium of the economy, is compatible only with first form of market attitude. Yet, as we have seen, the two forms interweave in the process of economic development of a capitalist economy.

In spite of Smith's opinion on the role of the sympathy sentiment, the bourgeois attitude helps in preserving only some features of the social order, certainly not the structure of the economic system. Yet it has been this attitude that has made economic evolution possible. Evolution, being characterised by structural changes, requires and produces disequilibria.

The structural changes, through which evolution occurs, are mostly produced by entrepreneurial activity that – as it has been clearly understood by Schumpeter (1912) – presupposes some power by the firm, the power being used to induce changes in the economy. In Schumpeter's analysis, credit is required to make it possible for the innovative entrepreneur to implement his plans. Therefore, the evolution of the system is the result of the interplay of the two forms of market cultural motivations: no equilibrium model can explain how a market economy works.

2.2 Equilibrium of the Economy and Equilibrium of the Social System

The capitalist market appears structurally unstable when we consider its cultural content. The fact that some kind of equilibrium – seldom of the Walrasian type – has always been restored after crises in the capitalistic economies, does not imply that there exists some kind of mechanism (market or market plus appropriate institutions) that has, as its essential feature, the role of maintaining the order of society. In fact, we should reflect on the nature of the equilibrium and of the process by which it is restored. The process is often the result of some political decisions provided neither by the market nor as the consequence of normal activities carried on by the existing institutions.

Apart from these considerations, we must notice that the positive essential role of the market is not to keep and restore equilibrium (as a necessary condition for the social order), but to create the most favourable conditions for economic development. As is well known, economic development implies evolution. Therefore it necessarily entails structural changes in the economy, and in the very long run, even in the social system.

Even the problem of price formation cannot be solved in the context of Walrasian equilibrium theory. In order to conceive as possible a normal – and thereby rational – structure of the economy, we need to assume that no agent has the power to affect prices: prices are established by the market whose role was interpreted by Walras's *logical* rule of the auctioneer. No scientific explanation has thus been provided of how prices are effectively determined. Nor has the shift from the first to the second meaning of *market* produced satisfactory solutions for the problem.

2.3 The Power of Economic Agents and the Interplay produced by their Decisions

It was only in 1944, when von Neumann and Morgenstern's *Theory of Games and Economic Behaviour* was published, that an alternative approach to the traditional general equilibrium approach was put forward. The new approach is based on the assumption that economic agents have power. In pursuing their divergent interests they interact with one another. Does such an interaction lead to equilibrium? The theory of games tells us that such a question can have a positive answer under particular conditions; that equilibrium situations can be different according to the different contexts in which interplay occurs. In fact, co-operative solutions are different from competitive ones. The set of possible co-operative solutions may be very large indeed: it depends on the procedures (and institutions) by which information can be provided and exchanged, and on the bargaining power of the players.[3]

In fact – as it is assumed in *differential games* – strategies must be defined in a dynamic context. Then to assume that each player knows in advance, what the alternatives of the others are, and how they are evaluated, is an heroic assumption indeed. A game entails a process of learning and a process of adjustment of the strategies. A situation of equilibrium may then be possible only if the objective conditions for the game remain unchanged while the processes develop. But can we conceive of objective conditions being independent from the subjective evaluations?

The objective conditions change in the course of time: the change is not independent of agents' decisions. When agents' expectations are wrong, their decisions will change the objective conditions in an unforeseeable way. For all agents the learning process must then start afresh. Nobody can tell in advance whether the process will converge to a well-defined situation that can be considered as a rational one (or to a path that can be considered efficient). A player can start a game in order to change the initial conditions and, thereby improve the set of strategies available to him.[4]

In an oligopolistic market the number of logically possible games is too large to have any operational meaning. We then need to define a subset of games that can actually be played. Such a subset depends on certain features of the economic as well as of the socio-political systems.

Game theory has been developed to explain the firm's behaviour in face of other firms operating in the same market. In fact a firm plays several games at the same time: a game with its rivals in the market, a game with the banking and the financial system, a game with the trade unions, a game with the government. All these games are interconnected. The theory cannot provide a set of criteria that can be applied by the firm to attain a rational solution for all these games. In fact the solution can be improved by wrong messages sent to other agents.

The criterion of economic rationality on which the theory of games is built is more specific than the one that is at the basis of the theory of general equilibrium, since it entails a specific assumption on how agents behave under uncertainty.[5]

We do not want here to discuss the possible theoretical development and the fruitful application of the game theory, nor, more generally, of the decision theory. What we must stress is that agents' behaviour depends not only on economic conditions, but also on sociological and institutional systems. A market economy requires some peculiar social and institutional frameworks. Its working cannot be independent of such frameworks. The social cultural system affects the ways problems are framed and solved even in a market economy.

2.4 Market and Strategies of Firms

Even if we disregard the complications that must be faced when we consider the interactions between firms, we cannot but consider the neoclassical model inadequate. Market conditions do not determine the firm's behaviour in a unique way. The profit criterion entails different choices according to the context in which the problem is posed – in particular the horizon[6] – and the ways uncertainty is perceived and taken into account by the various agents.

Economists usually consider uncertainty an undesirable feature of the real world. In fact, entrepreneurial innovations and speculative activities that have contributed to accumulation[7] could not have materialised in a context of certainty. Some essential features of the social and economic system are associated with uncertainty: the variety of individuals' expectations and their different risk aversion. Expectations dynamics increase the destabilising role of money and credit.[8] The economy will inevitably undergo structural changes, both because the power structure changes – through changes in the firms' strategies – and because of the effects of changes in expectations on individual choices. It is worth noticing that expectations can be of two kinds: active or passive. The expectations of the innovative entrepreneur are active, while our expectations of future prices are passive. Active expectations cannot be considered as given in framing agents problems. They are, in fact, both an input and an output.

Most of government expectations are of the active type. Active expectations of an individual cannot be shared by other individuals unless they are annouced. A reason for planning is the advantages that occur to various agents because of the announcement of government actions (active expectations) (see Meade, 1971).

Now it is sufficient to notice that strong political pressures for risk reducing government interventions may endanger the market mechanism as has occurred in various countries in the last decades. Conversely, too great uncertainty may hamper the market mechanism by inducing the firms to increase their market power through coalitions, mergers and agreements of various types.

3 MARKET AND THE STATE

3.1 The Market and the Democratic System

The competitive market has some resemblance to the democratic system. Both are supposed to satisfy individual needs: the former those needs that can be expressed on the market through demand, the latter, indivisible needs that can be expressed through the political aggregation of the individuals wishes by majority voting (see Lombardini, 1983). Both are deemed to be rational inasmuch as individuals, having antagonistic interests, are powerless: consequently it is possible for the market mechanism or the voting procedure to conciliate their choices.

Even if we confine ourselves to theoretical models, market and democracy show relevant differences. In the economic system, making choices entails acceptance of all their consequences if we exclude externalities. It is not so in the political system. A person may vote for limitations of car speed and yet drive his own car at a speed higher than the one allowed. A more serious shortcoming of the democratic system is the divorce between the role of tax payer and that of recipients of government benefits (see Olson, 1968; Lindblom, 1977 and Offe, 1980).

The divergence between market mechanism and democratic procedures looks even more substantial if we consider actual markets and specific democratic systems that are both far from their ideal models. The market can perform its role (to promote economic development) because firms have economic power. Yet the use of economic power may lead to market structures (monopolies, oligopolies, monopolistic competition) that may hinder the rational allocation of resources.

The working of a democratic system produces the formation of political parties. The political parties have power. They have their own goals that cannot be reduced to aggregations of the needs of people voting for them. The first goal of a political party is survival. Parties need financial support that can be provided only by some individuals and groups: those individuals and groups can thus exert a particular influence on the goals of the parties that can be made appealing also to other individuals and groups, even if they have divergent interests, through processes of ideological sublimation (or, more simply, by sheer propaganda).

In the abstract, not only are the resemblances between market and democracy emphasised, but the two systems are also supposed to operate independently of each other. The political system affects the market only indirectly through taxes and public expenditure. The market mechanism needs to be preserved: special laws (like the Antitrust Acts of Parliament) may be required. Most of the neoclassical economists are convinced that once the laws are approved and the judicial body is given the task of enforcing them, the social system can be partitioned into an economic and a political system. Let us consider some of the reasons why such a dichotomy cannot be affirmed.

3.2   Market Structures and Political System

According to quite a few classical and neoclassical economists, the only state interventions required to maintain a market economy are those aiming at preserving competition. In fact, no antitrust law was ever able to restore and preserve competition as it is conceived in the neoclassical theory. The Sherman Act was passed by the United States Congress in a period in which the small producers and traders had sufficient political power to contrast the strategies of a few budding giants of industry and finance. When the power structure became unstable, the law – together with others that were passed by the Congress – was used to preserve the power of some firms that could have been hampered by the strategies of other firms. But when the power structure attained sufficient stability, the law became ineffective, as it has been remarked by Dewey (1959, p. 149). We cannot but agree with Stocking (1964) when he writes 'the chief reason the antitrust laws have not been more successful is that no political powerful economic group wants them to be generally enforced'.

The Sherman Act – as Dewey (1959, pp. 156–7) reminds us – has been used

for attacking evils for which no specific statutory remedy exists. Thus over the years, it has been invoked to send labour racketeers to prison, induce the American Medical Association to grant hospital privileges to physicians who join group health insurance programmes, and compel the country's largest news agency to offer its facilities to all newspaper owners on equal terms.

These reflections offer ground for three statements that are fundamental for our argument:

1. The state (parliament and government) is not that omniscient agent supposed in some theoretical models of welfare economics and of the economics of public choice. It has limited information on the economy and on the political system (in particular on the possible political reactions to its decisions).
2. The state cannot be assimilated to other agents that can be assumed to be coherent in taking their decisions. The choices are arrived at after processes of conciliating diverging views and interests. The conciliation is often only formal. Then the concrete implications of the state decisions (laws, administrative acts) depend on how they are actually implemented, that is, how the laws are enforced or the administrative power is wielded.
3. The state is not capable of efficiently governing the market mechanism. It interacts with it in pursuing its own goals that cannot be considered independent of those pursued by other agents. To such a relation we must now turn our attention.

3.3   Collusive Behaviour between Industry, Finance and State

As we have already remarked, firms, in deciding their strategy, ought to consider the possible actions and reactions of the state as well as of the other agents who operate in the market. The state, by deciding on some kinds of public works rather than others, favours some industries more than others. In fact, any big push for economic development has always been given by state policy through interventions that have created the conditions for new activities. Suffice to recall the construction of roads in the UK and the building of the railroad in the United States.

The favourable effects for the various firms depend on the kinds of interventions decided. Therefore, as we have already noticed, one of the games the big firms have to play, is with the state. The firm or the group may decide to influence directly the members of parliament or public servants who make the decisions or implement them. The need for finance of the political parties makes it easy for the big firms or groups to exert their influence. Sometimes the influence is produced only indirectly: it occurs through the influence that the big firms can exert on mass media. The ideological debate can favour the 'cultural' processes that can be fostered through the mass media.

No dichotomy can be established between the economic system (market) and the political system (democracy). There are two factors that can explain the interrelations between the market economic system and the democratic political system:

(a) the role that political decisions play in shaping the economy and its working,
(b) the connection between the power structure of the economic system and that of the political system. It is because of this connection that some political decisions are motivated by the benefits – more or less openly granted to specific social groups or individuals – and that the firms, in deciding their strategies, take into account the influence they can exert on the political system.

We have mentioned some of the reasons why an economic system is unstable: the specific role of money and credit and potential changes in the power structure. The political system too is structurally unstable.

In the market economy some change in the power structure may be motiva ted by the need for less uncertainty, uncertainty being, to some extent, associated with instability. In the political system some peculiar power structure which can exert influence on the economy, possibly thanks to a perverse use of laws, may be obtained in order to reduce the instability of the economic system. Conversely, some evolution of the power structure of the economic system may have the effect of making the political system more stable. We can thus say that the connections between the market economy and the democratic political system may increase the overall stability. Yet in some circumstances the instability of the economic system, that can be fostered by monetary mechanisms, being associated with that of the political system, leads to a greater global instability.

3.4 Some Changes in the Relations between Economy and Government

Up to now the agents with a decisive influence on economic policy were the big firms and the financial system. In some countries (like Italy) the strongest influence came from industrialists. In others (like West Germany) it was the banks that could more easily affect economic policy by controlling industry. In the pre-war period in England, government policy (through the revaluation of the pound) appeared to be more sensible to the interests of financial groups rather than those of most of industries. In the post-war period trade unions have gained momentum. This occurred because in the consumer phase of development of the capitalistic system some convergence of interest between capital and labour is more easily perceived.[9]

The relations between capital and labour display a cyclical pattern. When entrepreneurs fear a recession because of a deficiency of internal demand, a convergence can more easily be established between workers and industrialists. The quest for interventions aimed at reducing uncertainty becomes stronger. In fact the orientation of economic policy can then be easily decided. Since it aims at sustaining global demand, a relevant increase is produced in the deficit of the state budget. Agreement between trade unions and industry can also be easily obtained, as it occurred in Italy at the beginning of 1974, when the prospects of the economy worsened.

When new perspectives of growth are perceived for their firms, either because of technological innovations or because of expansion of world demand, industrialists may feel that their interests are in contrast to those of labour. Then the political system becomes unstable and the power structure of the economic system is changed.[10]

4 DESIRABLE RELATIONS BETWEEN MARKET AND STATE

4.1 An Ideal State for an Ideal Economy

Let us now consider which relations should be established between market and institutions in order to have a rational political system and an efficient economic system.

Political rationality can be defined on the basis of either an atomistic or a holistic conception of society. Utilitarians have provided ground for the first alternative. We shall not dwell on the reasons why the utilitarians' approach – as it has been resumed by Harsanyi (1955) – embracing individual evaluations of social situations, cannot be accepted as a basis to define rationality. Individual longing – as Rawls (1972) has stressed – cannot be interpreted on the basis of a mere utilitarian principle. But it is difficult to define *principles of justice* without either coming back to the utilitarian principle (interpreted in a more sophisticated way), or proposing some primitive principle that can be justified only on the basis of some holistic conception of society.

A common premiss of contractualism (which is one ingredient also of Rawls's theory of justice) is the configuration of an *original position* in which the psychological attitude of, and the information available to, various individuals are such as to induce them to choose a constitution that assures some essential conditions for rationality of social choices. The Rawls approach is, in some respects, more realistic than Harsanyi (1955) and Buchanan and Tullock (1962), inasmuch as it admits some differences in the initial conditions of individuals. In other respects it is more open to criticism because of the maximin principle it entails,[11] the conception of a society polarised in the two groups of rich and poor, the ideological premiss that enables it to state the priority of the first principle of justice ('each person is to have an equal right to the most extensive basic liberty compatible with a similar liberty for others').[12]

The individual's innate aspiration for justice is not sufficient to bring forth a rational political system. The assumption of such a *veil of ignorance* that will make all individuals incapable to predict their position and benefits under a given set of principles is indeed a very heroic assumption. Let us disregard the fact that all individuals are born in a family, live in a community, acquire certain beliefs. Even if we consider the minimum essential features that qualify an individual, it is not possible to speak of an *original position* establishing a status quo of universal equality from which a social contract can be written. The individuals differ in certain qualities that are relevant when we discuss the role of institutions. These differences are:

(a)   The telescopic capacity as compared with the myopia characterising some economic as well as political behaviour;

(b)   the importance attributed to the various dimensions of alternative choices. In fact, the result of a choice is not an homogeneous magnitude that can be interpreted as purchasing power or utility.

The kind of labour activity offered to us may be more important than the level of the purchasing power we may obtain by working. The social relations in which we are involved enter into our evaluation of the various alternatives;

(c) the final goals that make increases in purchasing power appealing. For some people it is consumption, for others power. When power is the motive that makes it desirable to increase purchasing power, control of business, establishment of given social relations, and the power to affect political decisions may be a surrogate for money;

(d) the attitude towards risk. We have already stressed the relevance of such a quality in individuals. There are people with an entrepreneurial attitude and people with a conservative one. Should all people be of the first kind the social system would explode. If they were all be of the second kind, the system would never evolve.

To understand the Rawls principle let us follow Mueller (1979, p. 228) and

think of a group of individuals sitting down to draw up a set of rules for a game of chance, say a game of cards, in which they will subsequently participate. Prior to the start of the game, each individual is ignorant of the cards to be dealt to him, and uncertain of his skills relative to those of the other players.

The veil of ignorance thus assumed cannot cancel the different attitude towards risk that may lead to different preferences among alternative sets of rules. Individuals having the entrepreneurial attitude are not likely to accept the maximin principle.

The alternative sets of rules need to be evaluated by all individuals in all the possible consequences they might once have implemented. This is possible for a simple society but not for our modern society.

The meanings of various alternatives are different according to the level and kind of information that the system allows to be exchanged among individuals, and to the procedure by which the choice can be made. Saving, for instance, may be the result of individual decisions and be motivated by individual needs. Should saving be the result of collective decisions, individuals may be more capable of assessing its effect on economic development and more willing to sacrifice current consumption (see Lombardini, 1954).

Collective decisions may make it possible to consider all the likely consequences of the various alternatives. Individual decisions may favour innovation. Therefore it is not easy to assess the advantages of centralisation versus decentralisation (see Hurwicz, 1977).

The assessment of the various alternatives, as defined by those adhering to the contractualistic approach, is usually of a static nature. In a dynamic process a pattern of income distribution, which may seem unjust from a static viewpoint, may appear to be a prerequisite for economic development and therefore for efficiency (see Okun, 1975).

If we are informed that present unequal income distribution, by favouring entrepreneurial activity, may have future favourable effects for the poor, we may discard the minimax principle also on the basis of ethical considerations. Conversely, if we realise that the unequal distribution of income is an obstacle to the increase of demand, we may favour a more equal distribution, not only for ethical reasons but also for economic motives.

4.2 A Game Theory Approach to Institutions

A more fruitful approach to the analysis of the genesis and working of institutions and to their connections with the economy has been proposed by Andrew Schotter (1981). According to Schotter

> economic and social institutions are primarily informational mechanisms that complement the information contained in competitive prices when these prices fail to totally coordinate economic activities. In so doing they help to add structure and order to what would otherwise be a more chaotic situation of strategic interdependence. (Schotter, 1981, p. 143)

In fact 'there are circumstances where the information contained in market prices is not sufficient to efficiently decentralize the actions of agents. To compensate for this missing information, it becomes necessary for agents to create non market institutions' (p. 147).

Schotter is thus not limited in his analysis by the conviction that the economic and political system are separate, and can play different roles, whose different decisions are connected only by the fiscal and monetary policy. According to him, economic and social institutions can be considered as a product of co-operative games that may eventually be the outcome of a learning process through which commonly-held norms of behaviour are built up. Game theory is applied, not in the limited context of determination of the rational structure as can be obtained through the decisions taken by agents on markets, but to determine the more complex context in which markets operate.

In fact, as we have remarked, the same agents (individuals) contribute to shape the economic system as well as the political system, both with regard to individuals and social needs. The Schotter approach can help us understand how the process by which the structure of the economic system is determined interacts with that by which social institutions are created.

Our reflections have led us to stress the role that the power structures, characterising both the economic and the political system, plays in determining such interactions. If we assume a power structure at the beginning of the learning process, then the game may be more complex and different from the one envisaged by Schotter.

In fact the state may be the result of a survival game imposed by the agents who have more power. They operate in order to obtain institutions confirming and preserving their power, not completely to destroy the power of the other agents. In fact they cannot ignore the need of other agents who cannot be ruled effectively if they do not identify themselves – to a certain degree at least – with the state. We shall not try to develop this idea further. What we shall try to do is to envisage some of the features of a state that, because of a sufficiently stable consent of the various agents, may be assimilated to the result of a co-operative game played in an adequate predetermined institutional context.[13]

4.3 A Workable State for Efficiency and Justice

A democratic procedure for collective choices is not sufficient to assure a *workable state*, that is, a state that has sufficient autonomy to set up and implement a strategy in order to conciliate the interest of various social groups in such a way as to assure economic development. All depends on the *political ideology* of the various political parties, on the exogenous perspectives of the economy, and on the socio-cultural system. The main functions of a workable state are:

(a) to reduce uncertainty but to allow for those kinds of uncertainty which are required to foster entrepreneurial activities and which are the results of these activities;

(b) to create the most favourable conditions for economic development;

(c) to contribute to individuals' welfare by providing social services;

(d)   to take care of persons whose position is worsened by the economic process, for example the unemployed.

There may be conflict between these goals. It is true that in the long-run perspective the antagonisms are likely to lessen, yet in the short run, entrepreneurial activities, which are required for economic development, may make an increase in unemployment inevitable. But lasting unemployment is a symptom of inefficiency in the system. In fact, in the short run certain disequilibria appear as necessary conditions for economic development. In the long run equilibria are required to maximise efficiency. Equilibria can be obtained only through those changes in final (private or public) consumption as are required to compensate for the changes that have occurred in productive coefficients. (see Pasinetti, 1981).

The state has to promote economic development and efficiency. Such a role can be reconciled with the role of promoting justice if the political horizon is sufficiently wide, and it the social cultural system is such as to prevent people from being too myopic. The capacity of the parties to produce adequate political ideologies, namely their capacity to offer proposals of prospective societies in which it is easier to reconcile efficiency with justice, may help to produce an adequate cultural system.

The market is both a prerequisite and a result of a *workable state*. It is a prerequisite since an arena is required for entrepreneurial capacities to develop. It is a result since only efficient management of uncertainty by the state and efficient political choices concerning the prerequisites or economic development can make it possible for the market to work satisfactorily.

In some countries corruption is an obstacle for an efficient identification of people with the state. It appears to be desirable, if possible, to regulate the participation of the political leaders in income distribution by permitting side payments in their favour to be made openly according to certain rules.

As we have seen, it is not possible to divide the social system into a political and economic system. What can be achieved is to rule the relations between the two systems in such a way as to reduce their negative effects on efficiency as well as on justice.

Notes

1. Suffice to recall the *Walras's auctioneer's rule* (Arrow and Hahn, 1971), the *non-Walrasian equilibrium models* (Benassy, 1977; Malinvaud, 1977), the *search equilibrium approach* (Diamond, 1984) and the so-called *conjectural equilibrium* in which assumptions – similar to those made in the theory of monopolistic competition – on the firm's power to affect prices are made (Hahn, 1977; Negishi, 1968).

2. As P. Bohannan and G. Dalton (1962) have remarked, the prices that are established in such markets do not play the role of allocating resources efficiently. In fact, the site of the peripheral market is not integrated with the productive decisions.

3. Referring to the Nash model, Luce and Raiffa (1957, p. 134) have remarked:

   > one of the basic assumptions of game theory, and of the bargaining model in particular, is extremely doubtful, namely: that each player knows the true tastes – the utility functions – of the others. For example, suppose that in a bargaining situation the players agree to submit to an arbiter who is committed to Nash's assumptions. To resolve the conflict, the arbiter must first ascertain their utility functions; hence the situation deteriorates into a game of strategy where each player tries to solve the problem of how best to falsify or exaggerate his true tastes.

4. A game of this type is a *game of survival*. As Shubik (1959, p. 204) states, 'the goal of each player is to ruin his opponent: hence his payoff consists of the valuation he places upon survival and ruin'.

5. See Marschak (1950). For a criticism of the expected-utility principle see McLennen (1978). A more thorough examination of the nature of uncertainty leads to more critical assessments. In fact, when we assume uncertain prospects, reasoning may not be sufficient to shape a decision. Intuition, application of rules of thumb, adherence to given beliefs, processes of learning, contribute, together with reasoning, to decision formation, as it has been remarked by the father of cybernetics, Wiener (1964).

6. Soon after the war the automobile industry in the United States did not raise prices to the extent that would have been considered convenient on the basis of the neoclassical theory of optimising behaviour. Various explanations have been proposed:

   1. An increase in price and, thereby, in profits, would have induced trade unions to ask for an increase in wages. After some time the likely change in the conditions of the market, caused by the adjustment in production, would have induced a downward adjustment of the price, and, because of the stickiness of wages, in profits.
   2. The automobile industry was afraid of a government intervention grounded on the antitrust laws.
   3. Unfavourable reactions by consumers could have been induced by

price increases as soon as competition would have been established in the world market.

Whichever of these explanations we consider more convincing, what such a story tells us is that firms do not establish their prices on the basis of the current market conditions: they take into account the changes that are likely to occur, and all possible reactions to their price policy.

7. Speculation in the stock market – by which the fortune of some of the people that have started new business has been created – leads, sooner or later, to a fall in the stock prices entailing losses for a conspicuous number of savers. Since the injured savers are obliged to reduce their propensity to consume, accumulation can increase.

8. As Minsky (1975) has stressed, even a state of equilibrium is intrinsically unstable since its lasting will cause expectations to change for the better.

9. In the classical phase of development all increase in wages were in favour of the labour class and had negative effects for industry (since costs were increased). In the consumer phase increases in wages may favour in certain circumstances, not only workers, but also some industries (more precisely the industries producing consumer durables or commodities that are employed in their production).

10. Trade unions and industrialist associations may contribute, together with the political parties, to keep the instability of the political system within tolerable limits. We must remind ourselves that the class structure of the social system has been superseded by a *corporate structure*. The instability of the political system – in the Schwartz sense – is thus increased. It may then be that, only thanks to more or less conscious collusion between political parties and social groups, a minimum degree of structural stability of the social system can be assured. In Italy we can notice phases of more or less collusive behaviour between labour and capital (1948–63, 1965–8, 1973–5, 1980–4) alternating with phases of antagonism. The last of these phases has accelerated processes of restructuring the economy. Yet it has increased the danger of social instability by weakening trade unions and thus increasing the space for the action of small interest groups.

11. It is on the basis of this principle that choices improving the conditions of the poor can be justified, or at least accepted by the rich. Rawls (1972) expresses the principle by saying

the person choosing has a conception of the good such that he cares very little, if anything, for what he might gain above the minimum stipend that he can, in fact, be sure of by following the maximin rule [i.e. by choosing the option with the highest minimum payoff regardless of what the other payoffs are, no consideration being given to their different probabilities]. It is not worthwhile for him to take a chance for the sake of a further advantage ... .

In the consumption phase of development of the capitalistic system the level of aspiration of an individual is likely to move upwards with the increase in income (see Lombardini, 1957). Therefore the Rawls assumption could be grounded only on an ethical basis and certainly not on a psychological basis.

12. It is not clear how to evaluate the role of some institutions on the basis of this first principle of justice. Private property, for instance, can be considered both an obstacle for the first principle to be implemented, and the inevitable consequence of its implementation (to be free means to have the right to dispose of the yield of one's own work).

13. If we want to explain the institutional context as the result of a co-operative game, we are entangled in a *regressum ad infinitum*. In fact the establishment of Schotter's institutions of the first and of the second type (the former being imposed and the latter being produced by co-operative games) can be explained only by some kind of cybernetic model.

References

Arrow, K. J. and Hahn, F. H. (1971) *General Competitive Analysis* (San Francisco: Holden-Day).

Benassy, J. P. (1977) 'On Quantity Signals and the Foundations of Effective Demand Theory', in Strom, S. and Werin, L. (eds) *Topics in Disequilibrium Economics* (London: Macmillan Press).

Bohannan, P. and Dalton, G. (1962) *Markets in Africa* (Chicago: Northwestern University Press).

Buchanan, J. M. and Tullock, G. (1962) *The Calculus of Consent* (Ann Arbor: University of Michigan Press).

Dewey, D. (1959) *Monopoly in Economics and Law*, 2nd edn, 1964 (Chicago: Rand McNally).

Diamond, P. A. (1984) *A Search-Equilibrium Approach to the Micro Foundations of Macroeconomics* (Cambridge, Mass.: MIT Press).

Hahn, F. H. (1977) 'Exercises in Conjectural Equilibria', in Strom, S. and Werin, L. (eds) *Topics in Disequilibrium Economics* (London: Macmillan Press).

Harsanyi, J. C. (1955) 'Cardinal Welfare, Individualistic Ethics, and Interpersonal Comparison of Utility', *Journal of Political Economy*, 63.

Hurwicz, L. (1971) 'Centralization and Decentralization in Economic Processes', in Eckstein, A. (ed.) *Comparison of Economic Systems* (Berkeley: University of California Press).

Lindblom, C. (1977) *Politics and Markets. The World's Political-Economic Systems* (New York: Basic Books).

Lombardini, S. (1954) *Fondamenti e Problemi dell'Economia del Benessere* (Milano: Giuffrè).

Lombardini, S. (1957) *L'analisi della Domanda nella teoria Economica* (Milano: Giuffrè).

Lombardini, S. (1983) 'Democrazia e mercato', in Lombardini, S., *Il Metodo della Scienza Economica*' (Torino: Utet).

Lombardini, S. (1985) 'At the Roots of the Crisis of Economic Theory', *Economia Internazionale*.

Lombardini, S. (1986) 'Economia e Società nell'Unione Sovietica', *Rivista Milanese di Economia*, 18.
Luce, R. D. and Raiffa, H. (1957) *Games and Decisions, Introduction and Critical Survey* (New York: Wiley).
Malinvaud, E. (1977) *The Theory of Unemployment Reconsidered* (Oxford: Basil Blackwell).
Marschak, J. (1950) 'Rational Behaviour, Uncertain Prospects and Measurable Utility', *Econometrica*.
McLennen, E. F. (1978) 'The Minimax Theory and Expected-utility Reasoning', in Hooker, C. A., Leach, J. J. and McLennen, E. F. (eds) *Foundations and Applications of Decision Theory*, vol. 1 (Dordrecht: D. Reidel).
Meade, J. (1971) *The Controlled Economy* (London: Allen & Unwin).
Minsky, H. P. (1975) *John Maynard Keynes* (London, Basingstoke: Macmillan Press).
Mueller, D. C. (1979) *Public Choice* (Cambridge: Cambridge University Press).
Negishi, Y. (1968) 'Monopolistic Competition and General Equilibrium', *Review of Economic Studies*.
Neumann, J. von and Morgenstern, O. (1944) *Theory of Games and Economic Behavior* (Princeton: Princeton University Press).
Offe, C. (1980) 'The Separation of Form and Content in Liberal Democratic Politics', *Studies in Political Economy*.
Okun, A. M. (1975) *Equality and Efficiency* (Washington, DC: Brookings Institution).
Olson, M. (1968) *The Logic of Collective Action* (New York: Schocken Books).
Pareto, V. (1916) *Trattato di Sociologia Generale*, vols 1, 2 (Milano: Edizioni di Comunità, 1964).
Parsons, T. (1940) 'The Motivation of Economic Activity', *Canadian Journal of Economic and Political Science*, no. 6.
Pasinetti, L. L. (1981) *Structural Change and Economic Growth* (Cambridge: Cambridge University Press).
Prigogine, I. and Stengers, I. (1979) *La Nouvelle Alliance, Métamorphose de la Science* (Paris: Gallimard).
Rawls, J. (1972) *A Theory of Justice* (Cambridge, Mass.: Harvard University Press).
Schotter, A. (1981) *The Economic Theory of Social Institutions* (Cambridge: Cambridge University Press).
Schumpeter, J. A. (1912) *The Theory of Economic Development* (Leipzig: Duncker & Humblot) Translated R. Opie (Cambridge, Mass.: Harvard University Press, 1934) Reprinted (New York: Oxford University Press, 1961).
Schwartz, T. (1986) *The Logic of Collective Choice* (New York: Columbia University Press).
Shubik, M. (1959) *Strategy and Market Structure: Competition, Oligopoly and the Theory of Games* (New York: Wiley).
Smith, Adam (1776) *The Wealth of Nations* 1961 edn (Cannan, E.)

Spencer, H. (1867) *A System of Synthetic Philosophy, First Principles* (Thinker's Library Edition).
Stocking, G. W. (1964) 'The Effectiveness of the Antitrust Laws', in Mansfield, E. (ed.) *Monopoly Power and Economic Performance* (New York: Norton).
Tonnies, F. (1955) *Community and Association* (London: Routledge & Kegan Paul).
Wiener, N. (1964) *God and Golem, Inc.* (Cambridge, Mass.: The MIT Press).

Comment

Andrew Schotter
NEW YORK UNIVERSITY

1 INTRODUCTION

Let me start my comments today by saying that I found Professor
Lombardini's paper to be stimulating and suggestive, and one that led
me to think quite hard about a number of the ideas he raised. Hence, I
will use Professor Lombardini's paper as a base upon which to
elaborate on a number of themes he developed in his paper. More
precisely, in Section 2 I will discuss and define the terms 'market' and
'institution' which form the title of Professor Lombardini's paper. I
will do this by giving two definitions of the term 'institution' and using
them both to define what a market is. This discussion will lead me to
comment on Professor Lombardini's conception of a 'market culture'
(Section 3) and also his belief that economic and political systems are
inextricably linked to each other (Section 4). This link is caused, I
assert, because markets are mechanisms of denial which deny people
goods and services. Standard utilitarian theories of justice, while
useful in justifying what people receive from the market, are not as
useful in justifying what people are denied. Hence, in my final section I
investigate the consequences of this market denial for Professor
Lombardini's concept of an 'ideal state in an ideal economy'.

2 MARKETS AND INSTITUTIONS DEFINED

The first aspect of Professor Lombardini's paper that struck me was its
title, 'Market and Institutions'. What do we mean by those two words?
To answer this question I will propose two alternative definitions of
the concept of an economic or a social institution and use both of these
definitions to define the concept of a market.

2.1 Institutions of type I

My first definition of the concept of an institution comes from the work
of Professor Hurwicz (1973) on the theory of mechanism design and
implementation, and the work of Professor Reiter on what he called

50

the (New)[2] welfare economics (1977). In this tradition, an economic institution is a set of rules which constrain the behaviour of economic agents and determines outcomes on the basis of the choices they make. In short, an institution is a 'game form' which is designed by an exogenous planner and given to the agents to play. The rules *are* the institution under this definition. In order for such an institution to exist it must define a game that is playable by *real* people. In other words, the institution must define a full extensive form game stating the order of moves, the information that people have when they choose, and the outcomes existing at the terminal mode of the game tree. The aim of such research is to design games which yield pre-specified outcomes as an equilibrium.

2.2 Institutions of type II

An alternative definition of an institution is one that I have presented previously (see Schotter, 1981). Here an institution is defined as a regularity in the behaviour of economic agents which allows them to solve a set of recurrent problems that they face as the economy they are in develops. These institutions are almost identical to the 'conventions' of Lewis (1969) or the 'norms' of Ullman-Margalit (1978). To illustrate, primitive economies often develop a commodity money which helps them solve the problem of efficient trade. Such a money is in essence a regularity in behaviour or convention which dictates that a certain commodity is universally acceptable in trade. When such a regularity is common knowledge, and when incentives exist to conform to it, an institution exists.

Under this definition, then, an institution is not an abstract set of rules designed by a planner, but rather the Nash equilibrium to a game placed on the agents by a recurrent problem. Here the institution is a solution to an exogenously given game – *it is a feature of the equilibrium*.

2.3 Markets Defined

It is ironic that despite the fact that economics has been studying markets for nearly 200 years, it has not developed a clear definition of them. This fact is illustrated by Professor Lombardini when he starts his paper with five alternative definitions of what we *could* mean by the word market. The reason it is difficult to present a definition of a market is that markets (at least neoclassical textbook ones) are not type I institutions. Remember, to be a type I institution we must have a set of rules which define a game that is playable by *real* people. Perfectly competitive textbook markets with price-taking agents, however, require a fictitious auctioneer in order to function. In fact, no set of rules specifying a playable game in extensive form exists which defines the 'game of perfect competition', since the market is not a type I institution.

One of the accomplishments of experimental economics (see Smith, 1976, and Plott and Smith, 1978) is the investigation of exactly what types of rules (i.e., institutions of type I) lead to 'competitive outcomes'. What they find is that a number of sets of rules are successful in yielding 'competitive' outcomes, although none of them look like our textbook version of the market. Hence we are left with a situation in which, although no one can specify a type I institution called 'the market', experimentalists can at least define a set of rules or game forms (the double oral auction, for example) each of which yield outcomes which have the textbook characteristics of perfect competition.

If markets are not institutions of type I, what are they? I will answer this question indirectly by defining not what markets are, but rather what advocates of free markets claim they are. In other words, markets are what people who believe in them think they are. My definition will therefore reflect a rather libertarian view of what a market is. More precisely, people who advocate the free market reject the imposition of any set of rules on a voluntary exchange between agents, that is, they reject the imposition of type I institutions. They are anti-institutionalists of the first type. For them, a market exists when there is an implicit agreement among a population of people not to adhere to any institution of type I in order to exchange goods. The market is then an institution of type II, but a strange one since it is a commonly held agreement not to engage in an institution of type I. The thrust of the market is negative, involving a rejection of the imposition of any constraints on voluntary exchange. The basis for this rejection is, of course, the invisible hand belief of Adam Smith, which claims that if no constraints are put upon the voluntary exchange of goods, 'optimal' outcomes will result. This negative mentality is a characteristic of the market culture Professor Lombardini is talking about in his paper.

3 MARKET CULTURE: THE MARKET MENTALITY

The market culture discussed by Professor Lombardini is supported by a set of other beliefs (in addition to the self-centredness mentioned by Lombardini), all of which are necessary to support its nihilist attitude. They are:

1. Individualism and self-interest
2. Rationality
3. Belief in the invisible hand
4. Belief in process

In short, if you believe in the market, you implicitly believe that the only thing that should matter in determining social outcomes is the individual preferences of society's agents. Social choices are merely aggregated individual preference, nothing more and nothing less. (This is what Sen, 1979, has called welfarism.) However, in order for this view to be supportable, it must be true that people are rational, since aggregating the preferences of the insane may not be easily supportable (despite the attempts of libertarians). When it is then assumed that society is made up of rational individuals who are self-interested, the invisible hand belief comes into play, claiming that the voluntary outcomes determined by self-interested rational agents will always be 'optimal'. Finally, the market culture involves another belief in the market which does not rely on the optimality of equilibrium outcomes, but rather on the process engaged in to determine these outcomes. The argument here is that if rational agents are not constrained by the rules of any type I institution, they will be left free to exploit their own creative resources and seek out entrepreneurial opportunities whenever they see them. This attitude is alluded to in Lombardini's reference to the innovation of the producer class (or classical active classes) and is also present in the neo-Austrian view that the market's main advantage is that it encourages entrepreneurship and the seeking out of opportunities (Kirzner, 1973).

4 ECONOMIC AND POLITICAL INSTITUTIONS: THE JUSTIFICATION OF DENIAL

It is at this point in Professor Lombardini's paper that the economic system gets inextricably tied to the political system. In fact, Professor Lombardini is correct in pointing out that the two cannot be separated as neoclassical economics has historically tended to do. The reason for such an intimate link between our economic and political system is that while the market may be viewed as an allocative process which *provides* goods to people, it is also a device which *denies* people things and this denial must be justified. For example, people are denied goods and services when the market price and their own utility maximisation forces them to demand zero quantity. The market *culture*, and the attitude of self-centredness associated with it, has inspired a number of arguments that can be used to justify what an agent *receives* in a market allocation. But no duality exists between these arguments and those that are appropriate to justify the *denial* of a good or service to someone. For example, a utilitarian argument justifying the allocation of kidney dialysis to a wealthy banker on the basis of the fact that his salary appropriately reflects his marginal contribution to society, loses its moral punch when it is realised that such an allocation may deny it to an innocent child whose marginal product to society is still a fact of the future. Such utilitarian arguments used to justify market allocation must often be supplemented by political institutions in order to justify the denial inflicted on economic agents. For instance, the outcomes of a majority rule vote do justify not so much what the majority receives as what the minority is denied. They are denied what they want because it is the will of the *majority*.

5 THEORIES OF JUSTICE

The view of the market as a mechanism of denial leads to an examination of the various concepts of justice to see which best captures the essence of the problem. I find it no coincidence that Professor Lombardini pays most attention to Rawls's theory of justice, since that theory is most sensitive to the plight of that group in society which is denied the most. In fact, Rawlsian social welfare functions puts maximum weight on the welfare of the most denied group by maximising the welfare of that group in society that could potentially be denied the most under the veil of ignorance. It is my claim then that the intimate connection between economic and political institutions comes from the need to legitimate the set of denials defined by market outcomes. The exact type of political institutions we choose will, in turn, depend upon the theories of justice we use to justify this denial. Hence, Western democracies using utilitarian theories of justice choose majority rule because it most closely captures the essence of that welfare standard. However, utilitarian ethics are best used to justify what agents *receive* from the market and not what they are *denied*. The more a society cares about what it denies people, the more it will move away from the type of political institutions which, at present, seem so nicely tailored to support market outcomes.

6 CONCLUSIONS

In summary, I see the areas of concern to Professor Lombardini, *the culture of the market* and its relationship to our sociocultural and political institutions, to be intimately tied to the fact that the mentality of the market is a negative one and that markets are mechanisms of denial.

References

Hurwicz, L. (1973) 'The Design of Mechanisms for Resource Allocation', *American Economic Review Proceeding*, vol. 63, May, pp. 1–30.

Kirzner, I. (1973) *Competition and Entrepreneurship* (Chicago, Ill.: University of Chicago Press).

Lewis, D. (1969) *Convention: A Philosophical Study* (Cambridge Mass.: Harvard University Press).

Plott, C. and Smith, V. (1978) 'An Experimental Examination of Two Exchange Institutions', *Review of Economic Studies*, vol. 45, February, pp. 133–53.

Reiter, S. (1977) 'Information and Performance in the (New)[2] Welfare Economics', *American Economic Review Proceedings*, vol. 67, February, pp. 226–34.

Schotter, A. (1981) *The Economic Theory of Social Institutions* (Cambridge: Cambridge University Press).

Sen, A. (1979) 'The Welfare Basis of Real Incomes Comparisons: A Survey', *Journal of Economic Literature*, vol. 17, pp. 1–45.

Smith, V. (1976) 'Bidding and Auctioning Institutions: Experimental Results', in Amihudo, Y. (ed.) *Bidding and Auctioning for Procurement and Allocation* (New York: New York University Press).

Ullman-Margalit, E. (1978) *The Emergence of Norms* (New York: Oxford University Press).

Discussion

Rapporteur: Jenny Corbett
UNIVERSITY OF OXFORD

Mr Kaser remarked that we should recognise that different rules apply to an administered economy such as the USSR and one such as the USA, and that the objective of this conference was to establish what the rules governing real economies actually are. He questioned whether Schotter's distinction between type I and type II institutions was correct since it concentrated still on a broad definition of institutions. Kaser preferred to treat subsets of broad groupings. Administrations, which might extend across the whole economy as in the command economy, are a subset of organisations which might or might not be administered, and these in turn are a subset of understandings or conventions, such as the profit motive. Thus there is an implicit institutional structure which comprises sets of institutions and conventions, and the institutions may themselves impede the working of the conventions, as in the case of tax structures which interfere with the profit motive. Kaser also questioned Schotter's view of markets as a mechanism of denial rather than of provision. Such an interpretation could only be used if supply or demand were completely inelastic. Otherwise the existence of unsatisfied demand would raise prices and induce supply increases or cause consumers to buy substitute goods.

Professor Hurwicz questioned Lombardini's remark that a consideration of the USSR and China was outside the topic of the conference. If we broadened our view to include the spectrum of market economies, rather than the polar cases of pure market economies and their complete opposite, then our understanding of the reintroduction of markets in parts of the USSR and Chinese economies might be strengthened. He also commended the important contribution of the paper and commentary in raising the question of the appropriate definition of markets and of institutions. Economists have failed to give an adequate definition of institutions.

A possible first definition is of institutions in the sense of organisations or legal persons such as the Bank of England. A second definition is of institutions as sets of rules or behaviours or specifications of enforceable actions. Schotter's interpretation of the game theoretic literature as rules which define normative behaviour comes in this second category. Schotter, however, interprets the game theoretic literature as rules defining normative behaviour. In fact, the game form, or Hurwicz's 'outcome function', describes what will actually happen, that is, it represents the inescapable outcomes of actions or behaviour. With this understanding of what an outcome function or game form is, it is possible to define the *laissez-faire* market in a sense close to Schotter's type I institution, namely as the set of legal rules enforcing exchange contracts between individuals as well as the individuals' production decisions. This definition, however, excludes any state intervention and only describes a purely *laissez-faire* market. Our definition should be generalised as noted above.

Professor Dosi considered that the fundamental points raised by Lombardini's paper concerned the relationship between institutions and rationality. The question arises whether economics can explain the existence of institutions using only the traditional tools of economic models. In Dosi's view the existence of institutions cannot be derived endogenously using only the knowledge of the fundamentals of the economy, such as its technology and tastes, and a rationality principle, such as profit or utility maximisation by agents. This problem arises regardless of what definition of institutions we use. Take the definition of institutions as a set of rules for games and consider the problem of deriving the rules of a certain interaction as the outcome of a higher-level game specifically about those rules. One cannot avoid an infinite regress problem. To avoid the problem one must assume the existence of a super-rational being. If one takes the second definition of institutions, as behavioural regularities, these regularities might be taken to be approximations of rational behaviour only if the environment is stable so that agents are able to learn rational behaviour as a result of repetition of events (on this point see, for example, S. Winten in the special issue of the *Journal of Business*, 1986). Several research works, from Simon to Tversky, Kahnemann, etc., including a recent one by Dosi and Egidi (Dosi and Egidi, 1987) show that many problem-solving tasks may not entail unique rational strategies even when there is no difficulty about the computational skills required. Dosi concluded with three points on Lombardini's paper. First, institutions precede and shape the rationality of agents. That is, they inform the vision through which each agent perceives the world. Secondly, institutions in the sense of either definition evolve simultaneously with the actual market processes. An example is the parable of the fox and the sour grapes (discussed also in Elsters's *Sour Grapes*). When the fox is unable to reach the grapes and decides that it does not want them because they are sour, that is a particular case of a general characterisation of economic environments in which preferences and behaviour cannot be treated as exogenous with respect to outcomes of actual actions. Thirdly, actual behaviour is not necessarily rational in the sense that it is generated by explicit individual 'rational' computational procedures. Dosi suggested that if these points were correct then our research agenda should be first, the explicit analysis of the cognitive procedures leading specific institutions and second, the explicit representation of the process in which institutions and markets interact in a dynamic world. For both tasks, the prior assumption of rationality on the part of agents is not necessarily helpful.

Professor Malinvaud commented that the paper made the important point that it is impossible to disconnect economic systems from political systems. This is particularly apparent in considering our ability to understand the evolution of economies. It is clear that we cannot reach a full understanding if we limit our study to economic factors alone. However, these observations do not imply that the rigorous study of an economic system by itself is useless or impossible. Such a study is valuable as long as the system represents a useful simplification of the complex reality. There are two ways to proceed in the research into economic evolution if one wants to go beyond purely economic factors. One may be classified as belonging to Institutional Economics. It starts with easily identified economic factors and then extends to studies of the non-economic factors. This is the approach of Kuznets and Abramovitz. An alternative approach is the rigorous reflection on links between political and economic systems as in the papers by Lombardini and Schotter. This, in Malinvaud's view, is what the Economics of Institutions tries to do.

Professor Kay considered that Schotter's comment overstated the dichotomy between type I and type II institutions. In Japan, for example, a strict dichotomy between externally imposed rules and mutually agreed rules would seem very strange. In fact there is an evolution from behavioural regularities to rules. Competitive markets involve positive as well as negative rules (e.g., that trading will take place with all partners on the same terms and that co-operative relations are permitted between vertically related participants but not between horizontally related ones). Thus the libertarian concept of a market as involving no rules is a misunderstanding, and a misunderstanding which is widely held in the business world. Further, we have made an artificial distinction between the firm and the market. That distinction has been based on the Coasian concept of a firm as an organisation which internalises external market transactions. Recent theory of large organisations suggests we need to analyse them as if market-type transactions were taking place inside as well as outside firms.

Replying to Hurwicz and Kaser, *Professor Schotter* said it would be misleading to confuse physical institutions such as banks and stock markets with the underlying behaviour and conventions. The physical manifestations are simply manifestations of the solution to a problem. For example, banks emerged out of a need for the provision of credit in the early development of economies. His view of markets as a mechanism for denial was based on the idea that if your demand lay below the intersection point of the demand and supply curves, then you were denied the good by the market mechanism of price. He agreed with Dosi that he had assumed recurring problems in a constant world environment. He accepted that dynamic considerations would alter this observation and noted that institutions were regularly created for problems which no longer existed. In response to Kay he pointed out that once a regularity of behaviour became established, and was followed by the development of a rule, then the next generation would be taught that this was a rule. For that generation there would be no dichotomy between rules and behavioural regularities. However, that was because they were learning the proper behaviour at an equilibrium point. For generations in transitional periods there may be a greater dichotomy.

Professor Lombardini accepted that his paper lacked a clear discussion of what constituted an institution. When we talk of institutions we mean some structural features of the system which we can treat as structurally stable in our analysis. This is not to say that there will be no change in institutions, but their evolution is beyond the goal of economic analysis. He found Schotter's type I and type II institutions a useful device to analyse institutional change, but cautioned against accepting that these are two different kinds of institutions. There are no institutions which are established only through the behaviour of individuals on the one hand, and on the other there is no constraint or set of rules which can be considered to be completely externally imposed, since these kinds of institutions must take into account individual reactions. In the Soviet economy one could observe the interaction of the two types of institutions. One might begin with type I institutions but as type II institutions were introduced their existence would change the conditions for type I institutions. This makes clear that it is not just rules, but also the structure of political power, which determines institutional change. It is here that the second approach outlined by Malinvaud is necessary and further, it is clear that to understand changes in power structures or institutions we will have to take the approach suggested by Tsuru.

Reference

Dosi, G. and Egidi, M. (1987) 'Substantive and Procedural Uncertainty: An Exploration of Economic Behaviours in Complex and Changing Environment', Brighton, Science Policy Research Unit, University of Sussex, DRC Discussion Paper, prepared for the Conference on 'Programmable Automation and New Work Modes', Paris, 2–4 April 1987.

3 The Changing Pacific Rim Economy, with Special Reference to Japanese Transnational Corporations: A View from Australia

Edward L. Wheelwright and
Greg J. Crough
UNIVERSITY OF SYDNEY

1 INTRODUCTION

There is little doubt that the world economy has been undergoing a fundamental process of structural change in recent decades. This process is having a profound effect on the entire world institutional framework. The realignments of the international economic order resulting from this structural change are forcing governments, corporations, trade unions, and other organisations, as well as, of course, individuals, to come to terms with some of the most far-reaching, and potentially destabilising, forces seen this century. Many writers have warned that the world economy is entering a prolonged period of international economic disorder,[1] particularly if the trade relations between some of the major countries continue to deteriorate, and the financial and stock markets continue to experience the instability that they have in the past few years.

At the heart of these changes are a number of key developments. Quite clearly the internationalisation of banking and finance has been a major factor in the economic and financial integration of the world's major economies. This has been facilitated by the increasingly global nature of the communications industries. In combination with the developments in world transportation, particularly in the airline industry, these factors have enabled the key institutions of modern capitalism, the transnational corporations (TNCs), to undertake activities on a scale unprecedented in modern history. The size of many of these companies now rivals that of some of the world's medium-sized countries and, indeed, in a few sectors, such as communications, these companies are now undertaking activities that were once thought to be the domain only of governments.

In all sectors of economic activity, be it manufacturing, mining, agriculture or services, the international nature of these industries is now an undisputed fact. It is this internationalisation of the industrial and infrastructural base of the world's economic system which is posing major problems for the entire institutional framework of nation states. As Raymond Vernon has suggested:

> Nations are no longer very manageable as economic units. Their external economic links have become vital to their national existence; and those economic links lie beyond their control to manage, except jointly with other nations. (Vernon, 1985, p. 25)

The existing modes of behaviour of many of the nation states' institutions are being forced to confront rapid change and, indeed, for many of these institutions, to confront a particularly uncertain future. Of course, many of these issues have arisen in the past, but it is the rate of change, and the fact that many of these changes are occurring simultaneously across broad sectors of human activity, that is perhaps the single most important feature of the period in which we live.

Australia is a country which neatly encapsulates many of these developments. It is a relatively open economy, and is reliant on global markets for a significant proportion of its economic activity in key sectors, notably minerals and agriculture. Its manufacturing industries, important sectors of which are dominated by TNCs, have been severely eroded in recent decades, and the level of state protection is continuing to fall. One consequence of the weakness of world commodity markets, and the high level of imports of manufactured products, has been a severe deterioration in the country's terms of trade, together with a current account deficit larger than virtually any of the other OECD countries.

The 'domestic' financial system has been deregulated, and is now a small but integral part of the world's financial system. The heavy reliance on foreign investment in the past, and more recently on foreign borrowing, has resulted in a massive foreign debt that will be a millstone around the country's neck for many years to come.

The country's trade union movement is structured in a way that makes it increasingly unable to respond effectively to the challenges it is now facing. Trade unions in all sectors of economic activity are confronting changes that many would have thought impossible, even ten years ago.

Finally, the political system itself, and all of the institutions of the modern state, are perhaps on the brink of a fundamental realignment of forces in relation to the 'private' sector. As noted above, private companies are undertaking activities that were once thought to be the sole prerogative of governments. The movement to privatisation, in a broadly-defined sense, will have a profound effect on the role of the state in modern capitalism.

It is the intention of this paper to examine some of these changes from an Austrialian viewpoint. It will become apparent that these changes cannot be assessed without also examining the developments in a number of the larger countries in the global economy, particularly Japan and the United States. The future direction of these countries, more than any other, affects the lives of every Australian in a way that is still not yet fully understood by those same Australians.

2 THE PACIFIC RIM ECONOMY: A BRIEF HISTORICAL PERSPECTIVE

The concept of a Pacific Rim economy was discussed in a book by the present authors, *Australia: A Client State* (Crough and Wheelwright, 1982), some years ago. We are particularly pleased that a Japanese translation of the book, with a new introduction, has just been published. In discussing the evolution of the Pacific Rim economy, an historical approach is essential.

In this book we argued that successive waves of foreign investment, primarily from the United Kingdom and the United States in the post-war period, had locked Australia, and indeed many other countries in our region, into a new corporate world economic order,[2] which had essentially been created by the expansion of a few hundred TNCs from a small number of developed capitalist countries. The characteristics of this new order are the centralisation of production, technology, marketing and finance in key areas of economic activity on an unprecedented scale.

An important aspect of the new corporate order is that it internalises the market, in effect negating it for each conglomerate oligopolist.

This new kind of 'market' responds much more to the procedures developed to maximise global profits by the parent company than to traditional market signals, or the administrative fiats of national governments. Hence a new form of 'international capitalism' has been born, which was very much less susceptible to traditional market forces and to control by national governments.

By the early 1980s a particular manifestation of this new corporate order had been operating in the Pacific Rim region for almost 20 years. The Pacific Rim is an important international subsystem of the world capitalist market. It contains a number of countries which have experienced some of the highest rates of economic growth in recent decades, five of the world's largest food producers, and a large proportion of the capitalist world's production of important minerals and energy commodities.

It was clear that, until the Second World War, most TNCs, operating in the region were owned and controlled by the European colonial powers, with the notable exceptions of the Japanese operations in Taiwan and Korea, and the United States' operations in the Philippines and Hawaii. Most TNC activity in the region was in plantations, mining and merchanting, with the exception of significant US investment in petroleum. In the 1960s US investment increased rapidly, and Japan began to re-emerge as a major power.[3] International business on both sides of the Pacific began planning the development of the Pacific Rim, and the international flows of capital were undoubtedly stimulated by the business boom generated by the Indo-China war.

By the 1970s Japan had replaced the United States as the major trading partner of, and the major source of foreign investment for, many Asian countries, and began to dominate the trading patterns of South-East Asia, although the USA was still an important investor in the region. There were a number of factors that encouraged the rapid economic penetration of the region by Japanese TNCs. These included the strong desire of many of the national governments to counterpose Japanese competition to the old colonial monopolies; Japan's greater competitiveness in Asian markets due to its closer proximity, low production costs, high productivity and knowledge of local conditions; and the Japanese ability to adapt the forms and methods of economic penetration to suit particular locations. Subsequently the rapid growth of the Japanese economy and its external orientation via TNCs has contributed strongly to the 'internationalisation' of the Pacific Rim economy.

By the beginning of the 1980s the Pacific Rim economy had essentially been restructured into four broad tiers. The first tier consisted of the USA and Japan (see Table 3.1) which dominated the flows of international capital were responsible for a significant proportion of the world's technological development, and were sophisticated producers and consumers of a wide range of products and services. The second tier comprised the major middle-income countries of Canada, Australia, and New Zealand, whose major function remained the supply of primary commodities and important markets for manufactured products and services. The third tier comprised the former colonial areas of South-East Asia, and some South American countries, which supplied relatively cheap agricultural products and labour-intensive manufactured products. The fourth tier included some of the socialist countries of the region, particularly China, which was clearly being reintegrated into the world capitalist market.

Table 3.1 Net flows of foreign direct investment by major countries and regions, 1981–5 (in billions of special drawing rights)

	1981	1982	1983	1984	1985	Total
Developed countries of which:	−6.8	6.1	−0.4	−4.0	−16.3	−21.4
USA	13.5	10.4	8.7	17.1	2.6	52.3
Western Europe	−9.9	−4.3	−5.0	−13.0	−7.8	−40.0
Japan	−4.0	−3.7	−3.0	−5.8	−5.7	−22.2
Developing countries of which:	12.0	12.4	9.7	11.5	11.9	57.5
S. & S.E. Asia	4.3	3.7	3.8	4.8	4.4	21.0
Latin America	6.0	6.4	3.7	3.6	4.3	24.0

Note: The table was compiled by the UN Centre on TNCs using data from the IMF and OECD.

Source: Derived from: Commission on Transnational Corporations, Economic and Social Council, *Recent Developments related to transnational corporations and international economic relations* United Nations, New York. Reference E/C 10/1987/2) Table 1.

In short, the Pacific Rim economy had been organised into a loosely structured economic subsystem centred increasingly on Japan's growth rate, and with an extremely close interaction between the US and Japanese economies.

By the mid-1980s the Pacific Rim economy was experiencing the effects of a number of major developments in the world economy. Of particular importance were the structural imbalances resulting from the massive current account surpluses of Japan, and the even larger trade deficits of the United States. The 'trade war' that is now simmering between the USA and Japan is the most obvious manifestation of the effects of these balance-of-payments imbalances.

There is little doubt that the trade surpluses of Japan, and the resulting dramatic increase in the value of the yen, is having major impacts on the Japanese economy and society. Despite the dramatic nature of these changes, however, they are similar to the changes that have affected many of the other developed capitalist countries in recent decades. The Japanese economy and society, for so long relatively immune to the forces of international capitalism, is quite rapidly having structural change forced upon it. It will be interesting to observe the reaction of the Japanese institutional framework to these forces. As one writer has observed in the prestigious American *Foreign Affairs* journal:

> The Japanese political-economic system fosters inward-looking attitudes. It is incapable of selfless gestures, but it can react with alacrity once it is imbued with a pervasive sense of crisis. In the growing conflict with America no significant Japanese adjustments can be expected until the entire establishment has been thoroughly imbued with the idea that there is a new reality to which it must adjust, like the reality created by OPEC. (Van Wolferen, 1986, p. 302)

3 THE INTERNATIONALISATION OF JAPANESE INDUSTRY

An important feature of this structural change has been the continuing internationalisation of large sections of Japanese industry, both in manufacturing and non-manufacturing activities. Japanese TNCs are rapidly spreading their activities throughout the world, particularly into the United States, which is now the recipient of 40–50 per cent of the world flows of foreign direct investment (UN Commission on Transnational Corporations, 1987). Japan is now the world's largest individual source of foreign investment (see Tables 3.2 and 3.3) with a record outflow of US $22.3 billion in 1986, and

predictions for the current account surplus suggest that Japan is likely
to be in this position for some years to come.

Table 3.2 Outflow of foreign direct investment from Japan, 1980–5 (in
billions of $ US)

	1980	1981	1982	1983	1984	1985	Total
Developed countries	2.6	3.8	4.2	3.9	5.6	7.9	28.0
of which:							
North America	1.6	2.5	2.9	2.7	3.5	5.5	18.7
Western Europe	0.6	0.8	0.9	1.0	1.9	1.9	7.1
Developing countries	2.1	5.2	3.5	4.3	4.6	4.3	24.0
of which:							
Western hemisphere	0.6	1.1	1.5	1.9	2.3	2.6	10.0
Asia	1.2	3.4	1.4	1.9	1.7	1.5	11.1
Total	4.7	9.0	7.7	8.2	10.2	12.2	52.0

Note: Despite the differences, both tables indicate the increasing importance of Japan as a source of direct investment.
Source: As for Table 3.1. A note in the source points out that the figures in
this table differ from those in the previous one because they are
based on different sources; in this case the source is the Japanese
Ministry of International Trade and Industry in various issues of its
Japanese Multinational Facts and Figures.

Large parts of the Japanese manufacturing industry are being forced
dramatically to restructure their activities at the present time, and in
key sectors foreign investment into other countries is rising rapidly.
Some industries, such as aluminium smelting, were forced off shore a
decade ago by rising energy costs, but the recent revaluation of the yen
is now affecting the 'heartlands' of the industrial sector. Unemployment and social dislocation are rising, just as it has in the other
developed countries in the past decade, and this will pose a major
challenge to the country's political and economic stability (Drucker,
1987). The word 'de-industrialisation',[4] now commonly used in the
other countries, is being referred to more widely in Japanese economic
and political debate.[5] Japan's employment structure will probably
come to resemble more closely that of most of the other developed
countries (with the possible exception of West Germany), with a
relatively smaller manufacturing sector and a very large service sector.

Table 3.3   The world's largest industrial enterprises by country of origin, 1962–82

Country	Numbers of firms			Sales (US $ millions)			Distribution of sales (%)		
	1962	1972	1982	1962	1972	1982	1962	1972	1982
USA	292	256	213	203	475	1,402	67.6	58.5	49.2
Japan	29	65	79	11	82	346	3.6	10.0	12.1
UK	51	45	47	25	61	227	8.3	7.5	8.0
UK/Netherlands	2	2	2	10	23	107	3.4	2.8	3.7
West Germany	34	30	29	20	57	190	6.8	7.1	6.7
France	26	25	24	10	37	147	3.3	4.6	5.2
Italy	7	7	7	5	13	60	1.5	1.6	2.1
Canada	13	11	15	4	9	45	1.4	1.2	1.6
Switzerland	6	7	9	4	12	41	1.2	1.4	1.4
South Korea	—	—	9	—	—	37	—	—	1.3
Sweden	7	9	7	2	8	31	0.8	1.0	1.1
Netherlands	4	5	4	3	12	30	0.8	1.5	1.1
Others	12	21	38	3	23	188	1.3	2.8	6.5
Total	483	483	483	300	812	2,851	100.0	100.0	100.0

Note: The data for the table comes from various issues of Fortune; the sales figures have been rounded to the nearest million.
Source: Derived from John H. Dunning and Robert D. Pearce, The Word's Largest Industrial Enterprises, 1962–83 (Aldershot, UK: Gower Publishing, 1985) p. 52.

This process of internationalisation and rapid structural change is, of course, not a new process, and has been experienced by many of the major developed capitalist countries in the past. Indeed, there is now an extensive literature on the effects of the internationalisation of economic activity on both home and host countries, although only a small proportion of this literature explicitly refers to Japanese TNCs. This is partly because the development of Japanese TNC activity on a large scale is a relatively recent phenomenon (apart from the extensive international operations of the Japanese trading companies), and partly because of the obvious language differences.

This body of literature has identified many of the potential implications of the internationalisation of economic activity. The issues that have been examined include a wide range of 'development' issues, such as: the role of TNCs as sources of capital, technology, management and access to markets; the balance of payments effects; the effects on the level and structure of employment; industrial relations, and trade unions; the impacts on market structure and corporate concentration; the effect on the taxation base; the effect on the political system and sovereignty; the effect on social classes, and the impact on the environment.

Clearly the effects of the internationalisation process will differ between countries, depending on the individual circumstances of those countries. The actual impact of foreign investment depends crucially on a broad variety of factors, including the extent to which state power is used to influence the direction of economic activity, and the strength of the trade union movement. In the context of Japanese TNCs, it is an area of research that will be fruitful for many years to come.

Japanese manufacturing companies now have a significant foothold in the economies of many Pacific Rim countries, including South Korea, Thailand, Singapore, the United States and, increasingly, Australia. These investments are spread across the entire manufacturing sector, from labour-intensive industries located in the cheap-labour economies, such as China, to investments in the higher-income markets such as the United States, which are often occurring as a response to threatened protectionist measures, or because of the large size of the domestic market.[6] Japan itself is now reliant to a greater extent on manufactured imports than in the recent past, and this trend is likely to continue (Tadao Matsumoto, 1987).

It is, of course, important to remember that the processes of restructuring and internationalisation are not confined to manufacturing and primary production activities. The service sector, broadly defined, is also undergoing rapid restructuring. Indeed, recent research indicates that, with the growth of TNCs, the demarcation between services and manufacturing is quickly eroding, and both activities are being amalgamated into one corporate activity.[7] The Japanese trading corporations, with their long experience with the conglomerate form of activity, and their sophisticated international communications systems, will probably remain at the forefront of these developments for many years to come (Clairmonte, 1981, pp. 16–18) (see also Table 3.3). The internationalisation process has already strongly affected banking and finance, insurance, property and real estate, and it is now spreading into the 'professional' services, including engineering and architectural sevices, accounting and book-keeping, and legal services (Thrift, 1986a).

Japanese banks and other financial institutions are the largest in the world, and the financial resources at their command are immense by any measure. The pattern of investments and financial flows of these institutions critically influence stock markets, foreign exchange markets, and government bond markets in many countries, even in a country as large as the USA. Tokyo has rapidly developed as a major international financial centre (despite some remaining government restrictions), along with London and New York (see Table 3.4) and these three markets are surrounded by a set of smaller satellite centres, including the Pacific Rim centres of Singapore, Hong Kong and Sydney.

Japanese construction and property development companies are now taking important footholds in real estate markets around the world. Much of this activity has been concentrated in the above-mentioned financial centres, although tourism developments are an increasing source of business in countries such as Australia.

From the Australian point of view, in recent years foreign investment controls have virtually been eliminated. As a result, very large flows of foreign investment are coming into the country. Although much of this investment is short-term in nature, attracted by the very high real interest rates prevailing in Australia in recent years, and is being used to finance the current account deficit, significant flows of foreign investment and borrowed funds are being channelled by TNCs into key sectors of the economy.

One interesting impact that has been identified in a recent study by the Australian Bureau of Statistics is on the balance of payments of the host country. The study found that Japanese-controlled corporations accounted for some 10.6 per cent of Australia's total imports in 1984–5, and that these companies were far more heavily reliant on

Table 3.4 Stock Exchange statistics (US $ millions)

City	Total market value (end May 1987)	Stock trading value (December 1986)	Number of listed companies (December 1986)
Tokyo	2,837,760	1,013,260	1,499
New York	2,489,280	1,374,349	1,516
London	634,560	140,974	2,101

Notes: (i) All US dollar figures were derived from a rate of exchange of US $1 = Yen 150.
     (ii) Financial instititutions, banks and insurance companies owned over 80 per cent of total market value at the end of March 1987. These holdings belonging to 'keiretsu' business groups and are rarely traded; hence only about 20 per cent of stocks are freely tradable.
     (iii) The big four Japanese securities houses – Nomura, Daiwa, Nikko and Yamaichi, control about 70 per cent of daily share trading (Nomura and its associates control about 40 per cent), according to Ivor Ries, *Australian Financial Review*, 23 October 1987, pp. 1–2.
Source: *Australian Financial Review* (AFR), Sydney, 26 October 1987, Japan Survey, p. 17; advertisement inserted by Nomura Securities Co. Ltd, Melbourne, using data provided by Tokyo Stock Exchange, and the Nomura Research Institute.

imports from Japan than the subsidiaries of TNCs from other countries were on imports from their home countries (Australian Bureau of Statistics, 1987).

These results confirm those of an earlier study by the United States Department of Commerce, which also found that although one of the apparent objectives of Japanese foreign investment is to circumvent actual or potential barriers to imports, foreign affiliates of Japanese companies in the USA imported considerably more than they exported. It would appear that the pattern being followed by Japanese corporations in the USA is similar in many ways to that adopted by US corporations in developing countries, notably Latin America, two or so decades ago: foreign investment, comprising capital and relatively mature technology, is being used to penetrate a sizeable protected market for consumer goods.[8]

Japanese investment in Australia is particularly apparent in tourist development, property development, and some infrastructural pro-

jects (Ries, 1987; Daly, 1985). In recent decades, Japanese investment
has tended to concentrate in mining and energy projects, and in certain
sections of the manufacturing industry. Although such investment is
still occurring, notably in the automobile industry, the business and
financial service industries are now accounting for a larger proportion
of the total investment. As with the USA, the Australian government's bond issues are also strongly influenced by the inflow of
Japanese institutional investment.

Australia has been heavily reliant on the inflow of foreign
investment in the post-war period, especially from the USA and
Britain. While this has resulted in increased living standards for much
of the period, as the country enters the late 1980s, the structural
deficiencies caused by some of this foreign investment and TNC
activity are becoming painfully obvious. It remains to be seen to what
extent the increased volume of Japanese investment in Australia will
have longer-term beneficial effects.

4   DEREGULATION AND INTERNATIONALISATION

Closely associated with the internationalisation process has been the
deregulation, by the state, of significant sectors of economic activity.
Indeed, it is this very process of deregulation that has stimulated much
of the internationalisation that has been occurring, and as this
internationalisation proceeds, further deregulation is required. There
is a very interesting process operating in many areas of the economy, in
which the institutions of modern capitalism and the market interact to
produce quite intriguing results.

The extraordinary growth of international banking and finance in
the past decade has been stimulated by deregulation. In virtually every
major capitalist country banking and financial regulations have been
removed, and capital markets across the world have been integrated
together into one continuous global system.

As noted above, the Pacific Rim countries have played an important
role in this process, although the role of London should not be
underestimated. The Pacific Rim economy is now the location of some
of the world's most important financial centres, including Tokyo,
Singapore, Hong Kong, Sydney, and a number of cities in the USA.[9]
The world's largest banks are now from Japan, and it is increasingly
being recognised that their activities have a profound impact on the
entire world economy.

The process of the deregulation of Japanese financial markets has been slower than in other countries, and indeed has been a source of strong criticism of the Japanese government by the governments of some of the other developed countries. The large transnational banks and financial institutions from the USA and Western Europe have had great difficulty in penetrating the Japanese financial system and stock markets, but the pace of change in Japan is undoubtedly accelerating. The financial system in Japan has played a key role in that country's strong growth performance in the post-war period, and the changes now occurring as a consequence of deregulation and internationalisation could produce the same negative impacts being observed in some other countries.

While banking and financial corporations have manifestly benefited from the process of deregulation, other sectors of economic activity have also experienced major changes as a result of changes in state policy. The communications industry is another obvious example. Although banking and finance is the most important part of the service sector, the transnational business system is dependent on a steady flow of information to co-ordinate its widely-dispersed manufacturing, service and marketing operations.

All of the evidence suggests that the world is undergoing a revolutionary transformation of its communication, information and media industries, particularly through their concentration and central-isation in a small number of giant global conglomerates. These so-called 'cultural industries' are now said to be at the centre of the transnational corporate economy, and are dominated by companies from the USA and Britain (Wheelwright and Buckley, 1987).

As with banking and finance, the globalisation of communications has forced the breakdown of regulatory barriers, and the further these barriers are eroded, the more internationalised the industry becomes. The new technologies of communications, particularly satellites, have also had a major impact on state controls over the transmission of information and the media.

The implications of the deregulation of large sectors of economic activity are profound, but still as yet largely unresearched. Some manifestations of a decade of deregulation, in terms of increased instability in financial flows and exchange rates, major corporate restructuring and takeovers, and the boom in speculative activities, can be clearly identified. But the longer-term effects are not so readily apparent as yet. What can be said, however, is that the role and importance of the nation state is being fundamentally challenged by these developments. The more transnational corporate activity is deregulated, the more the role of the state would appear to be circumscribed.

5   THE ROLE OF THE STATE AND PRIVATISATION

Deregulation is impacting on state activity and governmental responsibility in many countries. A related development that is having perhaps a more direct effect is the move to privatisation. Privatisation is occurring in a variety of forms in different countries. These forms include the partial or complete sale of government assets to private companies, the contracting out of government services to private operators, and in some cases the provision of large-scale infrastructure by private corporations.[10]

One of the clearest results of the internationalisation of economic activity and deregulation has been the development of giant conglomerates which operate on a global scale. Many of these companies have financial and economic resources at their disposal which rival even some of the world's larger governments. These companies now have the ability to undertake activities that were once thought to be solely the domain of governments. In addition, the companies are seeking to expand their areas of activity, and have been active participants in the public debate about the appropriate areas of responsibility of governments.[11] Privatisation is thus both an economic and ideological issue.

In country after country the erosion of the role of the state can be seen, apparently irrespective of the political persuasion of the government in power at the time. In the case of Australia and New Zealand, in fact, it has been Labour Party governments which have presided over such changes in recent times. The Japanese government has recently privatised the Japan Tobacco and Salt Public Corporation, the Japanese National Railways and the Nippon Telegraph and Telephone Public Corporation. According to Professor Hiroshi Kato of Keio University: 'The major reason for these reforms is that the public corporations have become incapable of responding quickly to economic and social changes' (Hiroshi Kato, 1987, p. 6).

Another important reason for the willingness of governments to consider such policy changes relates to a concept raised more than a decade ago by an American economist, James O'Connor, that of the fiscal crisis of the State (O'Connor, 1973). This refers to the increasingly inability of the state to maintain expenditure levels, particularly on social welfare, in the face of a relative decline in taxation revenues. An important part of the undermining of the revenue base of the state has been the internationalisation of economic activity, as well as deregulation. International corporate tax planning has now reached an unprecedented degree of sophistication, and has resulted in declines, in relative terms, of corporate taxation revenues in many countries for at least a decade.

Governments have thus found it more and more difficult to fund adequately the complete range of activities and services that they have undertaken in the past. This is especially so with larger infrastructural projects.[12] When this is combined with the aggressiveness of large corporations in seeking expanded business opportunities, it is not difficult to see why privatisation has reached such prominence as a policy issue.

The combination of deregulation and privatisation is crucial for the future role of the state in modern capitalism. It is likely that in the next few years the role of state activity will contract, while that of the 'private' sector will expand. It may well be, however, given the present international economic uncertainties, that an expanded role for the state may be necessary.

6 CONCLUSION

The institutional framework of the entire world economy is undergoing a process of change, the pace and extent of which is probably unprecedented in modern history. The globalisation of production, distribution, finance, communications, and even labour, is seriously challenging the entire basis of the world's institutional framework, the nation state and all of its political, social and economic structures. Japan, as the world's largest creditor nation and most recently-arrived economic superpower, will play a crucial role in these developments, and its TNCs will probably dominate large sections of economic activity for decades.

Smaller countries such as Australia have opened themselves to the full forces of international capitalism, in the hope that they too can benefit from the developments now occurring in this system. The effects of a greater involvement in the global economy are only now beginning to be felt in Australia, and these effects are profound in their implications. Market forces have generally worked to benefit the strong, and this is no more apparent than in the workings of the international economic system. It is to be hoped that the institutional framework of Australia, be it the trade unions, or the corporate sector, or the state, can be modified and strengthened to cope with the forces now at work in the world economy.

Notes

1. See, for example, Thrift (1986b).
2. The term 'new corporate world economic order' should not be confused with the demands for a New International Economic Order which have been on the international agenda for a number of years, although some of the issues are closely interrelated. For a critical discussion of the NIEO, see Addo (1984).
3. An excellent overview of foreign investment and transnational corporate activity in this period is to be found in Utrecht (1978).
4. There is a very extensive body of literature on de-industrialisation and the internationalisation of economic activity, including Bluestone and Harrison (1982), The Business Week Team (1982), and Frobel *et al.* (1980).
5. As an example, see Yukuo Ajima (1986).
6. For a discussion of some of the impacts on employment and trade unions in Japan, see Kenmochi Kazumi (1987) pp. 30–33.
7. See, for example, Clairmonte and Cavanagh (1984).
8. The 1983 United States study is summarised in United Nations Commission on Transnational Corporations (1987).
9. For a detailed discussion of banking and finance in the Pacific Rim region, see Daly and Logan (forthcoming).
10. There is now an extensive literature on privatisation in a variety of countries (see, for example, Domberger and Piggott, 1986, pp. 145–62; Dunleavy, 1986, pp. 13–34; Hensher, 1986, pp. 147–74).
11. Some writers have, in fact, referred to this involvement in public debate in the context of an 'ideological management industry' (see, for example, Carey, 1987, pp. 156–79).
12. In Australia, for example, large private companies are involved in the construction of a second Sydney Harbour crossing, including the Japanese construction company Kumagai-Gumi; and are involved in planning a major new rail link between Sydney and Melbourne.

References

Addo, H. (ed.) (1984) *Transforming the World Economy?* (London: Hodder & Stoughton).

Australian Bureau of Statistics (1987) *Foreign Control of Imports into Australia, 1984–85* (Canberra: Australian Bureau of Statistics).

Bluestone, B. and Harrison, B. (1982) *The Deindustrialisation of America* (New York: Basic Books).

The Business Week Team (1982) *The Reindustrialization of America* (New York: McGraw Hill).

Carey, A. (1987) 'The Ideological Management Industry', in Wheelwright, E. L. and Buckley, K. (eds) *Communications and the Media in Australia* (Sydney: Allen & Unwin).

Clairmonte, F. F. (1981) 'The Expansion of Japanese Sogo Shoshas', *Raw Materials Report*, vol. 1, no. 1.

Clairmonte, F. F. and Cavanagh, J. (1984) *Transnational Corporations and Services: The Final Frontier* (Sydney: Transnational Corporations Research Project).

Crough, G. J. and Wheelwright, E. L. (1982) *Australia: A Client State* (Ringwood: Penguin).

Daly, M. T. (1985) *Australian Urban Development and International Finance Capital* (Sydney: Transnational Corporations Research Project).

Daly, M. T. and Logan, M. I. (forthcoming) *The Brittle Rim* (Ringwood: Penguin).

Domberger, S. and Piggott, J. (1986) 'Privatization Policies and Public Enterprise: A Survey', *The Economic Record*, vol. 62, no. 2, June.

Drucker, P. (1987) 'Japan's Choices', *Foreign Affairs*, Summer.

Dunleavy, P. (1986) 'Explaining the Privatization Boom: Public Choice versus Radical Approaches', *Public Administration*, vol. 64, no. 1, Spring.

Frobel, F., Heinrichs, J. and Kreye, O. (1980) *The New International Division of Labour* (Cambridge: Cambridge University Press).

Hensher, D. A. (1986) 'Privatisation: An Interpretative Essay', *Australian Economic Papers*, vol. 25, no. 4, December.

Hiroshi Kato (1987) 'For sale! The Phones, the Trains, Salt and Tobacco', *Look Japan*, March.

Kenmochi Kazumi (1987) 'The Hollowing: A New Threat to Japan's Super-economy', *AMPO: Japan-Asia Quarterly Review*, vol. 19, no. 4.

O'Connor, J. (1973) *The Fiscal Crisis of the State* (New York: St Martin's Press).

Ries, I. (1987) 'Tokyo's Property Lion puts its Faith in Australia', *Business Review Weekly*, 19 June.

Tadao Matsumoto (1987) 'In the Wake of the Rising Yen', *South*, July.

Thrift, N. (1986a) 'The Internationalisation of Producer Services and the Integration of the Pacific Basin Property Markets', in Taylor, M. and Thrift, N. (eds) *Multinationals and the Restructuring of the World Economy* (Kent: Croom Helm).

Thrift, N. (1986b) 'The Geography of International Disorder', in Johnston, R. J. and Taylor, P. J. (eds), *A World in Crisis?* (Oxford: Blackwell).

United Nations Commission on Transnational Corporations (1987) *Recent Developments Related to Transnational Corporations and International Economic Relations*, UN Document E/C 10/1987/2, (New York: United Nations).

Utrecht, E. (1978) (ed.) *Transnational Corporations in South East Asia and the Pacific* (Sydney: Transnational Corporations Research Project) vol. 1.

Van Wolferen, K. G. (1986) 'The Japan Problem', *Foreign Affairs*, Winter.

Vernon, R. (1985) *Exploring the Global Economy* (Harvard: Centre for International Affairs).

Wheelwright, E. L. and Buckley, K. (1987) (eds) *Communications and the Media in Australia* (Sydney: Allen & Unwin).

Yukuo Ajima (1986) 'Electronics Makers Move Offshore', *Economic Eye*, December.

Comment

Moriaki Tsuchiya
UNIVERSITY OF TOKYO

There are three important messages in this paper – important not only for the future of the world economy but also for economic theory.

The main message of the authors is to point out the ongoing process of fundamental change in the institutional structure of the world economy, and one of the most important factors in this structural change is the rapidly-growing Japanese foreign investment. Australia is called a 'client state', a term which is the title of a book by the authors. Australia has received successive waves of foreign investment, mainly from the United Kingdom and the United States. These inflows of foreign investment have resulted in increased living standards for Australians in the post-war period. However, it would be questionable if the rapid growth of Japanese investment in Australia would have long-term beneficial effects. The Japanese are also very much concerned with the outcomes of today's crazy foreign investment on the Japanese economy, and there is much more to discuss about this problem.

The second message is about the power and role of the nation state and the nature of the corporation. To the authors, some of the transnational corporations have enormous power. These companies now have the ability to undertake activities that were once thought to be the domain solely of public governments. The authors pose the problem of the balance of power between transnational corporations and nation states.

Thirdly, a very important theoretical question is raised. Today in many countries deregulation and privatisation are being promoted. More portions of the economy are entering the market economy. The authors conclude that market forces have generally worked to benefit the strong, and this is most apparent in the workings of the international economic system. What do the authors mean by the strong? They seem to mean the existing giant transnational corporations of Japan, USA and the UK. To us Japanese, the trend of deregulation and privatisation seems to be beneficial to small and medium-sized companies much more than to the existing and bureaucratic giant companies.

The authors discuss these problems from an Australian viewpoint; I would like to make comments from a Japanese viewpoint.

To return to the first problem; we Japanese are also very much concerned about the outcomes of the rapid growth of foreign investment. If more appreciation of the yen is inevitable in the coming years, Japanese foreign investment will still be growing. Of course this is very risky for the balanced growth of the world economy. It is also very risky for Japanese investors because the real value of the investment would be depreciated by the appreciation of the yen. Japanese investors would like to invest their money in domestic projects in Japan. Thus it is one of the urgent tasks of the Japanese government to stimulate domestic demands by some fiscal policy or other means. To the Japanese investor, Australia looks like a dream country with plenty of opportunities for investment. It would not be bad for Australian people to welcome Japanese investment. When the authors mentioned the four broad tiers of the Pacific Rim economy at the beginning of the 1980s, they did not refer to the new waves of new industrialised countries like Korea, Taiwan, Hong Kong, Singapore and others. They are no longer the former colonial countries which supply relatively cheap agricultural products and labour-intensive manufactured products. They are now formidable competitors in some aspects, as well as reliable partners in other aspects, to Japanese manufacturing industries. Newly-industrialised countries could succeed in taking advantage of foreign investment from USA and Japan to increase their living standard. I hope the Japanese investment in Australia will have beneficial effects in increasing the living standard of Australian people.

The second message I mentioned was the balance of power between large transnational corporations and the nation state. It is sometimes true that the annual sales of some big corporations surpass the budget of some nation states. It is also true that some corporations are very powerful in terms of technology and entrepreneurial vitality. However, the power of private corporations is very fragile compared with that of the nation state. If a corporation could not be managed rationally, or could not cope with its own strategical mistakes, it would easily lose power and fade away. We have seen instances of big corporations which vanished gradually or suddenly. The nation state could never vanish if people could change the regime of the government. Japanese governments sometimes force top officials of big corporations to resign.

One aspect of the nature of the Japanese corporation is that, though it is private, we cannot find the real owner. Ownership of big corporations is widely dispersed; the majority of shares are owned by other multiple corporations, which are owned by other corporations. Private individual shareholders own less than one-third of the capital of all the corporations listed at the Tokyo Stock Exchange. Of course, many foreign institutional and individual shareholders come to the Tokyo market. In the future we shall not be able to identify Japanese corporations by the criteria of ownership. Transnational corporations have multinational employees, and top management teams. How can we identify Japanese corporations in the future? Probably by the official language of the company but the Japanese language could be used as just one of the official languages in the company board.

The most important message in this paper is about the economic effect of deregulation and privatisation on the market economy. The authors argue that deregulation and privatisation would promote more competition in the market place, and I agree. In the USA and even in Japan, deregulation stimulated more dynamic business activities and competition. Deregulation is giving many small and medium-sized businesses new opportunities to enter markets which were formerly monopolised by a few big corporations. Of course, further deregulation is still to be promoted in Japan. Japan especially should open the door to more and more foreign agricultural and industrial products. If smaller countries such as Australia have opened themselves to the full force of international capitalism, why could not Japan open its domestic market to foreign products? Any regulations and barriers to foreign capital and products should be eliminated. We Japanese expect that this kind of deregulation would promote beneficial competition in the domestic market.

However, the authors proceed to the argument that deregulation and privatisation in general would be beneficial to the strong in the market place. As far as the domestic Japanese market is concerned, we cannot agree. But they may be right when they are talking about the market of a client state, Australia. As they point out, contemporary economists should carry out more research into the economic effects of deregulation and privatisation, including theoretical models and empirical findings in the various kinds of market.

Discussion

Rapporteur: Jenny Corbett
UNIVERSITY OF OXFORD

Professor Noguchi commented that half the Japanese foreign investment is carried out by small- and medium-sized enterprises and therefore the impact of these multinational corporations cannot be regarded as similar to the case of investment carried out by large corporations. He also pointed out that if foreign investment involves the introduction of adequate new technologies this may be a positive factor in regional development in the recipient country.

Professor Imai noted that there was a missing link between the major theme of the conference and this paper. The paper emphasised internal global management of large multinational corporations, but more attention should be given to network operations across the boundary of firms. Interorganisational networks may be thought of in concrete terms such as joint ventures and technology tie-ups, or in abstract terms. In the abstract, networks are institutions which lie somewhere between pure markets and hierarchical organisations. Imai suggested that the network in this sense is an emerging new flexible institution in a dynamic environment, and that information is of crucial importance to them.

Professor Pajestka disagreed with Imai's interpretation. He felt that the paper did deal with the subject of the conference. Transnational corporations are a 'new economic animal' and we must consider the question of relations between them and the state where they originate and where they operate. If we do not address this question we weaken our claim to be addressing problems of the future.

In reply *Mr Crough* accepted the point that much of Japanese foreign investment is carried out by small firms, but pointed out that their paper concentrated explicitly on large transnational corporations. With respect to deregulation it is true that the initial effect is to increase the opportunities for small firms in the short term but, in the long-term, experience suggests that effects are mixed. It is often the case that in the longer term concentration is increased. He also agreed that networking and joint venture arrangements were very important and that this was an area which needed further study. In considering joint ventures the question of the role of government arises. In Australia regulations on joint ventures with foreign companies were enacted to protect local business and to ensure a share of technology

82

and skills. These regulations are now eroding in Australia and in Canada, and many countries are finding that where joint ventures were common in the past some areas are passing completely under foreign control. Finally he noted that in a similar way to the internationalisation of capitalism in the industrial sectors we are now seeing a spreading into all sectors of the economy. This is affecting the world's institutional framework. For example, whereas the GATT was originally about manufactured goods trade, it is now having to deal with the service sector, and is finding this very difficult.

Professor Wheelwright noted that the English word 'client' is hard to translate. The term is meant to imply dependency even if the client is a rich country. Dependency implies a loss of sovereignty so that the discussion concentrates on the link between economic power and the loss of political sovereignty, an area neglected by both economics and political science in the past. It used to be argued that it made no difference to political power if transnational corporations controlled large sectors of the economy. Now we are beginning to study particular cases and find that the results don't always depend on the size of the state, but may depend on the state's own experience with its own firms. South Korea, for example, has been able to shape transnational corporations to its own needs. Finally, we find that most transnational corporations are owned in, or controlled by, the largest and richest countries. This links to Tsuru's point about institutional economics. The phenomenon was described in Dickinson's 1930s book, *Institutional Revenue*. We now see that institutions are getting their institutional revenue from technology rents.

Part II

Economic Theories and Institutions: Economic System, Planning and Transition

4 Mechanisms and Institutions

Leonid Hurwicz*
UNIVERSITY OF MINNESOTA

1 INTRODUCTION

Economists have long been interested in policies, systems, and institutions. But although normative issues arise in all three contexts, only narrowly-defined policy issues were considered open to formalised analysis. The famous battles between 'institutionalists' and 'classicists' provide some of the evidence. Atkins *et al.* (1931), in their *Economic Behavior, An Institutional Approach* (p. iii), make a point of the fact that 'no attention is given to hypothetical supply and demand curves...' and 'no treatment... given... to the factors of production – land, labor, capital, enterprise, as such – to subjective utility, to normal price, to marginal buyers and sellers....'

As for the other camp, it is enough to note that even the recent generation of textbooks of microeconomics include very little of what would qualify as institutional analysis.

A natural terrain for synthesis is the area known as 'comparative economic systems', and indeed steps in this direction are taken in such works as those by Neuberger and Duffy (1976), significantly sub-titled 'A Decision-Making Approach', as well as that by Holesovsky (1977), whose sub-title 'Analysis and Comparison' also indicates a belief in harmonising the study of systems which is institutional in nature with the insights provided by modern theory.

But what does theory have to offer? In its classical (or neoclassical) version, it either abstracts from the institutional aspects (as, for instance, in the formulation of necessary conditions for Pareto optimality), or it is almost completely focused on market-type economies, whether perfectly competitive or exhibiting various types of imperfections such as oligopoly, monopoly, or price discrimination. The theories associated with the names of Hotelling, Lange and Lerner, despite the socialist label, are still those of certain types of market economies (at least outside of the capital investment sector), although – as in the case of marginal cost pricing under increasing returns – not necessarily requiring profit maximisation.

There do exist analytical models for particular non-market economies, e.g., to study Soviet type or worker-managed systems, but these still do not provide a framework for studying the phenomena regarded as central by institutionalists. To create such a framework one must develop a model of sufficient generality to encompass a broad spectrum of institutional structures and economic arrangements, including markets (both perfect and imperfect), but also various types of centralised or command economies. If one becomes ambitious, one may also wish to encompass feudal and even primitive economies.

2 MECHANISMS

Efforts in this direction have been made in recent years in what is sometimes called the theory of mechanisms, with a normative branch known as the theory of implementation or realisation. The concept of a mechanism is intended to be broad enough to cover markets, command economies, etc., as special cases. It cannot require that there be prices (since the system might be based on direct quantity allocations and rationing) but it must have room for prices. Since there may not be prices, it cannot assume that profits constitute a well-defined notion. But even if prices exist and profits are meaningful, it need not be the case that profits are being maximised: prices might be required to equal marginal costs, or might be formed on the basis of criteria unrelated to cost or demand.

Of course, some of these theoretically formulated mechanisms may lead to gross inefficiencies and others may be unrealistic for political or other reasons. But inefficiency or other undesirable characteristics are not objectionable in a framework for positive (descriptive) theory. On the other hand, important aspects of reality must be built into the model to make it interesting.

Two aspects of reality have been given particular emphasis in existing work, informational and incentival. Historically, the informational aspect became the earlier focus of attention, due to Mises-Hayek objections raised against the notion of centralised planning, and the Lange-Lerner response to these objections. The essence of the response was to accept as desirable the informational properties of the perfectly competitive market process, but to separate them from institutional arrangements associated with private ownership of the firm and the incentive of profit maximisation. The incentive was replaced by rules to be followed by the enterprise manager: to treat prices parametrically, to minimise costs of the output produced, and to equate prices with marginal costs. (In the absence of increasing returns this amounts to profit maximisation under perfect competition.) Furthermore, prices were to be adjusted so as to equate supply and demand.

It is not necessary to have a formalised model of information processing to see that the informational requirements of a Lange-Lerner ('market') socialist economy are the same as those of the competitive (Walrasian) market economy familiar from microeconomics textbooks, especially in the auctioneer version. (For the special case of a linear economy, an explicit model was constructd by Koopmans, 1951, pp. 93–5.) If one were to compare an 'ideal' Lange-Lerner economy (i.e., one in which rules are assumed to be obeyed), it has point of superiority over what we may call a 'natural' market. By the latter we mean one in which small numbers or increasing returns result in monopolistic or oligopolistic behaviour. Such behaviour will, in general, result in non-optimal resource allocation while, in the absence of externalities, indivisibilities and satiation, the equilibria in 'ideal' Lange-Lerner economies will be Pareto-optimal. But, of course, to compare a 'natural' market economy with an 'ideal' Lange-Lerner economy is not appropriate. When incentives are taken into account, the issue becomes more complex. To undertake a comparative analysis of different systems one must consider (in addition to other dimensions of the problem) both their informational and incentive properties.

Initially, general models of mechanisms were constructed with the objective of studying exclusively their informational properties. To make this possible, the behaviour of the economic agents was postulated to follow specified rules, without a commitment as to whether such behaviour was motivated by 'natural incentives', by tradition, external authority, or anything else. In such a setting it is possible to compare various mechanisms with respect to the degree of informational decentralisation, the required amount of communication between agents (typically measured by the dimension of the message space), and the complexity of calculations required of agents (see Hurwicz, 1960, 1972b; Mount and Reiter, 1974). In practice, most of the research work has been centred on the static properties of mechanisms under consideration. That is, the informational requirements studied are those of a 'verification scenario', in which agents are presented with specific components of an equilibrium solution and each agent's task is to carry out calculations to determine whether the proposed solution satisfies certain conditions verifiable in terms of that agent's individual characteristics. Although this approach is in line with much traditional economic analysis (e.g., comparative statics typically deals only with equilibrium conditions), it is clearly unrealistic, for at least two reasons.

For one thing, equilibrium conditions and other relations can be verified only with limited accuracy, and the same is true of specifying proposed equilibrium values of the various economic variables. For this and other reasons one must expect that any mechanism will at best give only approximate answers. Hence alternative mechanisms must be compared in terms of their likely degree of error (see Hurwicz and Marschak, 1985, for a study of error and approximation aspects of mechanisms).

What is at least as important, the verification scenario – although methodologically a natural early step (and one implicit in much contemporary economic analysis) – is far from a plausible representation of economic processes. These processes are dynamic and can more naturally be modelled by iterative procedures, say systems of difference equations, and the immediate question is whether or how fast their solutions converge to the equilibrium values. (We are assuming that the systems do possess equilibria. In modelling phenomena such as inflation this cannot be taken for granted.)

Now whether there is convergence at all is the well-known problem of stability of solutions. We know that certain classical dynamic versions of the competitive process (the Walrasian *tâtonnement*) is stable for some environments but not for all. This raises the question whether there exist alternative mechanisms (satisfying decentralisation or other desired requirements) that converge for a sufficiently rich class of environments. This has been studied by Reiter (1979), Mount and Reiter (1983), and Jordan (1986, 1987), mostly with negative conclusions. However, such results may depend on the class of mechanisms under consideration so that broadening the class might lead to more optimistic results.

In practice, convergence may not be the most interesting dynamic property. Typically there is a limit, either on the number of iterations, or on the time period the iterative process is permitted to last. As a rule, even a convergent process will not have reached or perhaps even got close to the equilibrium values. Hence again one must be reconciled to incorrect, and at best approximate, outcomes. Systems may have to be judged on their performance under such time limits. It is conceivable that a mechanism with better equilibrium values would turn out to be worse under stringent time limits. (This is often an argument in favour of quantitative controls and rationing under war or other emergency conditions. An alternative argument is based on uncertainty concerning relevant parameters, see Weitzman, 1974.)

A number of other purely informational properties of mechanisms have been subject to recent studies. Of particular interest are those concerned with the hierarchical properties of decision structures. (Note that here, since incentive aspects are being ignored, decisions are not distinguishable from verifications or calculations – see Marschak and Reichelstein, 1986; Sah and Stiglitz, 1985; as well as Williamson, 1967.) Some of these models deal with the relationship between the probability of errors of judgement inherent in decisions and the hierarchical nature of the organisational structure (Sah and Stiglitz, 1984.) Others focus on the relationship between the structure and the managerial abilities (Geanakoplos and Milgrom, 1985).

Once we have formulated a general model of the informational aspects of the economic process, we note two types of new knowledge that this generates. On the one hand the model has in it room, not only for previously known special cases (e.g., perfect competition), but also an infinity (indeed a continuum) of mechanisms that have never previously been considered. Hence there is a broadening of the investigator's horizons. On the other hand, because the restrictions to which the model is subject are rigorously formulated, one also discovers what is not possible given those restrictions. (The restrictions may be either informational, e.g., informational decentralisation, or mathematical in nature, e.g., smoothness of the various functions in the model.) A number of important findings have been obtained. These mainly involve the dimension of the message space. On the one hand it has been shown (Mount and Reiter, 1974; Osana, 1978; Hurwicz, 1977) that Pareto optimality cannot be realised with message space of dimension lower than that used by a version of the Walrasian process. On the other, when convexity is absent (e.g., in the presence of increasing returns) no finite-dimensional message space will do (Calsamiglia, 1977; Hurwicz, 1977). Similarly, intertemporal welfare is not susceptible of non-*tâtonnement* realisation with a finite number of verifications or with a finite-dimensional message space (Hurwicz and Weinberger, 1987).

So far we have been discussing models of message exchanges followed by actions based on equilibrium (or terminal) messages. Here the term 'mechanism' seems highly appropriate, since given the basic elements of the model (the message space, the response functions, and the outcome function) everything proceeds automatically and could in fact be programmed into computers. It should be noted that much more general mechanisms could be considered, with actions taking place without waiting for equilibrium (or for the terminal message). The model can further be enriched by features pertaining to commitments, contracts, and enforcement (see Hurwicz, 1987). The essential feature in this class of models is that all rules are assumed to be obeyed truthfully and completely.

3   GAME-THEORETIC MODELS

When rules prescribed by the model are in fact to be put in effect by individuals, groups, or organisations, this can no longer be taken for granted. It may be to the participants' advantage to misrepresent their characteristics or in other ways to violate the rules prescribed by the model. Such possibility was pointed out by Samuelson (1954, 1955) in his analysis of the Lindahl solution for allocating public goods in economies with public goods. Similarly, in a Lange-Lerner type economy it may be to the manager's advantage to misrepresent marginal costs or other parameters. These considerations have led to the introduction of game-theoretic aspects into economic models. Initially this approach was formulated in the context of direct revelation mechanisms, i.e., those where the participant is supposed to provide information concerning his/her characteristic, and the outcome function then computes the appropriate actions (e.g., allocations). In a pure message exchange model it is taken for granted that the information is provided truthfully. But in a game-theoretic model the information to be provided becomes a strategy variable, with its true value only one possibility.

In the standard game-theoretic model there are only two elements to be supplied by the designer: the strategy domains for each of the participants ('players') and the outcome function (often called 'game form') prescribing the element of the outcome space (action space, allocation space) given the respective strategy choices made by the players. Although the outcome function together with the strategy domains are sometimes called 'rules of the game', they differ from the rules of the mechanism as embodied in the response functions of the message exchange process, since the latter prescribe behaviour, while in the game-theoretic model the rules of the game only specifiy possible behaviours (strategy domain) and its consequences (outcome function). Thus rules of the game correspond to the message space and outcome function of a (message exchange) mechanism. But the response functions are replaced by relations determined by the preferences of the players.

The game-theoretic approach has made it possible to explore significant issues and has yielded interesting results. Its models no longer deserve the name of mechanisms (although this term is frequently applied to them) because the strategy aspects carry them beyond the purely automatic and because they do take incentives into account. For reasons to be given in a moment, they do not yet – at least in their standard form – qualify as models of institutions. But their accomplishments are already of considerable value. Motivated particularly by the classic problem of efficient resource allocation of public goods, and influenced by the Lindahl-Samuelson formulation, the focus was on designing a direct revelation game where truthful Nash (and hence dominance) equilibria would yield Pareto-optimal allocations. A number of results (including the early one due to Ledyard and Roberts, 1974, as well as the very general one of Walker, 1980) showed this to be impossible. Groves and Ledyard (1977) opened new vistas by abandoning the restriction to direct revelation, admitting arbitrary strategy spaces and settling for Nash equilibria rather than requiring dominance. They then constructed an outcome function yielding Pareto-optimal Nash equilibrium outcomes. However, the nature of these equilibria raised questions of their domain of existence, and the outcomes turned out not always to be individually rational.

Such findings led to new issues. Hurwicz and Schmeidler (1978) asked: Under what conditions do there exist Nash equilibria, with all of them being Pareto optimal? Hurwicz (1979) showed that outcome functions guaranteeing Pareto optimality and individual rationality have equilibrium sets containing all Lindahl (i.e. Walrasian) allocations. But the tradition of focusing on Pareto optimality and individual rationality as pre-eminent social goals was excessively narrow. A new broader concept entered the analysis, that of a mechanism's performance function (or, more generally, correspondence – see Reiter, 1977). Given a mechanism the performance function relates the outcomes to economic environments. But if the performance function is taken as given (i.e., regarded as specifying the social goals), then it is natural to ask whether it is possible to design a mechanism yielding the outcomes prescribed by that function. If so, the mechanism is said to 'realise' the given performance (goal) function. (We use here the term 'realise' rather than 'implement' and reserve the latter term for game-theoretic contexts.) There will always exist (message-exchange, not game-theoretic) mechanisms realising a given goal function, namely direct revelation mechanisms. But they may require huge message spaces or response and outcome functions so complex as to be of limited practical interest. A central problem is that of realising a given goal function with minimal message space or other informational requirements.

When the game-theoretic approach is taken we again want to get away from focusing exclusively on Pareto optimality and individual rationality. Hence the question is (as in the just-discussed case of message exchange mechanisms) whether and how to design rules that would yield equilibrium outcomes in accord with a given goal function (or, more generally, correspondence – often called social choice correspondence). An outcome function (together with strategy domains) that does this is said to implement the goal function. Maskin (1977) obtained a necessary condition ('monotonicity') for a goal to be (Nash equilibrium) implementable, and also (stricter) sufficient conditions ('monotonicity' and absence of 'veto power' for groups with at least three participants).

3.1 Implementability

Results such as those of Maskin (1977) and Hurwicz (1979) show the limitations of Nash implementability. These are not as forbidding as those of dominance (truth-telling) implementability but very serious nevertheless. Actually, the situation is even worse because the constructive proofs of implementability often involve outcome functions using huge (in fact infinite-dimensional) strategy domains which must also function as message spaces. But even if one were to ignore these informational difficulties, the limitations on which goals are implementable pose a problem. Should one interpret them as real constraints on social planning and intervention or rather as weaknesses of our models, in particular of the Nash equilibrium concept? My own view is that the assumption as to an appropriate equilibrium concept is empirical in nature, i.e., that alternative behavioural types might opt for Nash, or maximin, or other strategy choices, and so generate corresponding equilibria.

Whether or not one accepts this point of view, it is of interest to investigate how alternative game-theoretic equilibrium concepts affect the implementability of various goals. Important contributions in this area have recently been made by Moore and Repullo (1987) and by Palfrey and Srivastava (1986, 1987). By restricting the class of admissible Nash equilibria to subgame perfect or undominated respectively, as well as by other modifications, they find the implementability conditions to be greatly relaxed.

As mentioned earlier, the outcome functions used to prove the various implementability results use very large message spaces. An individual message typically contains a profile (i.e., an n-tuple) of preferences plus additional components such as integers or real numbers. Moreover, when individual feasibility is involved, the message may also contain a profile of initial endowments or, more generally, production possibility sets (see Hurwicz, Maskin, and Postlewaite, 1980). Such messages would exceed the capacity of even the most powerful and advanced information processing systems – by contrast with the finite-dimensional ones (with price and quantity vectors) used to implement the Walrasian or Lindahl correspondences. From the work of Reichelstein (1982) and of Reichelstein and Reiter (1985) we know something about minimal space requirements for implementing the Walrasian correspondence, but here the choice is between different finite-dimensional spaces. Little is known as to the extent that one can dispense with the infinite-dimensional spaces in implementing other classes of goals. Should it turn out that exact implementation does necessitate the use of infinite-dimensional strategy spaces, realism would require that approximate or second-best solutions be considered.

The preceding description of strategy spaces of the profile type makes particularly clear that outcome functions used in implementation theory are very remote from what one could expect to observe or to advocate as an alternative to existing arrangements. Whatever the precise definition of 'institution,' these models do not provide representations of plausible institutions for resource allocation. But this is not only due to the excessive size of strategy spaces. The issue of modelling institutions would arise even if we confined ourselves to implementing (say) the Walrasian performance correspondence, with the message space consisting primarily of price and quantity vectors.

To see that this is so, it is enough to recognise some of the basic institutions that in practice make markets possible – the main one perhaps an enforcement system and the principles governing enforceability. One may start with the most elementary and ancient aspects, such as those concerning weights, measures, genuiness, and quality of goods traded, and end with highly-sophisticated contractual arrangements. Not to be ignored are the provisions against theft and robbery and the protection of personal safety. As the economies develop we encounter fairs and other (physical) market arrangements, culminating in modern commodity and stock exchanges and perhaps even electronic markets not having any physical location. How do we model these without abandoning the game-theoretic framework?

3.2 Enforcement

To begin with, it seems necessary to go beyond the normal form of the game and base the model on games in extensive form, so that the sequence of 'moves' can be taken into account. (This may encourage the adoption of more specialised equilibrium concepts as subgame perfect.) As for the enforcement aspects, there are two approaches open. The more ambitious, and in principle perhaps the only correct one, is to include the agents of the enforcement system (say, judges, police, etc.) among the 'players', and include the consequences of their actions in the outcome functions. (These would have to take into account the commitment of those agents to their duties, their honesty, and other behavioural characteristics.) Then the strategies of the other participants would involve the weighing of risks resulting from violations of the law as against the consequences of obeying it, and so on. The game-theoretic equilibrium solution (say Nash) would then predict the actual behaviour likely to be observed. It is important to note that – even though we often refer to outcome functions as the 'rules of the game' – it would be incorrect here to identify the outcome functions with law (whether statutory or customary). The outcome function must specify the actual consequences of strategic choices, not the 'official' rules. But this means that either the outcome functions merely reflect the facts of physics, psychology, traditions, customs, ethics and religion, or they also include those aspects of an enforcement system that can be regarded as reliable. But then it is natural to consider an alternative method of treating the enforcement aspect of an economic model and (admittedly at the cost of realism) simplify the problem by postulating the enforcement of the relevant rules to be either completely reliable or totally impossible. In Hurwicz

(1987) this second approach was the one adopted. (Here the enforcement agents to not appear as players.)

Obviously, in the second approach we have not attempted to model the institutions of the enforcement system. But suppose we pursue the more ambitious first approach, with enforcement agents as players. What aspect of our model can be said to represent the institution of an enforcement system? Since this is a difficult question, let us move on to a much simpler example that may help clarify the notion of representing institutions in the models under consideration. Let us look at a class of agricultural systems studied in Stiglitz (1974) and concentrate on the outcome function specifying the reward of the workers. The formula is linear and can be written as $y = aq + b$, where y is the reward and q the worker's output. The symbols a and b represent parameters; the parameter a is restricted to values between zero and one. It is seen immediately that if b equals zero while a is between zero and one, the worker is a sharecropper (and a represents the worker's share). If a is zero and b is positive, the worker is a wage-earner (and a is the wage per unit of output – and the piece rate system prevails). If a equals one and b is negative, the worker is a renter, keeping the whole output but paying to the landowner the rent b.

4 INSTITUTIONS – EXAMPLES, CONCEPT, MODELLING

Now it seems natural to think of crop-sharing, working for wages, and renting as three alternative institutional arrangements. (Of course, one could think of still others.) Let us think of the general linear formula $y = aq + b$ as a universe of institutional arrangements; it is simply a family of outcome functions (geometrically, the (a,b) parameter plane). As seen above, the institution of sharecropping does not specify a specific point in the parameter space (a,b) but only a subset, that of all points with $b = 0$. The institution of renting is defined by a subset of the (a,b) plane, namely of all points with $a = 1$ and b negative. Wage-earning corresponds to the part of the plane with $a = 0$ and b positive. Thus geometrically each institutional arrangement is defined by a subset of the parameter space which, in turn, represents a subfamily of outcome functions. This suggests formalising the concept of an institution within a game-theoretic model as a subset of *a priori* admissible outcome functions.[1] (Here we interpret outcome functions in a broad sense, including the specification of possible moves and hence strategy[2] domains.) It should be noted, however, that this notion of an institution at most represents an institutional arrangement but not what is usually meant by an institution as an organisation (e.g., the state, a firm, a family). (For a discussion of this distinction, see Ruttan, 1984. Ruttan follows the lead of Commons, 1924, 1934, 1951, and Knight, 1952, in defining an institution broadly enough to encompass both concepts.)

It may also be printed out that our definition of an institutional arrangement does not prejudge its genesis – whether it has arisen as a custom or through legislative action, and it does not require universality; different arrangements (say sharecropping and renting) may coexist in one economy. Although I cannot justify this in detail, let me just say that an enforcement system model with agents as players can be subsumed under this definition of a institutional arrangement. (This is not in contradiction to Schotter's 1981, p. 11, point that institutions may require policing, i.e., enforcement, whether internal or external; perhaps Schotter's notion of policing is included in our concept of an outcome function.)

Another application, and a very basic one, is the institution (or, in our language, institutional arrangement) of property or ownership. It is hardly necessary to note that differences in the patterns of ownership (especially of land and capital) are typically regarded as the major distinguishing characteristics of alternative economic systems, depending on whether individuals, groups, or the state, have a monopoly on owning resources, or whether a mixed system prevails. On the other hand, property rights do not play a prominent role in much economic analysis. In the Arrow-Debreu model, and in particular in Debreu's Theory of Value, the term 'private ownership economy' indicates that different consumers' incomes include profits from their shares in producer units whose decisions are motivated by profit maximisation; there is no explicit consideration of managers as distinct from shareholders. But if one thought of these firms as state owned, with managers programmed (or motivated) to maximise profits, only the distribution of income would change depending on how the state decided to distribute the profits. (With slight inaccuracy one might say that state ownership is merely a special case of this private ownership economy. It would in fact be so if lump-sum transfers were introduced into the model.)

We know that major battles, both ideological and power seeking, occur over rights of ownership. And there is a widespread belief that ownership does matter. The issue has been explored in some depth in the works of Williamson, especially in the *Economic Institutions of Capitalism* (1985), and in Grossman and Hart (1986). They attribute the impact of ownership on the phenomenon of residual control vested in the owner in the area of actions that are not susceptible to sufficiently precise contractual specifications. Now such residual control may be viewed as an attribute of the outcome function. That is, residual control simply means that enforceable decisions in this area will be those made by the owner. The above cited authors provide plausible explanations as to why this might be so. But one may take the fact of residual control as the important feature defining this institutional arrangement, regardless of its reasons. This way of looking at the problem helps unify the analysis of different types of residual control. While ownership may provide it in the capitalist system (in fact, much residual control may reside in managers rather than owners), in communist countries the part organisation within an enterprise may be the seat of residual control. (In detail, the 'rules of the game' are very different in the two systems, and there is no implication that the two forms of residual control have the same consequences.) It is interesting to observe that recent movement toward restructing the economy of the People's Republic of China places some emphasis on restricting the party's residual control in management decisions.

Schotter (1981, especially pp. 14–15) seems to identify a social institution with the von Neumann-Morgenstern concept of solution in a co-operative game (i.e., a set of mutually undominated outcomes dominating all outcomes outside the set), called by them also 'standards of behavior'. There is a similarity but also an important difference between this notion and that suggested in this paper. A solution is (to use the von Neumann-Morgenstern terminology) a set of imputations; in general, a solution does not predict the quantitative relations of rewards given to the various participants – e.g., price ratios may remain indeterminate. This resembles the situation where an institutional arrangement defined as a class of outcome functions may also leave the numerical values of rewards indeterminate. But the solution is a set of outcomes, while an institutional arrangement in our sense is a set of 'rules of the game'. While Schotter defines a social institution as a regularity in social behaviour, in our interpretation such behaviour is a feature of the (equilibrium) solution determined in part by individual characteristics (especially preferences), and in part by the outcome functions which embody the institutional arrangements.

A reason for favouring our concept is that it seems a better handle for analysing the design and purposive activity (as distinct from endogenous evolution) in the formation of institutions, and for interpreting the nature of conflict over institutional arrangements. But it must be admitted that a stronger tradition (including Commons, Knight, and Ruttan) is on Schotter's side!

It should be stressed that our concept in no way excludes or minimises the importance of the endogenous evolution of institutions. In fact, there is a way of reconciling the two approaches, at least to some extent. We may think of the prevailing outcome function, embodying an enforcement system and various social conventions, as the result of a 'higher order' game with a higher order outcome function. (There always must be an outcome function!) Then the 'lower order' outcome function is indeed part of a solution of the higher game, but it constitutes the set of rules of the game for the lower order game. (The relationship is somewhat analogous to that between the US Constitution and the ordinary laws passed by Congress.) In this interpretation there is room for institutional evolution influenced by changes such as technological innovation (see Ruttan, 1984).

It is not enough to define what an institutional arrangement is. We must still specify what we mean by saying that certain institutional arrangements actually prevail in a given society at a given time. Our interpretation is that, at any given time, the outcome functions in use in different parts of the economy are those selected from the specified sets of 'admissible' outcome functions. The admissible functions qualify under one of the prevailing institutional arrangements. Outcome functions from outside those sets cannot be chosen. (This is analogous to a situation in which groups of card players can choose to play bridge, or poker, or some other game listed (say) in Hoyle, but nothing outside of Hoyle.) There may already have been a higher order game played to select these admissible sets. Next, a game will be played to choose a particular outcome function from one of the admissible sets, and finally the lowest order game will be played according to the function selected. While the highest order game may be the battle over the basic system (the constitution, or, say, capitalism versus socialism), the lowest one may be just the process of bargaining over the particular wage.

A pioneering example of modelling institutions (specifically, a regulated economy) by means of a multilevel game is found in Reiter and Hughes (1980).

Notes

* Assistance from National Science Foundation Grants IRI-85/0042 and SES-8509547 is gratefully acknowledged.

1. Thus an institution imposes limits on the admissibility of outcome functions. There may also be limits due to laws of physics or other non-behavioural factors. A characteristic of limits defined by institutions is that they are due to human decisions or behaviour patterns. Also, they apply to a *class* of persons and outcomes – e.g., as noted by Schotter (1981, p. 11), to recurrent situations. This is a feature distinguishing an institution from a contract, which typically lacks the attribute of 'universality' or 'categoricity' and only applies to the contracting parties.

   The existence of price controls on certain commodities is an example of an institution. The institution of price controls *per se* does not specify the actual price ceilings. But for the outcome function to be well defined these ceilings would also have to be specified. This illustrates the fact that, in general, an institution defines a class of outcome functions rather than a particular outcome function.

   But even if an institution should specify uniquely the outcomes in a given sphere of activities (say economic), it still does not define a unique outcome function if (as is usually the case) it is silent on other activities (say personal). Thus for more than one reason it seems appropriate to think of an institution as corresponding to a *set* of outcome functions rather than specifying a particular one.

2. Generally speaking, strategies involve sequences of actions ('moves'). The latter may be contingent on the actions of others as well as on the nature of the economic 'environment' (various parameter values pertaining to technology, endowments, preferences, etc.).

References

Atkins, W. E. *et al.* (1931) *Economic Behavior: An Institutional Approach*, vol. 1 (by members of the Department of Economics, Washington Square College, New York University) (Cambridge: Houghton Mifflin).

Calsamiglia, X. (1977) 'On the Dimension of the Message Space under Non-convexities', *Universitat Autonóma de Barcelona*, Working Paper 16.76, Spain, January.

Commons, J. R. (1924) *Legal Foundations of Capitalism* (New York: Macmillan Press).

Commons, J. R. (1934) *Institutional Economics* (New York: Macmillan Press).

Commons, J. R. (1951) *The Economics of Collective Action* (New York: Macmillan Press).

Geanakoplos, J. and Milgrom, P. (1985) 'A Theory of Hierarchies based on Limited Managerial Attention', *Cowles Foundation*, Discussion Paper no. 775, Yale University.

Grossman, S. J. and Hart, O. D. (1986) 'The Costs and Benefits of Ownership: A Theory of Vertical and Lateral Integration', *Journal of Political Economy*, vol. 94, pp. 691–719.

Groves, T. and Ledyard, J. (1977) 'Optimal Allocation of Public Goods: A solution to the "free rider" problem', *Econometrica*, vol. 45 pp. 783–811.

Holesovsky, V. (1977) *Economic Systems: Analysis and Comparison* (New York: McGraw Hill).

Hurwicz, L. (1960) 'Optimality and Informational Efficiency in Resource Allocation Processes', in Arrow, K. J., Karlin, S. and Suppes, P. (eds) *Mathematical Methods in the Social Sciences* (Stanford: Stanford University Press).

Hurwicz, L. (1972a) 'Organizational Structures for Joint Decision-Making: A Designer's Point of View', in Tuite, M., Chisholm, R. and Radnor, M. (eds) *Interorganizational Decision-Making* (Chicago: Aldine). pp. 37–44; 2nd ed (Minneapolis: University of Minnesota Press, 1986).

Hurwicz, L. (1972b) 'On Informationally Decentralized Systems', in McGuire, B. and Radner, R. (eds) *Decision and Organization, Volume in Honor of Jacob Marschak* (Amsterdam: North-Holland) pp. 297–336; 2nd ed (Minneapolis: University of Minnesota Press, 1986). Also reprinted in Arrow, K. J. and Hurwicz, L. (eds) *Studies in Resource Allocation Processes* (New York: Cambridge University Press).

Hurwicz, L. (1977) 'On the Dimensional Requirements of Informationally Decentralized Pareto Satisfactory Process', in Arrow, K. J. and Hurwicz, L. (eds) *Studies in Resource Allocation Processes* (Cambridge: Cambridge University Press).

Hurwicz, L. (1979) 'On Allocations attainable through Nash Equilibria', *Journal of Economic Theory*, vol. 21, pp. 140–65. Also in Laffont, J.-J (ed.) *Aggregation and Revelation of Preferences* (Amsterdam: North-Holland).

Hurwicz, L. (1987) 'Inventing New Institutions: The Design Perspective', *American Journal of Agricultural Economics*, vol. 69, pp. 395–402.

Hurwicz, L. and Marschak, T. (1985) 'Discrete Allocation Mechanisms: Dimensional Requirements for Resource Allocation Mechanisms when Desired Outcomes are Unbounded', *Journal of Complexity*, vol. 1, pp. 264–303.

Hurwicz, L., Maskin, E. and Postlewaite, A. (1980) 'Feasible Implementation of Social Choice Correspondences by Nash Equilibria'. mimeo.

Hurwicz, L. and Schmeidler, D. (1978) 'Construction of Outcome Functions Guaranteeing Existence and Pareto Optimality of Nash Equilibria', *Econometrica*, vol. 46, pp. 1447–74.

Hurwicz, L. and Weinberger, H. (1987) 'A Necessary Condition for Decentralizability and an Application to Intertemporal Allocation', To be circulated as an Institute for Mathematics and Its Applications preprint.

Jordan, J. S. (1986) 'Instability in the Implementation of Walrasian Allocations', *Journal of Economic Theory*, vol. 39, pp. 301–28.

Jordan, J. S. (1987) 'The Informational Requirements of Local Stability in Decentralized Allocation Mechanisms', in Groves, T., Radner, R. and Reiter, S. (eds) *Information, Incentives, and Economic Mechanisms, Essays in Honor of Leonid Hurwicz* (Minneapolis: University of Minnesota Press).

Knight, F. H. (1952) 'Institutionalism and Empiricism in Economics', *American Economic Review*, Papers and Proceedings Supplement, vol. 42, pp. 45–55.

Koopmans, T. (1951) 'Analysis of Production as an Efficient Combination of Activities', in Koopmans, T. (ed.) *Activity Analysis of Production and Allocation* (New York: John Wiley).

Ledyard, J. and Roberts, J. (1974) 'On the Incentive Problems with Public Goods', Discussion Paper no. 116 (Center for Mathematical Studies in Economics and Management Science, Northwestern University, Evanston).

Marschak, T. and Reichelstein, S. (1986) 'Informationally Efficient Hierarchies', mimeo (University of California, Berkeley) May.

Maskin, E. (1977) 'Nash Equilibrium and Welfare Optimality', Working paper (Cambridge, Mass.: Massachusetts Institute of Technology).

Moore, J. and Repullo, R. (1984) 'Subgame Perfect Implementation', mimeo (May 1987 revision, original paper September 1985).

Mount, K. and Reiter, S. (1974) 'The Informational Size of Message Spaces', *Journal of Economic Theory*, vol. 8, pp. 161–92.

Mount, K. and Reiter, S. (1983) 'On the Existence of a Locally Stable Dynamic Process with a Statically Minimal Message Space', Discussion Paper no. 550 (Center for Mathematical Studies in Economics and Management Science, Northwestern University, Illinois) February.

Neuberger, E. and Duffy, W. (1976) *Comparative Economic Systems: A Decision-Making Approach* (Boston: Allyn & Bacon).

Osana, H. (1978) 'On the Informational Size of Message Spaces for Resource Allocation Process', *Journal of Economic Theory*, vol. 17, pp. 66–78.

Palfrey, T. R. and Srivastava, S. (1986) 'Nash Implementation using Undominated Strategies', mimeo, December.

Palrey, T. R. and Srivastava, S. (1987) 'Mechanism Design with Incomplete Information: A Solution to the Implementation Problem', mimeo, May.

Reichelstein, S. (1982) 'On the Informational Requirements for the Implementation of Social Choice Rules', handout for the Decentralization Conference.

Reichelstein, S. and Reiter, S. (1985) 'Game Forms with Minimal Strategy Spaces', Discussion Paper no. 525 (Center for Mathematical Studies in Economics and Management Science, Northwestern University, Illinois).

Reiter, S. (1977) 'Information and Performance in the (New)^2 Welfare Economics', *American Economic Review*, vol. 67, pp. 226–34. Also in Reiter, S. (ed.) *Studies in Mathematical Economics* (Washington, DC: Mathematical Association of America, 1986).

Reiter, S. (1979) 'There is No Adjustment Process for Two-Dimensional Message Spaces for "Counter Examples"', mimeo (Northwestern University, Illinois) December.

Reiter, S. and Hughes, J. (1980) ' A Prolegomenon on Modelling the Regulated U.S. Economy', Discussion Paper no. 424 (Center for Mathematical Studies in Economics and Management Science, Northwestern University.

Ruttan, V. (1984) 'Social Science Knowledge and Institutional Change', *American Journal of Agricultural Economics*, (1984) pp. 549–59.

Sah, R. K. and Stiglitz, J. E. (1984) 'The Architecture of Economic Systems: Hierarchies and Polyarchies', Working Paper no. 1334 (National Bureau of Economic Research).

Sah, R. K. and Stiglitz, J. E. (1985) 'Human Fallibility and Economic Organization', *American Economic Review*, vol. 75, pp. 292–7.

Samuelson, P. (1954) 'The Pure Theory of Public Expenditure', *Review of Economics and Statistics*, vol. 36, pp. 387–9.

Samuelson, P. (1955) 'Diagrammatic Exposition of a Theory of Public Expenditure', *Review of Economics and Statistics*, vol. 37, pp. 350–6.

Schotter, A. (1981) *The Economic Theory of Social Institutions* (Cambridge: Cambridge University Press).

Stiglitz, J. E. (1974) 'Incentives and Risk Sharing in Sharecropping', *Review of Economic Studies*, vol. 41, pp. 219–56.

Walker, M. (1980) 'On the Nonexistence of the Dominant Strategy Mechanism for Making Optimal Public Decisions', *Econometrica*, vol. 48, pp. 1521–40.

Weitzman, M. L. (1974) 'Prices vs. Quantities', *Review of Economic Studies*, vol. 41, pp. 477–91.

Williamson, O. E. (1967) 'Hierarchical Control and Optimum Firm Size', *Journal of Political Economy*, vol. 75, pp. 123–38.

Williamson, O. E. (1985) *Economic Institutions of Capitalism: Firms, Markets, Relational Contracting* (New York: The Free Press).

Comment

Mikiro Otsuki
TOHOKU UNIVERSITY

It is a pleasure to comment on Professor Hurwicz's paper, which is concerned with mechanism design theory, one of central issues in contemporary economics. My comments are threefold.

1 COMPARISON OF MECHANISMS

The first comment is concerned with benefits and costs of mechanisms. In the paper, the role of mechanism designers is defined as the invention of a mechanism whose outcomes exactly implement pre-assigned social goals. I think, however, such a mechanism may not be regarded as the best. This mechanism may be worse than another mechanism that would not exactly implement the identical social goals, say because of Pareto efficiency and so on, if the efficiency loss in the outcome of the latter is very small, or if the size of informational spaces and the complexity are reduced to a substantial degree in the latter. To make such a comparison between mechanisms for specified social goals we need to order the social goals so that a certain outcome is declared as better, according to the social goals, than another. As for Pareto efficiency, we may transform it into an ordering on the set of feasible resource allocations by using a measure of efficiency loss defined in Debreu's paper 'The Coefficient of Resource Utilization' (Debreu, 1951) or other measures of efficiency loss. If the transformation of social goals into an ordering is possible, we may define the role of mechanism designers as to clarify the relation between benefit and cost, that is, the relation between the exent of implementability, on the one hand, and the size of information spaces, the cost of complexity and the other factors on the other hand. (Of course, it is impossible to define the net benefits, because benefits and costs are not measured in any common unit.) Surely, the wealth of work on mechanism design theory so far accumulated has paved the way for the comparison of mechanisms in terms of cost and benefit.

2   DISTRIBUTIVE JUSTICE AND OWNERSHIP

Pareto efficiency may be one of the important social goals for almost every economic system, whether existing or designed. Much more important is distributive justice, which is a fundamental concept to any discussion on how economic systems ought to be organised. Clearly different systems of distributive justice are implemented in different legal systems of ownership. For instance, fairness in net trade may be implemented in a private ownership economy.

The paper discusses the problem of ownership whereas it seems not to clarify what type of ownership should be legitimated in order to implement pre-assigned social goals. This is because the discussion in the paper is confined to the problem of residual rights.

3   INSTITUTIONAL EVOLUTION

In the final section Professor Hurwicz suggests a game-theoretic approach to interpret a certain ongoing institution and changes in it. My comment will end with a representation of the model that may be somewhat different from that of Professor Hurwicz.

The highest order game, which is the political sphere of institution, sets up certain social goals, including distributive justices, for society. From among economic systems implementing these social goals, one system (rules of the economic game, laws of ownership and the other institutional factors) is selected in the second order game. The lowest game with the selected fabric is played to determine the resource allocation and income distribution within the society, and to mobilise part of its resources for enforcement. Thus, if the social goals are not accepted by a majority of the members of the society, the prevailing institution tends to change. Even if the social goals are upheld by the entire society, the tendency to institutional evolution develops if it is discovered that the prevailing institution fails to implement the fully accepted social goals.

Reference

Debreu, G. (1951) 'The Coefficient of Resource Utilization', *Econometrics*, vol. 19, pp. 273–92.

Discussion

Rapporteur: Jenny Corbett
UNIVERSITY OF OXFORD

Professor Schotter commented that we should not exaggerate the dichotomy between institutions which are planned and those which are unplanned. Both types exist and we need not choose one view. Further, it is possible that an unstructured mechanism may yield better results than a consciously defined or planned mechanism. For example, laboratory experiments by Schotter and Radner suggest that unstructured, 'face-to-face' bargaining may give superior results, that is, capture more of the gains from trade, than pre-determined trading 'rules'.

Professor Imai wanted to bring an empirical element to Hurwicz's theoretical discussion. He asked, who are the designers? In the highest level game the state, or government, may be the designer, but could the designer in the middle level game correspond to the entrepreneur who establishes new ways of doing business and new 'rules of the game'?.

ProfessorTsuru asked whether Hurwicz's concept of evolution subsumed Marx's concept of dialectic evolution of the socioeconomic system. Marx's view of the endogenous development of capitalist systems into different modes of production could not be described as designed change.

Professor Hurwicz responded to Otsuki on three points. First, Otsuki was correct to point out that a mechanism with lower efficiency but also lower cost might be preferred to the most efficient. This can be shown as follows. Let $F(X,M)$ represent the maximum welfare attainable given (X), the resources available excluding those required to operate the mechanism, and given (M), the rules of the mechanism itself. If the costs of the mechanism are denoted $B(M)$ then, with total initial resources A, we have $X = A - B(M)$. Thus the welfare attainable can be expressed as a function of the net resources available and the rules of the mechanism $W = F(A - B(M), M)$. (For more detailed discussion, see Hurwicz, 1972a, 1972b.) This formulation allows us to account for the costliness and other complexities of particular mechanisms. A paper by Hurwicz and Marschak (1985) explicitly examines approximate realisation or implementation of objectives where equilibrium is not attained precisely, but with some given accuracy. This does not take fully into account complexity, but it does show that we need to consider not only what the mechanism could accomplish ideally, but what approximations and errors are likely to be involved in a mechanism.

On Otsuki's second comment there were two points to be made: one about distributive justice and one about ownership. Hurwicz acknowledged he did not mention distributive justice or fairness explicitly, but the formulation of his problem was in terms of the implementation of any given goal function. Therefore it was not, in principle, limited to Pareto optimal goals. One could embody in the goal function desired minimum levels of standards or any egalitarian criteria. There is, however, the problem that if too many objectives are included, the mechanism may not be implementable. A great deal of research is going on in this area. It is also necessary to clarify what type of ownership would be appropriate. Hurwicz did not claim to have adequately elucidated all issues of ownership, property rights and so on. He mentioned it in a specific context to indicate that certain aspects of ownership, namely residual powers of control, are not unique to ownership but may also appear in socialist economies in the form of certain kinds of political bureaucratic controls. The question of which type of ownership is appropriate for pre-assigned social goals is important, but is in fact an aspect of the solution of the problem. Hurwicz was only trying to formulate, not solve, the problem. This is an area for future research, but one must have a modelling framework and rigorous definition of how ownership works, whether collective or private.

Thirdly, Otsuki had suggested an interesing modification to the game at the end of Hurwicz's paper. The paper was trying to show that there is no philosophical conflict between Schotter's view and Hurwicz, and to present one way of unifying the two conceptual frameworks. There could, moreover, be many more than two levels of the game as mentioned in the paper. Altough Otsuki's three-level concept might be very valuable, it might be possible to subsume the two lower levels into one broader game. Hurwicz had not thought through the implications of Otsuki's formulation but it seemed very appealing. However, Otsuki is perhaps being a little narrow in saying that when the social goals are not accepted by the majority of society the prevailing institution tends to change. There are a lot of counter-examples. This is an example of an implicit postulation of an institutional framework, namely an ideal democracy. Finally, Otsuki asks what if the goals are upheld by the entire society but the system doesn't work in that direction? That means that the mechanisms or institutions or games which prevail are not the ones implementing those goals. The question then is what happens? Tsuru's comment is relevant here. The Marxian picture of dialectic development in which the endogenous dynamics of the capitalist system contain the seeds of a system which will replace it, is precisely what Hurwicz meant by evolutionary development. Nevertheless, the deliberate choice aspect is also important. Hurwicz offered a subjective comment that historically the prevalence of the evolutionary view in the world socialist movement and the lack of sufficient attention paid to the deliberate choice of designer was part of the reason that socialism in China and Russia operated in an *ad hoc* fashion. They would have been better off with some design theory. Marx and Engels' contempt for 'utopian' socialists pushed us in an unfortunate direction. Utopian socialists did not necessarily have the explanation of the development of the evolutionary forces which it was necessary to develop, but there were valuable elements of the designer approach in Owens and others.

In response to Imai, Hurwicz concluded that when he first used the term 'designer' in his 1972 paper ('Organizational Structures of Joint Decision-Making, A Designer's Point of View') he was not stressing the existence of the designer but that the designer's point of view is normative. Further, it is normative not about policy parameters but about structural aspects. In the multilevel game, however, it is possible to identify people who play the role of designers. They may be committees, or constitutional assemblies, or private firms and entrepreneurs as Imai suggests. This is an empirical question worthy of research. Schotter mentioned an interesting example that less restrictive mechanisms may perform better than others. One would like to check whether this would also be true in the presence of externalities such as the public goods case but Hurwicz accepted that it could be true in the pure exchange case although there might be qualifications if Otsuki's point about distributional justice were taken into consideration.

Professor Uzawa asked whether 'evolution' in the sense used here included 'revolution', that is, sudden, rather than gradual, change. Hurwicz clarified that the key to his use of 'evolutionary change' was its endogeneity. Therefore revolution could also be subsumed.

Professor Dosi pointed out a class of cases where the Hurwicz definition and the Schotter definition of institutions are significantly different. The two tend to coincide when it is possible unambiguously to derive the actors' strategies from a knowledge of their preferences and of the solution concepts of a game. However, there may be cases when this is not possible. For example, in a dynamic situation it may be that a certain evolutionary path depends on the existence of a variety of strategies, including mistaken ones. It will then not be possible to derive the strategies of the agents from the knowledge of the equilibrium. The outcome will be the result of the interaction of agents and of the existence of various sorts of externalities or dynamic increasing returns to scale. An example of this problem is examined in Dosi, Orsenigo and Silverberg (1986) which considers the diffusion of technology. It is shown that the diffusion of a superior technology might well require 'irrational' actors to take on the burden of exploring the technology even though they would be better off to wait for someone else to do it. This is, of course, similar to the Schumpeterian notion of entrepreneurship. Dosi argued that, in these cases, Schotter's definition of institutions in terms of actual behavioural regularities could still hold, but a definition in terms of an equilibrium independent of the actual distribution of strategies might not be possible. Hurwicz responded that Schotter's stochastic evolutionary model with random components could be interpreted in the way Dosi suggested and is a very good example of what is meant by evolution.

Reference

Dosi, G., Orsenigo, L. and Silverberg, G. (1986) 'Innovation, Diversity, Diffusion: A Self-Organisation Model', Science Policy Research Unit, University of Sussex, DRC Discussion Paper: presented at the Conference on Innovation Diffusion, Venice, 17–22 March 1986.

5 Institutional Change for the Future: Socialist Experience and New Horizons

Józef Pajestka
ACADEMY OF SCIENCES OF POLAND

1 SOME INITIAL PREMISES

It is understandable that the socialist ideology and theory developed in the nineteenth and the beginning of the twentieth century was searching for changes in the socioeconomic pattern at a certain stage of the evolutionary process. The mutation of the dominant capitalist mode of production, which was advocated and considered to be the necessary outcome of the development process, was supposed to be effected by institutional change.

This way of interpreting and, also, of engineering historical change, was deeply rooted in the theoretical thinking of the classics of Marxism. The development process was considered to be a process of dialectic relations or feedbacks between productive forces on the one hand, and socioeconomic and political institutions on the other. It is astonishing to see how all the arguments have been revived in recent times under the name of the new institutional economics. To a man trained in classic Marxist literature, argumentation along the lines of 'property rights economics', 'institutional evolution', and even 'constitutional choice', sounds all too familiar. Indicating that, I wish only to stress that in studying institutional transformations it should be easy to find the common language of the various schools of theoretical thought.

It was to be expected that, based on the theoretical interpretation of interdependencies within the historical process mentioned above, a programme of institutional change would be worked out and advocated. This is what actually happened. Projection of institutional change required, however, one more logical step. It is necessary to

111

assume that human beings behave purposefully within the scope of national and international society. A few comments require attention in this context.

The idea of consciously shaping socioeconomic processes is widely acknowledged nowadays, though not in the not-so-distant past. Within the European culture, the age of enlightenment ushered in understanding of world processes in terms of rational behaviour. It was only one step further to the paradigm of moulding socioeconomic processes. This is how the socialist theory of planning came about. The paradigm has found wide acceptance in the twentieth century, and recently there has been a tendency to apply it to global processes.

Once one has started determining the paths of socioeconomic processes, the evaluation of institutional solutions may be used to pave the way for programmes of institutional adjustment or transformation, and this has led to institutionalised socialism. Not all the institutions of this system followed precisely the paths of former theoretical considerations, but it was a grand scheme of institutional change based on theoretical considerations.

The evaluation of the actual performance of the new institutional set-up is a vast field. We are able to discuss it within only a limited scope, concentrating on the main lessons delivered by historical experience.

2   INSTITUTIONALISED SOCIALISM: CHANGES IN INSTITUTIONAL SET-UP

In a most concise, though necessarily very simplified, way the main lines of institutional change introduced in the socialist countries of Eastern Europe can be described as follows by:

1. abandoning or shrinking traditional institutions connected with the market economy;
2. developing a new planning apparatus from the top to the bottom within the hierarchical structure;
3. developing a system of national plans – long, medium and short term, used for strict guidance of activities and for allocation of resources;
4. changing the role of the firm to the executive function of achieving the plan targets, an element in the hierarchical management structure;

5. strictly controlling prices and all instruments of income distribution;
6. leaving free consumers' choice and therefore also a kind of market for consumer goods;
7. leaving some kind of labour market, though with many reservations.

Those institutional solutions were considered to be necessary, even 'natural', consequences of the introduction of social or state ownership of the means of production. Theoretically, changing the ownership was considered most crucial, and determined the basis of the whole institutional system.

The institutional structure which was introduced proved functional in relation to certain basic societal objectives: it allowed for fuller utilisation of resources, particularly of manpower; it facilitated the raising of the saving ratio, and, *inter alia*, by that, brought about acceleration of economic growth; it was efficient in changing the economic structure on a macro-scale; it allowed for installation of greater social justice by way of full employment, development of social services and relatively equal income distribution.

In the further process of economic development the established institutional solutions were showing growing shortcomings. It can be seen that the positive impacts listed above related in great part to the initial stages of industrial development. They have been less conducive to progress at a more advanced stage of the development process. This was not realised for a long time, and the institutional structure acquired features of petrification. It is only now that a broad movement towards reforming the institutional set-up may be observed. If carried on successfully, it can lead to institutional change which will give a new face to institutionalised socialism.

A few additional comments on the existing institutional system described above merit particular attention because of their theoretical significance.

The practice of conscious shaping of socioeconomic processes seems a proper general model for development planning. Its characteristics should be that it is based first on a cognisance of reality which utilises all the available knowledge and experience, and on anticipation of the future; and secondly on value judgements, that is, judgements of what is just, rational etc. Anticipation and value judgements are concerned with aims and objectives on the one hand, and ways and means on the other. Thus one can state that to act consciously is tantamount to acting with cognisance of what one wants to achieve and how best to achieve it, by determining the material means to be used and the institutional and economic instruments.

It should be seen that practical planning, as institutionalised in the socialist countries, did not fully conform to the theory outlined above. It followed a narrower path.

In the initial theoretical premises, planning was conceived to operate mainly in the sphere of the 'exchange system' – as a substitute for the workings of the market and to solve the problems of allocation of resources. This allocative function of planning overshadowed other functions leading to neglect of certain important aspects of the development process and of socioeconomic change. It is my view that this was, at least partly, due to overemphasis on theoretical deliberations on the controversy of planning versus market. Both the theoretical thinking on, and the practical institutionalisation of, planning were gripped by the conceptual controversy to the great detriment of progress.

For a long time problems connected with the values and aims of society were largely forgotten. It is only in more recent years that they appear in development planning. After initial changes towards socialism in the institutional sphere, further changes in that field were checked and there appeared, as indicated above, a certain ossification of the established institutions. In consequence, one can state that the important characteristics of the way forward in development, with their implications as discussed above, were neglected or sank into oblivion in the planning system. Yet it may be observed that in the development process, socio-moral and institutional issues grow in importance. They reflect new tendencies in societal behaviour. Planning has necessarily to cope with them.

The main initial theoretical idea of socialist planning underlying institutional solutions may be seen in the concept of macroeconomic rationality, as opposed to the efficiency of the individual firm. This was considered a corollary of the social ownership of the means of production, and formed the basis of the political organisation of society, of the national planning system, and of the management system. It is my view that it is necessary in the socialist countries to attain a new balance between macro-rationality and micro-rationality, and this is what the various economic reforms being considered or carried on in a number of countries are about. Institutionalisation of macroeconomic rationality is indispensable, but it should not be carried on to the detriment of the necessary conditions for rational behaviour at the micro level. One cannot have sound development unless it is based on rational and dynamic behaviour of firms.

Creating conditions for micro-rationality requires appropriate institutional change. It can be presented in a simplified manner as consisting in acknowledging the three basic institutions – real money, the market mechanism and the independent firm. Though this may sound like a cliché, it is to be perceived that what is really involved is a radical change of the initial institutional set-up.

Current economic reforms being pursued in a number of socialist countries can be characterised by three elements: firm installation of the relevant institutions; their links with central strategic planning and guidance; acknowledgement of the principles of social justice in their guidance.

Institutional change along these lines encounters barriers and obstacles. The socialist countries do not easily accommodate institutional change, as is sometimes claimed. Indeed, institutional change seems difficult in the whole human world: transforming nature always needs endeavour, whether it consists in transforming material nature or human institutions.

3 SOME DETERMINANTS OF INSTITUTIONAL CHANGE

Anticipation of factors and forces operating in the field of socioeconomic relations and institutional solutions runs into difficulties and uncertainties. This does not mean, however, that one cannot work out some analytical insights into future conditions and tendencies, from which one can deduce conclusions allowing for more rational policies. It would not seem proper to be sceptical about the ability of the human mind to forecast in this field, since we have not devoted much conceptual effort to considerations of the future.[1]

Hypotheses and expectations of future tendencies must be continuously verified. This type of verification is necessary in every area of science and is the method by which capabilities for forecasting can be put on a firm basis. While this is true for scientific advancement, it is equally true for development policy if it is to be future-orientated. We have here an exceptionally difficult process of cognition where we find, not only highly diversified causative factors and feedbacks, but also characteristics of behaviour which may undergo modifications in the process of time. We cannot, of course, anticipate modifications which are not yet conceived of. But germs of change appear long before they acquire dominating strength.

The need for scientific analysis and anticipation of the future needs emphasis. It is necessary if we aim at increasing rationality of policy for programming various capital investment development projects. We cannot act rationally unless we consider future conditions. Similarly, in undertakings relating to the mode of functioning of the economy and society, maximum use must be made of knowledge concerning the most probable and the desirable future. Myopy is no less harmful here than in other areas of societal activity, since institutional facts and patterns of behaviour once established are reversible, but only with great difficulty and with a lapse of time.

We assume in this paper that a certain number of determinants of change in the economic system can be ascertained. By 'determinants' we understand here certain features of the development process leading to progress and having strong implications for institutional solutions. Some important determinants of institutional change can be formulated for present and anticipated conditions as follows:

1. Societal aspirations as well as political forces are expected to continue to exercise a strong drive for economic progress. It can be anticipated that – against the background of historical experience – this will strengthen the position of rational pragmatism. As a consequence, a very open attitude in search of the best institutional solutions making for efficiency is needed. One would also expect greater diversification of institutional solutions within countries and amongst them. Then acceptance of institutional change as desirable phenomena conducive to greater purposefulness and efficiency will spread.

2. Education and cultural advancement has already been the main driving force making for institutional and political change. Together with that, economic process brings growing importance to the qualitative and creative features of men. This line of change should be expected to intensify in the future. Both the operating societal force and the logic of the development process are going to demand new solutions. Conclusions should be drawn for shaping the management system and style. Whoever succeeds in introducing new management patterns allowing for better development and utilisation of the qualitative features of human beings will also succeed in economic competition. Reliance on

creative human forces cannot be limited to economic management only. People who are creative in economic life demand
active participation in decision-making processes on the various
political platforms also. One would expect a parallel development of new management methods and of the political system
towards democratic patterns.

3. The growing importance of scientific and technological advance
   and of innovative dynamism is commonly acknowledged and
   forecast for the future. This is going to have wide implications for
   the whole economic system, as can be seen from historical
   experience. The problem merits special study, which should be
   caried out by all interested in institutional change. The impact of
   technological change is expected to appear as a result of internal
   development factors, for example, the human factor mentioned
   above, as well as of changing characteristics of international
   markets and of the global situation. Far-reaching change should
   be anticipated.

4. In the past, creation of the basic conditions for self-sustained
   growth was considered to be the main policy orientation of the
   socialist countries. This should rightly be expected to change.
   Inclusion of the socialist countries in the international system is a
   cardinal requirement of their prosperous development now and in
   the foreseeable future. This dictates the need for adequate
   institutions and other instruments. Changing over from a system
   of almost closed economies to one of wide participation in the
   international system is going to demand some deep institutional
   adjustments.

5. The development process at more advanced stages leads to
   intensification of economic interdependence, with increased need
   for flexibility in economic relations, and brings diversification and
   complexity to human needs. All this requires adequate measures
   in the area of co-ordination of economic activities. Experience
   shows that this cannot be achieved by bureaucratic methods
   previously applied widely by socialist planning. They need to be
   replaced by a mechanism of self-regulation, that is, by a
   mechanism of the market type. A number of the socialist countries
   have already embarked on reforms aiming at using the market
   mechanism. Its organisation and adaptation, adapted to various
   internal requirements as well as to the external environment, is
   expected to be of crucial importance for improving efficiency in
   the socialist economies. Development of the market mechanism,

and of the related institutions, is also important for the inclusion of the socialist countries in the international system.

6. There are no premises to expect that aspirations of the people to participate in self-management and on the various political platforms will decrease or vanish. On the contrary, one anticipates further limitation of the various élitist institutions and procedures, and a strengthening of tendencies making for democratic solutions. The corresponding line of institutional change should be anticipated and advanced.

4 EGALITARIANISM, WELFARE STATE AND MOTIVATIONS FOR PROGRESS

Due to the initial ideological premises, though also as a result of certain policy lines connected with them, for example, in the field of employment and education, socialism brought fast growth of human aspirations affecting a wide social strata and leading to strong egalitarian tendencies. It is nowadays possible to evaluate, *ex post*, the effects of the revolution of aspirations developed by socialism on the basis of real historical experience.

It seems worth observing that the unleashing of wide societal aspirations was a most powerful factor in socioeconomic progress. Later, however, this element of socioeconomic mechanism changed – and this appeared strongly in certain countries such as Poland. A wide chasm developed between aspirations and their realisation. Aspirations were degenerating, operating more and more as demands addressed to the state. There appeared, resulting from the gap, great frustration and discontent, sociopolitical conflicts, weakening of the state in performing the function of protection of long-run societal interests, and, as a result, a slowing down of the rate of progress. This experience demonstrates that the policy was incapable of turning aspirations into strong motivation for progress. It is not the policies alone which are responsible for the final outcome, but also the ideology and the institutional mechanism influencing those policies.

These processes were not clearly perceived or understood by analysts or by policy-makers. Nevertheless, they have had a strong impact on social consciousness and on patterns of economic behaviour. It is the purpose of economic and institutional reforms to turn back the negative features which have developed. They should establish conditions which would prevent egalitarianism from undermining the motivation for progress; indeed, that would direct aspirations into strong motivation for progress. This, like any other serious change of patterns in human thinking and behaviour, cannot be achieved in a short period of time. It must become a long-term aim of reform, supported by appropriate conceptual and ideological premises.

Attempts to install a new link between social justice and the motivation for good and creative work have only just begun on the installation of the new patterns.[2] Human expectations still operate on the old pattern. They appear in the form of sociopolitical pressures rather than as motivations which bring dynamic enterprise, innovation and productivity. The conviction still prevails in social psychology that the success of an individual is determined more by the state than by his own creative activity. It is now clearly seen that human attitudes must be overcome by reforming institutions and economic rules to produce the intended long-term results.

All these problems are connected with the functioning of the main societal institution – the state. In conjunction with striving for social justice, the 'welfare state' developed. The battle for justice and the socialist state led by its nature to the state becoming the main enforcer of this justice. Justice has many aspects, of which some should be seen as equal opportunity in education, access to culture, care for handicapped people, decent living conditions for the aged, etc. Realisation of those social functions is embraced by the concept of the welfare state. There seem to be no reasons for radical criticism of those functions or of the nature of the socialist state.

Historical experience shows, however, that a certain critical attitude to the social and welfare functions of the state is justified. Two problems emerge in this context. The first is to take care that in performing its social functions the state does not undermine the motivation for work, as discussed earlier. The second is the appropriate division of duties between the state and the family.

However, while no deep adjustments in the functioning of the state seem to be necessary in these fields, a most serious change is required in another function of the state. A most important phenomenon of the institutional system should be seen in the development of functions of the welfare state, not only in relations between the state and the citizen, but also between the state and the firms and other organisations. No justification can be found for that in the principles of socialism. The socialist ideology put great emphasis on social justice but it never demanded 'justice' for firms. Much could be said on the rise of state patronage over firms. In my opinion, its origin lies in a specific syndrome of institutionalised interests. In Poland an important role was played by the peculiar institutional development in which the alignment of the branch ministries, which directly defended specific interests, gained in strength, while the institutions which were supposed to defend the general societal interests grew weak.

Leaving the historical evaluations aside, I am inclined to state that:

(a)	There can be no strong motivation for progress within economic organisations if their relations with the state are shaped along the pattern of a 'welfare state', since this institutional pattern tends to obscure the objective of efficiency, and directs the efforts of firms, not towards the struggle for efficiency, but towards various methods of influencing the state authorities.

(b)	A welfare state for firms is essentially a very soft state, and while it is soft in relations with firms, it must be hard on the people. In such a system a lasting sociopolitical balance cannot be ensured.

(c)	Experience shows that in these circumstances the state does not exert economic pressure on the efficiency of firms and, therefore, it is not in a position to programme and to realise sound structural transformation. These phenomena are clearly visible in the working of the Polish reforms, in that it not only failed to change the attitude of the state apparatus but may even have strengthened it.

(d)	Institutional transformation must be considered from the point of view of proper balance between the position of the state, supposed to protect long-term national interests, and the position of industries and territories or regions.

Experience shows that a wrong balance may upset the prosperous development of the country.

While there are many aspects of institutional change to be monitored carefully, the crucial problem is that of changing relations between the state apparatus and economic organisations by departing from the welfare state pattern. Without achieving this objective, not much can be expected from the reforms.

This assessment gives ground for certain more general observations. Guidance of institutional change is the most crucial field of planning for the future. In this guidance, two issues merit very special attention by:

1.	assuring the holistic coherence of the whole institutional set-up and of the leading concepts governing patterns of human thinking and behaviour;

2. assuming that the ability to create change is a basic feature of human behaviour, which should be built into the whole institutional system and into ideology.

5 CAPABILITY TO PARTICIPATE IN GLOBAL RATIONALITY

The arguments above were based on two important premises:

(a) that human progress consists in mastering nature and, therefore, that socioeconomic institutions should be adapted to that objective, taking into account changing conditions;
(b) that institutional evolution proceeds within the world of nations but safeguards the national interests.

However, looking into the foreseeable future of mankind, both premises have to be challenged. The human evolutionary process is undergoing deep change. The main lines of this change can be described as follows:

1. A growing number of people and the inherent tendency of contemporary civilisation to acquire more material goods for the satisfaction of human needs and desires have radically changed the rate of transformation of the material world, leading towards a precarious imbalance between mankind and the ecosphere.
2. The rate of change in technologies transforming the material world has been too fast for people to learn and comprehend its impact, let alone to control its possible destructive change inflicted on the psycho-physical constitution of human beings.
3. Mankind has developed arms and technologies capable of destroying the whole ecosphere. This is not only dangerous *per se*. It demonstrates a perilous inability of human beings to behave rationally: the top achievements of the human mind are used for absolutely irrational ends. Here again the rate of change has been too fast for people to comprehend and control its impact.
4. Patterns of technoeconomic change demonstrate growing polarisation tendencies. As a result, a great part of the inhabitants of this planet is left outside the scope of the beneficial influence of the progress of civilisation. Unbearable inequalities arise, undermining the unity of mankind and thereby creating dangers of sociopolitical destabilisation and military conflicts. It is, then, not

only that mankind has created means of destruction greatly overpowering the potential of the ecosphere, but it is also maintaining sociopolitical mechanisms to utilise them.

The changed set-up produced by the human evolutionary process has the following features: it is global, that is, it concerns all mankind and the whole planet; it endangers human existence; and to avert the danger, a change in human behaviour is indispensable. We put forward the proposition that the necessary mutation of the human species should not, and cannot, consist in rejection of the fundamental line of human development – towards greater individual and collective capability for rational action, including the field of mastering nature. It is not that human rationality should be challenged in its virtue, but it should be extended from its narrow scope of mastering the material world for the satisfaction of immediate needs and desires to a wider scope and a longer time horizon.

It would seem absurd to expect that such a mutation would not require adequate institutional evolution within the planet. Continuing institutional change along past lines would lead to growing polarisation and growing dangers to human survival. It is not my intention to outline the directions of institutional change which could serve global rationality. I will, however, undertake to consider a partial problem, that of the tendency of the Eastern European socialist countries to participate in global rationality.

Since socialism, institutionalised in the states of Eastern Europe, is still historically young, it would be expected to have been under strong influence from the initial ideological premises. It should be remembered that some of the crucial premises of socialist thinking have a strong relationship to what can be called global rationality. The following may be mentioned:

(i)   Liberation of the exploited, social justice and human brother-hood within the global scale.
(ii) The withering away of the state as the basic institution of the human world.
(iii) Introduction of planning, that is, of conscious guidance, as the main technique for guiding the socioeconomic processes.

With these ideological premises it might have been expected that the socialist countries would be the main partisans of the various schemes aiming at some kind of global rationality. This is not what has happened, in my judgement; these countries remained rather on the sidelines of global schemes. This judgement may be considered very controversial by some analysts. It seems necessary, therefore, to give it a certain interpretation.

Without excluding in any way the validity of some other arguments, particularly of a political character, it seems relevant to indicate certain factors influencing the position of the socialist countries in relation to the various global ventures:

1. Mutations appearing in the evolutionary process tend to be competitive, and this is how the socialist countries saw themselves and were seen by others. To expect competitors to join together with the aim of working out some common global rationality would seem a difficult proposition. For this to come about would require real arguments developed by historical process and also ideological reformulations. Such changes would take time.

2. Based on certain theoretical premises widely presented in economic literature, the socialist countries were experimenting with an economic system not compatible with the function of world markets, but devised rather for a country remaining in isolation or in a hostile environment. This had a deep impact on the whole institutional structure. It created real difficulties for those countries to take part in international exchange. After years of isolation or rather marginal participation, the socialist countries felt rather uneasy in the intricate world of international economic and financial institutions and relations.

3. Due to a number of historical factors, there was a tendency to strengthen the institution of the state and enhance the display of national interests, making the created new institutional set-up not easily compatible with the requirements of global rationality. At the same time, certain basic ideological premises were leading towards the same end. It is worth indicating that nationalisation of the means of production makes for particular strengthening of the institution of the state, while it also strongly institutionalises the national interests.

Considering present and anticipated tendencies, the above factors are undergoing remarkable change, leading to a growing readiness in the socialist countries of Eastern Europe to participate in the international system and in ventures aiming at greater global rationality, notably:

Peaceful Coexistence

The concept of peaceful coexistence, as developed over a number of years, is a crucial ideological concept accommodating real and sincere co-operation, aimed at solving the common problems of mankind with the participation of all countries. This can be understood as a reformulation of the ideological position which was inhibiting the acceptance of the goal of a common global rationality (point (i) above). Ideological and political repercussions of peaceful coexistence are increasing with the growing need for mankind to meet the looming global challenges. What we are witnessing in this field at present is expected to intensify in the future.

Economic and Institutional Reform.

The process of economic and institutional reform in a number of countries is intensifying, and can be expected to develop further in the coming years. It is anticipated that the ongoing change will bring, along with other results, increased readiness and capability in the socialist countries to join global economic interaction. It can be expected to increase the compatibility of the centrally planned economies with the functioning of the global system. A trend towards participation of the socialist countries in international financial institutions is already visible. Though the course of economic reforms may encounter certain obstacles and disturbances, the general line of change seems evident.

Seeing the indicated lines of change, one cannot fail to observe that they tend towards growing capability to participate in ventures making for global rationality. It should be realised that achieving global rationality is a long-term process, and it can be equally difficult to achieve for all elements of the global system. At the present juncture of the evolutionary process we are able to understand what we are aiming at, though we are certainly not well advanced in the comprehension of how to achieve it. It is the most crucial new frontier of institutional change.

Notes

1. See Pajestka and Feinstein (1980), especially Introduction, pp. xi–xv.
2. The phenomena and argumentation described relate mainly to the Polish

experience. Analysts from some other socialist countries might with reason not accept this interpretation.

Reference

Pajestka, J. and Feinstein, C. H. (eds) (1980) *The Relevance of Economic Theories* (London: Macmillan Press).

Comment

Masayuki Iwata
CHIBA UNIVERSITY

My comments on Professor Pajestka's paper are focused on the relations between conscious and unconscious elements in the formation and management of a socialist society. I wish to choose four points.

First, Pajestka says that the concept of 'engineering historical change was deeply rooted in the theoretical thinking of the classics of Marxism' (Section 1).

I have a somewhat different view on the theoretical stance of classical Marxists to the future history of mankind. It is well known that classical Marxists did not try to draw any exact blueprint of future society. Without a blueprint no kind of 'engineering' would be conceivable. At that moment they were confronted with only two possibilities, or more accurately, two concrete necessities, namely:

1. The unconscious processes of the restoration of the old regime.
2. The conscious construction of new socioeconomic institutions.
   Society abhors a vacuum in its ordering.

The successful revolutionaries were forced to acknowledge that they did not possess any ready-made blueprint for future socialist society. Generally speaking, they did not have any clear image of a new society which could be expressed in affirmative statements, but they had some vague image expressed in negative messages which signified a certain outline of a future society from which capitalist features had been withdrawn. It is very important that the theoretical and analytical propositions about capitalist society be given in the affirmative forms by the first generation of Marxists and be adopted by the second generation in many countries.

In those conditions, the leaders of the revolution could not but help making for themselves some clear blueprints for that future society. In this way the idea of 'engineering historical change' came to the forefront of their minds.

After 1917 in Russia, 1945 in Eastern Europe, and 1949 in China, concepts enshrined in *Das Kapital* such as commodity, money, capital, fetishism, profit, interest, rent, production price and so on, acquired a completely different theoretical status: the constituent elements of the grand designs of socialism had to become essentially elements of 'being negated', that is, antonyms without ideals.

Today, after the passage of 70 years in the USSR, or 40 years in the other socialist economies, the nature of those processes has diametrically changed. Almost all the socioeconomic categories characterising capitalism have turned out not to be negated, and have been rehabilitated. The issue has become how a new society should be constructed from the old components.

Secondly, Pajestka writes, 'the paradigm [of moulding socioeconomic processes] has found wide acceptance in the twentieth century, and recently there is a tendency to apply it to global processes' (Section 1).

Here, too, I have a different view from his on the recent tendencies, both in contemporary capitalism and in 'actually existing socialism'. In the past dozen years or so we have seen very strong currents of denationalisation and deregulation in both domestic economic policy and international financial activity. In parallel with these currents we have observed an accelerating trend of 'economic reform' in Eastern Europe, the USSR and China.

An emigré economist of Polish origin, J. G. Zielinski, discusses the theme of 'the communist system and the limits of social engineering' in his *Economic Reforms in Polish Industry* (1973, p. 321). He suggests that in Eastern Europe 'historically developed economic and social relations were replaced by "man-invented" mechanisms, to an extent and with a speed unknown in the history of mankind'. He stresses that 'man-invented' society is encountering many difficulties in economic, social and political spheres which make economic reforms inevitable. In his opinion, 'the essence of the reform movements is to reintroduce or to stimulate – in one form or another – historically developed economic and social mechanisms. The guided market model, profit incentives, etc., all point in this direction' (p. 323).

When Zielinski mentions the 'man-invented' society he bears in mind the étatist-centralisation-type of economy. There is, however, another type of 'artifically created' society – the anti-étatist self-management society – which has been tried since the excommunication of Yugoslavia from the Comintern in 1948, especially since the 1974 Constitution and the 1976 Associated Labour Act. Its main features are summarised by D. V. Marsenić, one of the sharpest opponents of the system. The system (a) denies a market in labour, (b) denies ownership of the means of production, (c) denies the contribution to income creation of factors of production, (d) denies the concept of the market as spontaneous flows of commodity exchanges, (e) proclaims that every instrument of income participation based on property is incompatible with a self-managed commodity economy, and (f) denies the concept of enterprise as the organisational form of a commodity economy'. In Marsenić's estimation, 'in this way Yugoslavia, intending to accelerate the development of self-management, overstepped the border line of objective potential and found itself in collision with the commodity economy' (Marsenić, 1986, pp. 65–8).

It is very interesting that both systems, diagonally opposite to one another, are blamed by their respective critics for negating the laws of the commodity economy.

Thirdly, Pajestka observes in Section 2 the phenomenon of 'a certain ossification of the established institutions' in the initial phase of transformation and writes that 'it is necessary in the socialist countries to attain a new balance between macro-rationality and micro-rationality'. The activation of micro-rationality requires the reintroduction of 'real money, the market mechanism and the independent firm'. In a word, the new balance is in the direction of Zielinski's 'historically developed social and economic relations'.

I do not understand why Professor Pajestka does not reconsider the most important problem of ownership of the means of production. In my opinion, a new interpretation of the state ownership of the means of production is necessary to render the institutions workable.

In the USSR, L. Abalkin, director of the Institute of Economics of the USSR Academy of Sciences, told the staff of Gosplan:

> The current reconstruction goes to the roots, to the deep fundamental bases of the economic system. The possible necessity of profound transformations in the very base of our economic system – in the ownership of the means of production – has never been raised before. Today this problem, which embraces all the complexity of property relations, has forced itself on our attention. (Abalkin, 1987, p. 10)

It is worth observing here that Yugoslav economists and system designers have always carried on controversies with each other about the subject of ownership, that is, the differences between state ownership and social ownership, the essence of social ownership, and whether the definition of social ownership in the sense of non-ownership is, or is not, theoretically and practically feasible. The official definition, which has been blamed by Yugoslav reformists for being the main obstacle against the reaction of market mechanisms, in the words of the 1974 Constitution, is that

> no-one has the right of ownership over the social means of production; nobody – neither socio-political communities, nor organisations of associated labour, nor individuals – may appropriate on any legal property grounds the production of social labour nor manage and dispose of the social means of production and labour, nor arbitrarily determine conditions for distribution.

Today the market mechanism is acknowledged to be common to any form of ownership, private, state or social, whence the next problem is which property rights can manifest its vitality to the greatest degree and in what combination.

Fourthly, I find important Pajestka's observation that the state within socialism as initially established was incapable of turning popular aspirations, exaggerated by the strong egalitarianism inherent in the centrally-organised system, into strong motivations for progress. A wide chasm between the aspirations inspired by socialist ideals and the party's promises, on the one hand, and actual accomplishments on the other, must lead in due time to great frustration, mass discontent and sociopolitical conflicts.

The coupling of high aspirations and weak motivations among the people is pointed out by Soviet economists: 'Under the guise of the coming together of two ownership forms (state and collective) a dependent way of life emerged' (Lukinov, 1987, p. 4). 'Let the leadership decide – so, let them be responsible (Abalkin, 1987, p. 13).

This problem turns out to be connected with the problem of distribution of rights and responsibilities among the agents of the centralised system. We see the centralisation not only of power but also of responsibility on the part of the leadership, and the deprivation of power and responsibility on the part of ordinary people.

When we consider the problem of motivation for work and progress, we need to classify three kinds of sociopsychological motivation: first, the contradiction between anxiety and certainty which is the main motivating force of business activities in the competitive market; secondly, the tension between discontent and satisfaction which is connected with structure of promises and expectations and works as the main motivating force of economic activities in centrally planned systems; and third, the collision between trust and sincerity which is found in community relations and serves as the main motivating force of socioeconomic activities in self-management societies.

People cast into each of these three sociopsychological conflicts have only two alternatives: they must either wither away, occasionally in the tragic forms of suicide, homicide or fratricide, or work harder to evade tragedy and to reduce the conflicts. Even so, one should remind oneself that there is no propelling power for progress filled with pure happiness in any socioeconomic system conceivable on the earth.

When Pajestka writes, ' ... the policy was incapable of turning aspirations into strong motivation for progress' (Section 4), he is discussing the character of the second kind of propelling force. In both the Polish centrally-planned system and the Yugoslav decentralised economy of 'social compacts', the motivation for progress is evidently lower. Accordingly, reform-minded economists recommend the competitive motivation of the first kind. They forget, however, that the most important buttress of competitive motivation is the danger of failure, symbolised ultimately in suicide. This is the tragedy of responsibility, self-discipline and risk-taking. In Japan, for example, roughly 10–11 per cent of suicides, totalling some 23,000 annually, are caused or triggered off by economic hardship such as business failure, bankruptcy and heavy indebtedness.

I would like to know how many managers, project designers, and planners have committed suicide in the midst of the economic crisis in the 1980s in Poland, one of the world's most seriously indebted countries.

I have suggested elsewhere a cyclical process which is peculiar to the centralised economic system (Iwata, 1981, pp. 87–107). One of the possible outcomes of the cyclical pattern is that the centralised economy has to be reorganised by *perestroika*. An example of this is the Polish reform carried out since 1982 as evaluated positively by Pajestka: 'In comparison with all previous experiments, this time, for the first time, we have a reform which is not being put aside after the lapse of three years' (Pajestka, 1986, p. 385). But at the same time, Pajestka feels misgivings about the future of economic reform in the 1980s, and judges that it stands 'at the crossroads' because he knows the nature of a centralised society, namely the 'syndrome of particularism', the 'allure of the privileges of power without responsibility' and the 'bureaucratic *homo oeconomicus*' too deeply to be optimistic (Pajestka, 1986, pp. 404–6).

Abalkin also emphasised the complexities of a decentralising reform:

Even scholarly analysts have concurred in the over-simplified apposition of supporters of independence and creative initiative in the enterprise on the one hand and, on the other hand, of bureaucrats resisting in every possible way enterprise independence and autonomy among the higher levels of administration. This is a very convenient schema which requires no effort of thought or analysis. The reality, however, has proved to be much more complicated. (Abalkin, 1987, p. 12)

References

Abalkin, L. (1987) 'The Reconstruction of the System and Methods of Planned Management', (in Russian), *Planovoe Khozyaistvo*, 5, Moscow.
Iwata, Masayuki (1981) 'The Centralised Economy in the Shadow of the Market Mechanism' (in Japanese), *Keizaihyoron*, I, Tokyo.
Lukinov, I. (1987) 'Paying One's Way and Showing Initiative under Today's Economic System', *Voprosy ekonomiki*, no. 6, Moscow.
Marsenić, D. V. (1986) *Sumnje u privredni sistem Jugoslavije* (Doubts about the Economic System of Yugoslavia) (Belgrade: Ekonomika).
Pajestka, J. (ed.) (1986) *Gospodarka w Procesie Reformowania* (The Economy in the Reform Process) (Warsaw: PWE).
Zielinski, J. G. (1973) *Economic Reforms in Polish Industry* (Oxford: Oxford University Press).

Discussion

Rapporteur: Jenny Corbett
UNIVERSITY OF OXFORD

Professor Hurwicz remarked that Iwata's observation about attributing success to one's own merit and problems to the state was common among American libertarians as well as in the socialist countries. There is a danger that the disillusionment with central planning in socialist economies, described by Pajestka, could lead to an unrealistic view of what can be achieved by market systems. There are real conflicts between the need for managerial incentives and the problems posed by oligopoly and increasing returns. The problems are demonstrated by the Lange-Lerner proposals for profit-sharing incentives when prices are parametric.

Mr Kaser agreed with Hurwicz's identification of the similar problem in both capitalist and socialist economies. He noted the pivotal place which Iwata accorded middle-level management in promoting innovation and efficiency and the need to remunerate them accordingly. Other work by Pajestka has shown that the middle strata in a socialist economy can hinder innovation and efficiency. Similarly, the problem of inducing civil servants to act in the public interest is identified by Kay. In a 'shortage economy' there may be preferential access to goods for senior management which is not accorded middle management. Pajestka had the management problem in mind in postulating that the 'institutionalisation of macroeconomic rationality-
... should not be carried on to the detriment of the necessary conditions for rational behaviour at the micro level'. His requirement of autonomy of the firm is a response to what Hicks (*A Theory of Economic History*) termed the need for 'belowness' to counter the need for 'aboveness' in economic institutions.

Professor Malinvaud accepted the importance of Pajestka's challenge that we turn our attention to what institutional change will be needed in future to achieve global rationality. He suggested, however, that politicians, not economists, would play the major role in designing institutional change. The economists' role should be to clarify the implications of these changes. Furthermore, as long as economists cannot come to a consensus view about major issues of institutional change, they will have little political impact. To achieve an effect on policy it would be better for economists to limit themselves to more modest tasks on which consensus is possible. Pajestka accepted Malinvaud's point and was only advocating that discussion should be begun to see whether a consensus did exist.

Part III

Technological Change and Institutions: Development of Information Technologies

6 The Japanese Firm as an Innovating Institution

Masahiko Aoki
STANFORD UNIVERSITY AND UNIVERSITY OF
KYOTO

and Nathan Rosenberg
STANFORD UNIVERSITY

At one level, this paper may be regarded as an exercise in comparative industrial organisation. We are primarily interested in accounting for the highly successful performance of Japanese manufacturing firms in the innovation process. In pursuing this goal, however, it will be necessary to 'unpack', and to examine critically, some intellectual baggage that has strongly shaped and influenced the approach to innovative activity in the recent past. To the extent that our approach is convincing, it suggests a reordering of focus and emphasis in the study of innovation.

It is not necessary to rehearse the whole story of Japan's extraordinary economic performance of the past 30 years. The essential features of that performance are generally familiar, although its causes may not be familiar. Our interest, rather, is in Japanese success in innovation and product improvement. Japanese firms have, on numerous occasions, been the leaders in the commercialisation of new products, in spite of the fact that the new product, or some essential component, was invented elsewhere. Thus, the United States is the acknowledged source of such inventions as the transistor and the integrated circuit. The sequence of scientific and techological events that culminated in these inventions was clearly based upon American leadership. Nevertheless, Japan was responsible for the large-scale commercialisation of transistor technology for the radio, and Japanese technical skills in the production of high quality colour television sets effectively destroyed America's earlier dominance in the market for that product. Similarly, although America dominated the early introduction of robotics, by 1984 Japan was actually employing more than four times as many operating industrial robots as the USA.[1]

Japanese successes in higher quality and design improvements over a wide range of products such as compact automobiles and consumer electronics are too highly visible even to require much comment. The video-cassette recorder (VCR) is a rather more complex and interesting case. It is currently one of Japan's largest export items, recently accounting for almost US $6 billion per annum in export earnings. Its successful commercialisation has been overwhelmingly a Japanese affair. Although the earliest conception and first development attempts were undoubtedly American, Japanese engineering, design and manufacturing skills were responsible for solving many of the basic problems that needed to be over-come before commercialisation was possible.[2] In this respect the video cassette recorder (VCR) may constitute an interesting case in Japan's transition from dependence upon foreign invention to the status of an independent practitioner in the invention of complex products.

1   THE CHAIN-LINKED MODEL

In order to develop an improved understanding of the impressive performance of the Japanese manufacturing firm with respect to innovation, it is first necessary to modify drastically a widespread conceptualisation concerning the sources of new technological knowledge. According to this view (sometimes called the 'linear model') new technologies can be regarded, at least to a first approximation, as representing the application of previously-acquired scientific knowledge – usually meaning 'recently-acquired' scientific knowledge. Thus, technological innovation is regarded as essentially the application of 'upstream' scientific knowledge to the 'downstream' development activities of new product design and new manufacturing processes (see Figure 6.1).

We do not wish to become entangled in a sterile discussion involving artificial dichotomies. Technological knowledge is not usefully illuminated by an insistence that it is an either/or matter. Indeed, it is central to our whole argument that, in any economy, *new and valuable technological knowledge comes from many sources*, one of which is certainly earlier scientific research.[3] We wish only to insist that the linear view offers a far-from-exhaustive representation of the sources of new technological knowledge. Our view, as we will see, has important implications, one of which is that America's generally acknowledged leadership in frontier science is far less of a *commercial*

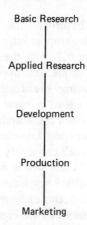

Basic Research

Applied Research

Development

Production

Marketing

Figure 6.1 The linear model

advantage than has ordinarily been supposed.

Where then are the primary sources of innovation? Our first answer, quite simply, is that they originate farther 'downstream', without any initial dependence upon, or stimulus from, frontier scientific research. These sources involve the perception of new possibilities or options for efficiency improvements that originate with working participants of all sorts at, or adjacent to, the factory level. These participants include professional staff, such as engineers, but especially those who have responsibilities for new product design or product improvement. But they also include – at least occasionally – any of a wide variety of blue-collar workers. Such knowledge typically has no specific antecedents in organised scientific research. New technological knowledge is 'produced' within the technological realm, and largely accumulated within the individual firm. It is often knowledge of a highly activity-specific, as well as a firm-specific nature.

The general thrust of our criticisms of the linear model so far suggests an alternative model of the innovation process where sources and stimuli to innovation originate farther 'downstream'. In such a model, therefore, feedbacks in which 'downstream' stimuli influence 'upstream' activity are far more common. More generally, the firm's research agenda is powerfully shaped by the motivation to exploit the accumulated stock of in-house engineering knowledge. This motivation exercises a 'pull' upon the research agenda that is, typically, far more significant than the 'push' initiated by new scientific knowledge that leads to the incorporation of such knowledge in new products or processes. In this model, therefore, new manufacturing knowledge (i.e., innovation) does *not* develop within a well-established hierarchical order, depicted in Figure 6.1, with the discovery of new scientific knowledge proceeding to sequential applications to 'downstream' engineering problems, leading eventually to the production and marketing of new products. Rather, new manufacturing knowledge receives its major stimulus from the search for new economic uses of the in-house stock of engineering knowledge, and from the normal commercial impulse to use such capability to design new or improved products. Sometimes, but by no means necessarily, this search will enlist the assistance of scientific knowledge and methodology.[4]

These perspectives can be better explored by reference to what has been called a 'chain-linked model' (see Figure 6.2).

The purpose of this diagram is to depict, in a stylised way, the variety of routes leading to innovation and product improvement. Three points warrant emphasis:

1. Instead of a single, well-defined sequence, there are a number of possible sequences.
2. Scientific research capability does not sit at the apex of a hierarchical process as *the* initiator of innovation. Rather, it exists *alongside* a number of sources of technological improvement, including the *existing* stock of knowledge. The scientific research capability is sometimes invoked, but only when other sources are unable to supply the necessary knowledge. In fact, the *frequency* with which the research capability of scientists has to be called upon is an excellent criterion by which to classify a firm or industry as 'high tech'.
3. Finally, feedbacks constitute a dominating feature. The acquisition of economically-useful knowledge is, by its very nature, the outcome of an interactive process.

This is so for three reasons. First of all, there is more than one criterion by which an 'improvement' has to be judged. An altered technology will normally be associated with some performance improvement, but cost constraints are always pertinent (at least, one is inclined to say in parenthesis, outside of the military and medical sectors). The choice *among* technological alternatives, and the decision as to *how much* performance improvement it is worth acquiring, involve commercial and economic judgements, and not only technological criteria. There are, typically, many ways of strengthening a bridge, or reducing the weight of a commercial

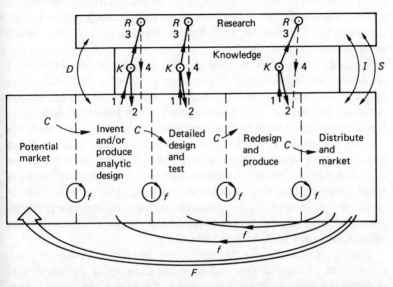

Notes: This model shows flow paths of information and co-operation. Symbols on arrows: C = central-chain-of-innovation; f = feedback loops; F = particularly important feedback.

K–R: Links through knowledge to research and return paths. If problem solved at node K, link 3 to R not activated. Return from research (link 4) is problematic – therefore dashed line.

D: Direct link to and from research from problems in invention and design.

I: Support of scientific research by instruments, machines, tools, and procedures of technology.

S: Support of research in sciences underlying product area to gain information directly and by monitoring outside work. The information obtained may apply anywhere along the chain.

Sources: Kline, S. J. and Rosenberg, N. 'An Overview of Innovation', in Landau, R. and Rosenberg, N (eds) *The Positive Sum Strategy* (Washington, DC: National Academy Press, 1986) p. 290. An earlier presentation and discussion appears in Kline, S. J., 'Research, Invention, Innovation and Production: Models and Reality', Report INN-1, Dept. of Mechanical Engineering, Stanford University.

Figure 6.2 The 'chain-linked' model

aircraft, or improving the conductivity of an electrical transmission system. The exchange of information among specialists in establishing the optimal trade-off is therefore a central part of the firm's decision-making process.

Secondly, and closely related, the acquisition of knowledge necessary for technological improvements is not a once-and-for-all matter. It is, rather, a continual process because available knowledge is always incomplete, and because market conditions are subject to frequent change. The performance characteristics of new products are full of uncertainties and commonly require redesign, as these characteristics become better understood through experience in use (see Rosenberg, 1982a). At the same time, a competitive environment involves frequent changes in response to the behaviour of competitors, in addition to feedbacks concerning product performance and the consumers' reactions to the cluster of characteristics embedded in any particular product design.

Thirdly, there is an extremely close interdependence between changes in product design and required changes in the underlying manufacturing technology. Alteration in the design of a final product, typically, carries implications, sometimes important ones, for the process by which these products are made. In fact, even this assertion does not fully convey the degree of interdependence between product change and process change. It will often be possible to bring about substantial cost reductions in manufacturing if certain alterations in product characteristics are accepted. Thus, there is a continual tension between optimisation with respect to design of the final product from the point of view of its marketing appeal, and optimisation with respect to designing the product in a way that will permit it to be produced at a lower cost.

Mediating these interdependencies between product designers and the manufacturing department can be extremely subtle, involving the consideration of multiple tradeoffs, and commercial success in the electronics industry since the Second World War has turned heavily upon the outcome of this mediation.[5] Indeed, after the invention of the transistor, American Telephone and Telegraph (AT&T) felt compelled to establish a system of branch laboratories at its major Western Electric facilities. The purpose of these branch laboratories has been to mediate between the new product designs emanating from Bell Labs and the natural preoccupation of Western Electric, the manufacturing arm of AT&T, with manufacturing efficiency and opportunities for cost reduction. Similar considerations are prominent in the current difficulties that are being experienced with the introduction of robots into industry. Given the limited capabilities of state-of-the-art robots in an activity such as assembly, their successful introduction will turn very heavily upon simplification in the design of complex products and their components – e.g., automobile parts.This simplification amounts to nothing less than explicitly designing a product in ways that will best accommodate an assembly technology subject to the peculiar constraints involved when robots are substituted for human participants. This requires extensive co-operation and intimate interaction between product designers and manufacturing engineers, and even blue-collar workers.

Thus, optimal product design necessitates frequent information exchanges among specialists with different competencies and different realms of responsibility within the firm. We have frequently used the term 'feedback' to describe these information flows, and we have, in the course of this paper so far, used the terms 'upstream' and 'downstream' with respect to the direction of information flows, although we have been sufficiently uncomfortable with these terms that we have regularly enclosed them within quotation marks. The reason for this discomfort should now be apparent. We visualise innovation as a continual, interactive process in which success requires an ongoing synthesis of changing information from a variety of sources, including potential buyers. Terms such as 'feedback', 'upstream' and 'downstream' carry heavy overtones of a rigid temporal sequence of events, and of a hierarchical ranking of significance of different information sources (with basic research at the top, technological and engineering toward the middle, and marketing at the bottom) which is quite irrelevant for the innovation process. These terms do indeed reflect the different status that is often assigned to different disciplines in the American academic world, but they have no particular relevance for the success of new products in commercial markets.

From this general discussion, we now turn to an explicit (although necessarily somewhat stylised) consideration of the large Japanese manufacturing firm and the context that it provides for innovative activity. We will argue that there are a number of important respects in which the Japanese firm possesses organisational, incentive and communications advantages over its American (and European?) counterparts. However, a full appreciation of these advantages (as well perhaps as some future limitation) must draw upon the more complex model of the innovation process that we have just presented.

We believe that this 'chain-linked' model helps to identify some substantial advantages of the Japanese firm in the innovating process.

2   THE JAPANESE FIRM AS AN INNOVATING INSTITUTION

To begin with, we must note both the size and the source of the growing commitment of Japanese resources to the research and development (R&D) process in recent years. R&D expenditures constituted between 1.70 and 1.72 per cent of Japanese gross national product (GNP) in the years 1975–8). This ratio rose to 1.80 per cent in 1979, but then rose sharply to 2.77 per cent in 1985. This last figure was higher than the comparable American figure for 1985. Furthermore, since a very large fraction of the US figure consisted of military R&D, Japanese *civilian* R&D percentages have become a far higher figure than the American one (indeed, if military R&D expenditures are removed from the figures for both countries, it turns out that the share of GNP devoted to R&D in Japan has exceeded the American figure since the early 1960s).

Furthermore, and contrary to a widely-held misconception, a smaller percentage of total R&D expenditures in Japan is financed by government than is the case in the United States. The share of R&D expenditures that were financed by the Japanese government was only 22.2 per cent in 1983, and this included grants-in-aid to national and private universities. The comparable figure for the USA in 1983 was 46.0 per cent. Of course, the large military R&D budget in the USA accounts for much of this difference, but the Japanese share of R&D financed by the private sector is larger than for the USA even if we consider only R&D for civilian purposes.

2.1   General Informational and Incentive Characteristics of Japanese Organisations

Since innovation is the production of new technological knowledge, it is to be expected that the basic nature and direction of the R&D process in the context of Japanese firms is determined by the ways in which information is processed and utilised within the organisation and the structure of incentives that supports such information processing. We first present three basic and commonly-observed characteristics of Japanese organisations, whether the manufacturing department of a firm or the bureaucratic organisation of a government ministry (see Aoki, 1986 and forthcoming). We then argue that there is a very strong isomorphism between these characteristics and those of the R&D organisation in the Japanese firm. This isomorphism suggests that the characteristics of the R&D organisation in the Japanese company is neither incidental nor easily changeable, and that the nature and direction of innovation in Japanese industry is very much shaped by such characteristics.

1. Reliance upon on-site information:
At the operating level, much less emphasis is placed on economies of specialisation in the Japanese organisation than is the case in its Western counterpart. Problem solving is integrated with, rather than separated from, the operating task. For example, the work team on the shop floor is delegated a wide range of responsibility for coping with local emergencies, such as breakdown of machinery, absenteeism, and defective outputs, without much reliance upon outside experts such as engineers, reliefmen and inspectors. Informationally, this aspect of the Japanese organisation may be interpreted as aiming at the better use of on-site information made possible through learning by doing at the operational level, as contrasted to the more intensive use of specialised skills acquired from formal training. Within the government bureaucracy, a similar characteristic appears as a tendency toward jurisdictional autonomy (the so-called 'bottom-up' decision-making process).

2. Semi-horizontal communications:
When problem solving must be dealt with co-jointly by multiple functional units, direct communication among the relevant units, without the clear direction of a common superordinate, is typical (for example, the 'kanban' system in the manufacturing process, the 'ringi' system in administrative organisation, etc.). Even when a superordinate does mediate, his role is more of an arbitrative than of a controlling nature. Politically the Japanese organisation may appear as a coalition of semi-autonomous component units rather than a coherent whole directed by the visible authority of the central office.

3. Ranking hierarchy:
If functional units are entrusted with semi-autonomous problem solving and semi-horizontal co-ordination responsibilities without clear hierarchical direction, each of them may develop its own

unit-specific interest and pursue that interest in ways that are inefficient from the point of view of the goals of the organisation. As a safeguard against the emergence of such localised interests, and as an incentive for learning to enhance semi-autonomous problem-solving capabilities, the Japanese organisation utilises a ranking hierarchy. In both manufacturing and bureaucratic organisations, personnel (workers and bureaucrats) are ranked according to seniority and merit. Over the course of their working lifetimes they compete within the organisation with respect to speed of promotion to higher ranks. Personnel are evaluated by their contributions to collective, semi-autonomous problem solving, learning achievements, and ability to communicate with one another, rather than by some more abstract measure of their individual skills. Promotion often takes the form of transfer to other departments. Obviously, the cross-jurisdictional transfer of personnel facilitates semi-horizontal communication among functional units, and also restrains the development and pursuit of localised interests within each unit. Because of the long-term nature of personnel evaluation and emphasis on cross-jurisdictional transfers, personnel management within the Japanese organisation is much more centralised than its Western counterpart. In other words, the tendency toward decentralisation with respect to information is offset by the tendency toward centralisation with respect to the incentive structure.

2.2   Characteristics of R&D Organisations

The R&D organisational process of Japanese firms shares these three general features of Japanese organisation:

1.   *The importance of the engineering department:*
Although the central research laboratory is gaining in importance recently in terms of internal budget allocation, prestige, etc., the engineering department of the manufacturing division in the large Japanese firm has traditionally played a significant role in the R&D process. The engineering department is physically located on the manufacturing site, and engineers assigned there normally have a good command of practical knowledge concerning the manufacturing process. Their primary responsibility is to develop and apply engineering know-how of the manufacturing division to related uses. The relative importance of the engineering department of the manufacturing division, located on the manufacturing site, strengthens the reliance upon the localised use of on-site knowledge.

In terms of the chain-linked model (Figure 6.2), it strengthens the likelihood of drawing upon the existing stock of knowledge rather than generating new scientific research. Perhaps most important, it facilitates a close interchange of information between those responsible for product design and those responsible for the manufacturing technology. At the same time, it facilitates an easy communication among professional specialist groups who have separate but closely connected responsibilities. The failure to provide for better communication among such groups, we believe, has been a common deficiency in large American firms.

Finally, it is essential to distinguish here between two different categories of innovation. There are two kinds of designs that may initiate innovation: 'invention' and 'analytic design'.

> An invention is a new means for achieving some function not obvious beforehand to someone skilled in the prior art. It therefore marks a significant departure from past practice. Analytic design ... consists of analysis of various arrangements of existing components or of modifications of designs already within the state of the art to accomplish new tasks or to accomplish old tasks more effectively or at lower cost. It is thus not invention in the usual sense. However, analytic design is currently a more common initiator of the central-chain-of-innovation than invention. (Kline and Rosenberg, 1986, p. 292)

The 'invention' path is the only one considered in the traditional linear model, but the chain-linked model departs from the linear model in this respect as well, in emphasising the importance of 'non-inventive' analytic design as a common initiator of innovative activity. This form of less-visible innovative activity is one to which the Japanese firm is well adapted by virtue of the prominent role played by the engineering department.

2. Transfers of researchers and engineers:

If a research agenda formulated by the engineering department requires more basic scientific knowledge than it possesses, the research may be commissioned by the central research laboratory. When a research project is commissioned, young engineers from the engineering department are normally dispatched to the central research institute to participate in the research team established there for that project. After the research team has solved the basic problems, the project is handed off at a relatively early stage to the engineering department of the commissioning manufacturing division. In this process, the dispatched engineers are transferred back to the original department. They are ordinarily responsible for the continuation of R&D as well as the implementation of the project, when completed, into a manufacturing process. By building good records at these successive stages, divisional engineers may eventually be promoted to managers in the manufacturing division and screened for further advancement in the career hierarchy within companies. Many top managers of large Japanese manufacturing companies have been selected from those divisional engineers who were promoted through this process. This confirms again the strategic importance of the engineering department in the Japanese company.

A researcher who is assigned to the central research laboratory on entry to a firm may also move to a divisional engineering department after reaching the age of 30, usually as a carrier of a development project in which he has been actively involved. He takes responsibility for moving the new product or modified product from the development stage to manufacturing. Considering the strategic position of the Japanese engineering department for career advancement, the transfer is normally regarded as a major promotion. Several years later, a further promotion may lead to entry into the upper managerial hierarchy.

The close connections between the central research laboratory and the engineering department that is facilitated by the transfer of personnel between the two, as well as the close connections between the engineering department and the manufacturing shops within a division, lend great effectiveness and strength to the Japanese firm's communications channels.

3. *Ranking hierarchy:*
Under the ranking hierarchy researchers and engineers share the cost of human investment when they are young and they reap returns to the investment only when, and if, they are promoted to higher ranks (possibly managerial ranks). Therefore, quitting a firm in mid-career is likely to carry serious financial penalties (the loss of seniority premia and retirement bonuses). As they are promoted according to their contributions to R&D projects and managerial leadership in the subsequent commercialisation of new products, they are motivated to contribute to company-specific projects rather than to develop individually-marketable research capabilities. On the other hand, in view of the impact of these arrangements upon the motivation of

researchers and engineers, the firm is less fearful of the free-rider problem (i.e., the mid-career departure of researchers in whom investments have been made, at least partially by the company). Therefore the firm will be likely to adopt longer-run perspectives in investing in researchers (by sending them to scientific conferences, or to graduate schools abroad at company expense, etc.). This in turn provides incentives to the firm to direct R&D activities in such a way that engineering and research expertise accumulated within the firm are maximally utilised.

2.3 The Chain-Linked Model

Finally, the chain-linked model may now be explicitly invoked to highlight certain distinctive characteristics of the Japanese firm in the innovative process.

In the central-chain-of-innovation path (C), the Japanese firm has been relatively more active in the downstream phases of the innovative process, such as the redesigning phase of existing products, rather than new invention. However, there have been some notable instances of, and an increasing emphasis on the importance of, innovative analytic design, as that term has been used here.

The Japanese firm has made highly effective use of short feedback loops (f), such as from marketing to production (feedback from consumers' complaints, opinions and suggestions leading to product improvement), from production to redesign (through value engineering and value analysis), from product design to analytic design (leading to new products), etc. Such short-loop feedbacks are activated and strengthened by the ease of semi-horizontal communications between adjacent functional units, often facilitated by rotation of personnel between them.

On the other hand, the Japanese firm has been comparatively weaker in utilising the long market feedback loop (F) for the perception and implementation of radically new products (although, of course, there have been some exceptions). We speculate that a major reason for this has probably been that such long loop feedbacks require major acts of entrepreneurial leadership, often involving a single individual who is prepared to spin off to establish a new firm; whereas Japanese management has, up till now at least, been generally more concerned with the efficient use of in-house human resources than with exploring possible new market opportunities and reorganising the R&D process to accommodate such possibilities.

With respect to the interactive paths that link the innovation process to science (K), the Japanese firm has been comparatively most skilful at developmental stage of innovation process – testing and redesign, small modifications of product based upon careful engineering attention to detail, etc. Engineers at the manufacturing division of the Japanese firm are very active in scanning outside scientific information and making use of such information to augment their own stock of knowledge, and to apply this new information to product and process improvement. One significant index of the greater priority and systematic nature of the Japanese approach to these downstrean development activities is a recent finding that the Japanese product development cycle is a great deal shorter than the American one – perhaps as much as 50 per cent shorter (Imai, *et al.*, 1985).

The links connecting scientific research to invention have been comparatively weak in Japan (D), although there is reason to believe that this will be strengthened in the future. As we have already seen, there has been a substantial growth in the share of Japanese GNP that has been committed to R&D, including the commitment to pure science. According to a recent report to the National Science Foundation, based upon the use of science citation indices, Japanese contributions to pure science have been distinctly rising in the course of the 1980s (Narin and Olivastro, 1986). Whether this increase will be associated with an increased Japanese capability to create truly major innovations based upon pure science remains to be seen.

3   INTERDISCIPLINARY RESEARCH AND ORGANISATIONAL INNOVATION

We have argued in the previous sections that the relationship between science and technology is interactive, not linear; and therefore that the nature and direction of innovation in an economy is affected by informational and incentive structures of organising this interactive process. We have tried to illustrate the point by examining the characteristics of the R&D process in Japanese industrial firms. In fact, we believe that our earlier discussion identifies certain advantages of the Japanese firm as an innovating institution. As a way of concluding this essay, we refer to some organisational and incentive issues associated with growing evidence that scientific knowledge, of a kind that is most likely to be useful to high technology industries, has to be pursued in an increasingly interdisciplinary fashion.

In recent years, medical science has benefited immensely, not only from such 'nearby' disciplines as biology, genetics and chemistry, but from nuclear physics (nuclear magnetic resonance), electronics, and materials science and engineering. Regarding the field of pharmaceuticals, there have been explosive advances in the related fields of biochemistry, molecular and cell biology, immunology, neurobiology and scientific instrumentation. In other fields, more productive seed varieties, such as the high-yielding rice varieties developed at the International Rice Research Institute in the Philippines, were the work of geneticists, botanists, biochemists, entomologists and soil agronomists. The trend for continued shrinkage in the size of electronic devices has created the situation where further technological progress requires a knowledge basis no longer of the kind in which electronics engineers have been trained; rather it is theoretical chemistry (and potentially even biology).

The increasing importance of interdiscplinary research creates serious organisational problems. Such research often runs counter to the traditional arrangements, training, priorities and incentive structures of the scientific and research professions. In the US context, this may imply the need for substantial changes in the university system organised on the basis of traditionally well-recognised disciplinary boundaries, if it is to make as great a contribution to technological leadership in the future as it has done in the recent past. At the same time, the American university system has developed a highly successful interface with the industrial world. Although this relationship is not without its problems and dangers, such as the potential loss of academic autonomy, a tendency to focus upon short-term problems of immediate interest to industry, and the sacrifice of basic education in favour of research, there is little evidence that these threats have, as yet, become a reality. In fact, the interface between the university and industry has been enriched by institutional innovations whose purpose is to bring about more effective interchanges between industry and the university community. The Center for Integrated Studies at Stanford is an interesting recent example of university-based research with industrial financing.[6]

In the Japanese context, where private industry has effectively exploited scientific and technological progress achieved elsewhere for the development of its own knowledge base, the growing need for interdisciplinary research poses different problems and challenges. One might think that the industry is more flexible in bringing people together from different disciplines than the academic world in which rigid disciplinary boundary lines have loomed so large; and therefore that the Japanese may have some advantage in the coming age of interdisciplinary research and development. But, as we have suggested, the Japanese firm has trained its own engineers and researchers in ways that make them especially useful for the development of in-house engineering knowledge geared toward specific business lines in which it already has a presence. It is less flexible in gathering specialists from different disciplines as the agenda for research and problem-solving requires. Recruiting ready-made specialists in needed disciplines would be in conflict with the basic imperatives of the ranking hierarchy as an incentive device: to employ engineers and researchers out of schools and promote them within the ranking hierarchy based on long-term in-house competition. One conceivable way of overcoming the internal limit of the knowledge base would be, as Western firms often do, to acquire, or merge with, another firm which possesses the needed stock of knowledge. Japanese firms have begun to be active in such attempts abroad, but domestically there has been only scattered evidence for acquisition or merger for any purpose. This is basically due to the potential difficulty of meshing two independent ranking hierarchies into one without spoiling the incentives of employees brought up in each of them.

One of the interesting organisational innovations emerging in Japanese private industry to cope with this problem is the growth of research co-operatives and projects organised by multiple independent firms from different industries (Agency for Science and Technology, 1985). This inter-corporate linkage through R&D effort differs from relational contracting in the traditional Japanese subcontracting group organised by the major manufacturers, or the ill-fated industry-wide research associations in Great Britain going back to the First World War, in that the linkage is across traditional industrial boundaries. It is also different from well-publicised research co-operatives organised by government agencies, such as the fifth generation computer project sponsored by the Ministry of International Trade and Industry (MITI), in that the formation of these linkages is entirely at private initiative.

It is still too early to evaluate whether or not the emerging inter-corporate linkage to generate new science-technology interfaces is a transitory phenomenon leading to the eventual rise of integrated firms, or suggests the possibility of a new type of viable industrial organisation replacing the old corporate grouping whose major function has been that of risk-sharing. Nevertheless, in order for such inter-corporate research co-operatives to be successful, it appears to be certain that mutual trust and commitment to such ventures by participating firms are absolutely necessary. In this respect the business morality that is traditionally found in Japanese industry may be a distinct advantage.

In any event, the crucial importance of innovation for improved economic performance poses forcefully the problem of institutional forms that are conducive to the effective interactions among different scientific disiplines and fields of technology. We believe that a careful comparative study of the informational and incentive structures of different countries (encompassing industry, universities and government) might yield high intellectual dividends.

Notes

1. Based on surveys by the Japan Industrial Robot Association and the Robotics Institute of America.
2. See Lardner (1987). The subtitle to Lardner's article aptly summarises his analysis: 'They didn't steal our VCR technology – They invented it'.
3. However, even when a new product does flow from prior scientific research, the technological knowledge required to produce the product is likely to draw upon entirely separate bodies of knowledge. Thus, synthetic fibres may be regarded as the outcome of scientific research. But the development of commercially-feasible methods for *manufacturing* synthetic fibres was primarily a matter of drawing upon an entirely different body of knowledge: engineering principles and methods, mainly of chemical engineering.
4. Sometimes, in addition, in firms with sophisticated scientific research capabilities, this search will actually produce new scientific knowledge (see Rosenberg, 1982b).
5. See Steinmueller (1987) for an illuminating discussion of some of these issues.
6. See Rosenberg (1986) for issues associated with interdisciplinary research at American Universities.

References

Agency for Science and Technology (1985) *Annual White Paper* (Tokyo).

Aoki, M. (1986) 'Vertical vs. Horizontal Information Structure of the Firm', *American Economic Review*, vol. 76, December, pp. 971–83.

Aoki, M. (forthcoming) *A Microtheory of the Japanese Economy: Information, Incentives and Bargaining* (Cambridge: Cambridge University Press).

Imai, K., Nonaka, I. and Takeuchi, H. (1985) 'Managing the Product Development Process: How Japanese Companies Learn and Unlearn', in Clark, K. *et al.* (eds) *The Uneasy Alliance: Managing the Productivity-Technology Dilemma* (Boston: Harvard Business School Press).

Kline, S. J. and Rosenberg, N. (1986) 'An Overview of Innovation', in Landau, R. and Rosenberg, N. (eds) *The Positive Sum Strategy* (Washington, DC: National Academy Press).

Lardner, J. (1987) 'The Terrible Truth about Japan'. *The Washington Post*, 21 June.

Narin, F. and Olivastro, D. (1986) 'First Interim Report: Identifying Areas of Leading Edge Japanese Science and Technology', submitted by CHI Research/Computer Horizons, Inc., to NSF, May.

Rosenberg, N. (1982a) 'Learning by Using', in Rosenberg, N. *Inside the Black Box* (Cambridge: Cambridge University Press) chapter 6.

Rosenberg, N. (1982b) 'How Exogenous is Science?', in Rosenberg, N., *Inside the Black Box* (Cambridge: Cambridge University Press) chapter 7.

Rosenberg, N. (1986) 'Some Reflections on the Interface between Science and Technology', mimeo, Stanford University.

Steinmueller, W. E. (1987) *Microeconomics and Microelectronics: Economic Studies of Integrated Circuit Technology*, doctoral dissertation, Stanford University.

Comment

Giovanni Dosi
UNIVERSITY OF ROME AND UNIVERSITY OF SUSSEX

I will comment on the paper by discussing, first, some general
implications of its approach to the analysis of the institutions
governing technological change, and secondly, the specific description
of the Japanese case.

1 TECHNICAL CHANGE AND THE NATURE OF THE FIRM

In a very general sense, firms entail three basic functions, namely (a)
they embody procedures and mechanisms for co-ordination/con-
trol/resource allocation; (b) they are associated with an incentive
structure; (c) they embody specific problem-solving capabilities. As is
known, most of the economic analysis tends to focus on the former two
functions (the classic references being, of course, Williamson 1975 and
1987 respectively), while treating the latter, if at all, in terms of the
information structure which decision-makers face. On the contrary, in
my view, the paper shows the heuristic richness of explicitly
considering firms as institutions which certainly co-ordinate activities
and allocate resources, but are also *loci of learning*. Let me develop
this point. Whatever is the information structure facing each firm, in
the typical conditions of non-stationarity and environmental complexity in which firms operate, they have to *solve problems* which are
generally *ill-structured* (cf Simon, 1973, 1979) and demand 'special'
and often partly tacit capabilities in order to deal with them. Thus one
must make a distinction between the 'information' on the grounds of
which decisions are taken, and the specific knowledge and capabilities
which allow the solution of particular problems, for example,
technological problems related to the improvement in the efficiency of
a certain process, or the performance features of a product or even the
search for a different – more efficient – organisational set-up. Notice
the difference between this view of problem-solving as a fundamental
activity of the firm and the representation of the decision procedures in
traditional economic theory. In the latter, problems are typically
trivial. They might be computationally very complicated, sometimes
even incomputable, but they are still trivial in the sense that they are
represented as problems for which there is a general algorithm which

155

can automatically generate a solution (whether this algorithm exists or not is another matter, and I discuss it in Dosi and Egidi, 1987). The case is perhaps best illustrated by perfect information models (both competitive and strategic game-theoretic ones) where the availability of all relevant information leads 'automatically' to the appropriate equilibrium (and equilibrium strategy in game-theoretic frameworks). However, I would suggest that the typical problem-solving activity of business firms is akin to the activities of getting the Nobel Prize, solving the Rubik cube, playing chess, proving a theorem, etc., whereby the knowledge of the rules and of a solution concept does not entail any automatic (let alone 'optimal') derivation of the solution procedure. The knowledge about the solution is not implied in the information about the problem, irrespective of whether this information is perfect or not.

A growing body of literature, especially in the economics of technological change, has focused on the sources of that knowledge and the ways it is accumulated within firms or transmitted among them (I review some of this literature in Dosi, 1986). A general finding is that practically all the technologies that one empirically observes entail elements of context-specific, industry-specific and company-specific forms of knowledge (in the recent theoretical analysis, this point is stressed by Nelson and Winter, 1982). Moreover, it is generally found that the patterns through which knowledge grows within firms (as well as other organisations) are cumulative and path dependent. Not only is learning local in the sense that the improvement in the heuristics for the solution of a certain class of problems may not be of any help in the solution of problems of different natures, but also in the sense that a specific learning process – and a related organisational structure – may entail a powerful 'exclusion effect': you become good at something also by 'forgetting' something else, and by becoming, loosely speaking, relatively 'blind' on other directions of search and on other informational inputs. In terms of theory all this implies that the firm should be characterised as an institution combining co-ordination/control rules, an incentive structure, allocation rules *and* learning procedures. One is also likely to observe a continuous tension, and different tradeoffs, between the different functions of the firm. For example, one may find tradeoffs between the incentive structure, the efficiency in resource use, and the learning potential.Moreover, one may have significant tradeoffs between learning by the organisation and learning by the individual. The 'Taylorist/Fordist' firm is a good example, whereby, at least for a certain historical period, efficiency in resource use and *organisational* learning (related to the optimisation of production processes, mechanisation, exploitation of economies of scale, etc.) has been associated with a very little individual learning (possibly even 'de-learning'), and ultimately a weakening of the incentive structure.

I doubt whether it is theoretically, let alone empirically, possible to define what is an 'optimal' combination. However, one tends to observe in different countries, industries and historical periods a finite and relatively small number of 'typical' combinations and, indeed, it seems to me that an interesting and challenging theoretical question is the assessment of the viable combinations between different types of learning process and different types of corporate institutions. Notably, it has been suggested that these institutions may be different in different countries in terms of organisational arrangements, even when facing roughly similar problem-solving tasks (this is implied, for example, by the comparison between the USA and Japan of Imai and Itami, 1984, and underlies the Aoki-Rosenberg paper). In the long term, though, different institutional set-ups are likely to entail both different rates and directions of learning and, thus, possibly different degrees of evolutionary 'fitness', that is, competitiveness, profitability and chances of survival, in a changing international environment. Aoki and Rosenberg describe in the Japanese case the specific combination of organisational arrangements, incentive structures, and learning procedures which, they argue (and I am quite convinced by their argument), account for the impressive technological and competitive success of Japanese firms. Let me briefly discuss some issues related to the long-term viability of these arrangements. I will simply pose some questions. They are *not* rhetorical ones but, in my view, concern major theoretical and normative problems which are relevant to the Japanese institutional set-up as well as to that of other countries.

2 LEARNING INSTITUTIONS AND THE NATURE OF TECHNOLOGICAL CHANGE: SOME SPECULATIONS ON THE JAPANESE CASE

First, note that the nature of the process of technological learning which has typically characterised Japanese firms as well as other firms from most countries outside the USA has been related to what I call elsewhere 'normal' technological progress along relatively established 'technological trajectories' (Dosi, 1984). It is true that, in this, Japanese firms have often been extremely successful, and have sometimes achieved the world technological frontier, but it is also true that in general the original search for new 'technological paradigms' and knowledge bases has been done elsewhere (generally in the USA).

Now, the point is, that the typical search process for 'extra-ordinary' innovations that one has observed in the USA (e.g., in the early history of semiconductors, in bioengineering, etc.) involved a lot of trial-and-error, a variety of attempts in different directions, and so on. Putting it another way, the industry 'learned' also by means of selection amongst a relatively high number of firms. Is this variety, with an associated high rate of birth and mortality of firms, a necessary condition for innovative search in the early phase of emergence of new technologies? Clearly, if the answer is yes, one could question the long-term innovative efficiency of the Japanese organisational set-up, now that the catching-up process in several sectors is completed and sometimes replaced by a position of technological leadership.

I do not have anything more than conjectures on this point, but I tend to believe that, at least to some extent, it is possible to 'internalise' the variety of search processes within a single institution. Certainly, as Aoki and Rosenberg point out, this requires significant organisational changes. They mention the need for interdisciplinary research, but it applies as well to the requirement of more 'task-free' research and possibly, somewhat paradoxically, incentives 'to be deviant' and 'imagine things differently from what other people believe them to be'.

In more general terms, it seems to me that there are two broad questions to be addressed, namely:

(a) Are the institutions which are well suited to a process of technological catching-up with a leading country different from the institutions propelling technological innovation in a technological leader which has to explore partly unknown technological opportunities? and

(b) What are the combinations between intra-firm learning and *ex post* market selection between a variety of firms which guarantee a sustained rate of technological innovation in a technologically leading country?

To answer these questions one is likely to have to do much comparative institutional analysis, and also improve the theoretical representation of the processes through which institutions and technological learning interact. Certainly, in my view, the paper by Aoki and Rosenberg shows how the understanding of these processes is crucial also for the understanding of economic performance.

References

Dosi, G. (1984) *Technical Change and Industrial Transformation* (London: Macmillan Press, and New York: St Martin Press).

Dosi, G. (1986) *Sources and Microeconomic Effects of Innovation – An Assessment of Recent Findings* (Brighton: Science Policy Research Unit, University of Sussex) DRC discussion paper.

Dosi, G. and Egidi, M. (1987) *Substantive and Procedural Uncertainty: An Exploration of Economic Behaviours in Complex and Changing Environments* (Brighton, SPRU, University of Sussex) DRC discussion paper, prepared for the Conference on 'Programmable Automation and New Work Modes', Paris, 2–4 April 1987.

Imai, K. and Itami, H. (1984) 'Interpenetration of Organization and Market. Japan's Firm and Market in comparison with the U.S', *International Journal of Industrial Organization*, vol. 2, pp. 285–310.

Nelson, R. and Winter, S. (1982) *An Evolutionary Theory of Economic Change* (Cambridge, Mass.: Belknap Press of Harvard University Press).

Simon, H. (1973) 'The Structure of Ill-structured Problems', *Artificial Intelligence*, vol. 10.

Simon, H. (1979) 'Rational Decision-Making in Business Organizations', *American Economic Review*, vol. 69, pp. 493–513.

Williamson, O. (1975) *Markets and Hierarchies* (New York: Free Press).

Williamson, O. (1987) *The Economic Institutions of Capitalism* (New York: Free Press).

Discussion

Rapporteur: Jenny Corbett
UNIVERSITY OF OXFORD

Professor Borner noted the similarities between the Swiss situation and the Japanese. Both were not at the frontier but were in the catching up phase during a period of high economic growth and openness in the world economy. He asked first, how this process would be affected by changes in higher level institutional arrangements such as protectionism. Secondly, since people generally prefer stability to change, it is necessary to design new institutions both to initiate change and to compensate those damaged by change. In the Swiss case the dialectical counterpart to innovation and change carried out by firms has been a corporatist state. In Western society this process of balance can lead to a dichotomy where corporatist politics prevent dynamic change. Borner asked what were the analogous dangers in Japan where the compensation function seems also to be internalised?

Professor Noguchi pointed out that the paper dealt exclusively with manufacturing industry and gave insufficient attention to developments in software and biotechnology fields.

Acadamician Khachaturov noted that in socialist countries enterprises often resisted technical changes because they required the use of resources to restructure production methods. He asked how these difficulties are overcome in Japan and whether there is any difference between large and small enterprises.

Dr Corbett asked Professor Aoki to consider the broader questions raised by Professor Tsuru's opening remarks, that institutional economics is concerned with the impact of technical change on society and on power relations. Since Aoki's model stressed the relationship between the incentive structure of the economy and the type of innovation which occurred, did he consider that the new forms of institutional change he identified in Japan would alter the incentive structure or power relations in the economy? Secondly, was the role of government still important, as in the past, in bringing about 'designed' institutional innovation rather than the endogenous change described by Aoki? Does this help to make technical change politically and socially acceptable in Japan?

Professor Tsuru pointed out that in Japan in the past there had been cases where the link between basic research and applied research was constrained by the rigid hierarchical nature of the Japanese academic system where teachers expected their own disciples to carry on their

160

work. He asked whether this problem had been overcome in the more recent period?

Professor Pajestka asked where a consideration of quality circles entered into Aoki's model?

Professor Aoki responded to Dr Dosi's question of whether the Japanese system of internalised innovation would continue to be viable when Japan was at the frontier rather than in the position of a follower country. Aoki challenged the notion that Japan was a follower which would need to change its whole orientation. This view depends on the idea that all innovation comes from 'upstream' activities in a linear model. Rosenberg and he wanted to stress, however, that downstream activities could also generate innovation. This is the view in Rosenberg's 'Learning by Using' and 'How Exogenous is Science?'. They were trying to get away from the idea that the production function is exogenous and that the sequence of innovation is determined. They, therefore, argue that many of Japan's features will survive.

Aoki also noted that Dosi contrasted two systems and asked which was viable: the internalisation or selection model. Their paper described new forms of cross-firm co-operation and these are an interesting attempt to blend the two models. They go beyond the traditional extreme models. Aoki believed, however, that the answer to Corbett's question was that there would not be a fundamental change to the incentive structure of Japanese firms as a result of these new forms of organisation.

Aoki also claimed that the cost of innovation was not a major problem, but it was noticeable that most innovation took place either in very large or very small firms, not in medium-sized ones. He acknowledged that corporatism in Europe may have helped reduce unemployment, and that some observers regard Japan as a system of corporatism without labour. His own view was that Japanese firms should not be regarded as the property of their shareholders as in the West. Japanese managers have to take account of the interests of workers. As a result, the job security of those inside the firm is preserved, but those outside it are increasingly marginalised and dependent on the state as, for example, farmers in Japan. In response to Corbett's second question, he was pessimistic about the Japanese government's ability to manage this aspect of technological change.

Finally he admitted a difference of opinion between the two authors of the paper over the question raised by Tsuru. Aoki was not optimistic about the strengths of Japan in the interdisciplinary research increasingly needed but Rosenberg believed Japan had an advantage over the USA.

7 The Effect of Innovations in Information Technology on Corporate and Industrial Organisation in Japan

Masu Uekusa
UNIVERSITY OF TOKYO

1 INTRODUCTION

Throughout the last two decades high technology in fields such as microelectronics, telecommunications, new industrial materials, biochemicals and new energy,[1] has been making rapid strides in the industrialised nations. Above all, innovations in the first two fields mentioned have appeared one after another at a great pace: in microelectronics, the smaller size, higher integration, faster processing and lower prices of integrated circuits (IC), the smaller size, faster processing and lower energy requirements of electronic computers, and developments in microprocessors; and in telecommunications, developments and utilisation of microwaves, optical fibre cables, satellites, electronic switching, value-added network (VAN) services, cable television (CATV), integrated services by digital networks (ISDN), etc. These innovations in the technology for accumulating, processing and transmitting information have had enormous repercussions on the entire fabric of our economy and society.[2]

Particularly noticeable is the extent of organisational change in the information equipment and communications industries. This has involved rapid growth in the electronics industry; intensification of competition in the telecommunications industry through 'inter-industry convergence' and 'relaxation of government regulation'; the ment of intrafirm and interfirm information network systems; and the resultant increase in the relative importance of the 'primary and secondary information sectors' in all industries. These revolutions in corporate and industrial organisation have also brought forth various problems inherent in the process of revolution. It seems that the major requirements are a newly balanced price structure in the telecommunications industry, the standardisation of information hardware and software, and a method of dealing with cartel-like behaviour by interfirm information networks.

This paper focuses on the recent changes in Japanese corporate and industrial organisation caused by innovations in information technology, and on the policy issues which have arisen in consequence. The next section describes organisational changes in the telecommunications industry, and then considers the policy options with regard to telephone rate structure. The third section concentrates on the development of information network systems, and examines several problems which have occurred in relation to such systems. In the last section some conclusions are drawn.

2 ORGANISATIONAL CHANGES IN THE TELECOMMUNICATIONS INDUSTRY

One of the most important consequences of the recent innovations in information technology has been the organisational revolution of the telecommunications industry. Technological innovations have led to new information services promoting 'inter-industry convergence' between the telecommunications industry, and the related communications industry, and provoking the relaxation of government regulation in the former. In turn this has transformed the industry from a monopolistic structure into a competitive one.

2.1 Growth of the Information Sector

Technological innovations have been providing such a variety of attractive information equipment and services that this sector has been growing rapidly. According to the definition of Mark Porat (1977),[3] the information sector can be divided into the primary information sector and the secondary information sector. The former sector refers to that group of industries which produces and sells information equipment and services and includes (a) information goods, (b) information equipment, (c) information media, (d) social and public services, and (e) the wholesale and retailing of information goods and equipment (see Table 7.1 for more detail). The secondary information sector includes all of the information services which are consumed in industries other than those belonging to the primary information sector. Machlup (1962), Porat (1977), Jonscher (1983), and other scholars, have analysed the relative importance of the primary and/or secondary information sector(s) in all industries in the United States and found an upward trend in both sectors. There are some studies of Japan (for example, Imai, 1983), and these have detected the same trend as in the United States.

Figure 7.1 shows the percentage distribution of employees among the agriculture, manufacturing, service and information (namely, primary and secondary information) sectors in post-war Japan. Employees in the information sector already occupied the largest share in the early 1970s and have continued to shift upward. This upward trend in the Japanese information sector in the broad sense reflects a similar trend in the United States, although there is a time-lag of about one decade[4] in the case of Japan.

Through focusing on the primary information sector, and looking at the degree of growth in each information industry, we can get a slightly more detailed view of 'the informationisation of the industrial structure'. Table 7.1 shows changes in the inter-industry gross output structure during the 1970s, classifying industries into (A) the basic material sector (this includes the primary sector in Colin Clark's definition and basic material industries in the secondary sector), (B) the processing and assembly sector (this includes final manufacturing industries but excludes the information goods and equipment industries), (C) the information sector (this is almost equivalent to the primary information sector but excludes the wholesale and retailing of information goods and equipments), and (D) the service sector (includes the tertiary sector but not information services). It is apparent that the information sector rose rapidly in relative importance in the late 1970s. Particularly remarkable is the growth of gross output in the information equipment industry. This reflects the diffusion of electronic computers and other office and factory automation equipment.

2.2 Inter-industry Convergence

Inter-industry convergence refers to the process by which two or more industries which were mutually independent, and so did not have a significant competitive relationship with each other, come to compete together through the development of a substitutive commodity or service in one industry or more, and the consequent increase in cross-elasticity of demand. This phenomenon amounts to convergence or fusion of the multiple industries into one industry (sometimes partially and sometimes wholly).

Let us examine a typical case of inter-industry convergence. In the telecommunications industry, hand-operated and automatic telephone switchboards have been replaced by electronic computer switchboards. The computerised switching system has made it possible for telecommunications carriers to provide not only switched telephone services but also VAN services, including code conversion, protocol conversion, media conversion, document form conversion, multi-addressing and mailbox. On the other hand, the data-processing industry has developed through utilising electronic computers and has recently begun to supply VAN services by using computers and leasing private lines from the telecommunications industry. Thus, the development of electronic computers has partially fused the telecommunications industry with the data-processing one (the fused area being VAN services). If common carriers were able to enter the data-processing industry by using electronic switchboards or computers, and if the data-processing companies were able to provide public telephone services by using leased private lines (the resale of private lines is prohibited in Japan), both industries would wholly converge, forming one single industry.

Inter-industry convergence is not a new phenomenon. Technological innovation has generated this phenomenon in the past in a large number of industries (e.g., the convergence between the natural fibre industry and the synthetic fibre one). But between telecommunications and related industries, it has appeared on an unprecedented scale. In addition to the above-mentioned convergence with the data-processing industry due to the dual supply of VAN services, there is the convergence between telecommunications and the postal services industry, through the provision of facsimiles and personal computer communications by the former, and the provision of electronic mail by the latter; the convergence between telecommunications and the broadcasting and newspaper industries through the supply of CATV, videotex, video-response systems and teletext; and the convergence between telecommunications and VAN, data processing, data-base services, computer software services, and computer manufacturing industries, through overlapping in the supply

Table 7.1 Changes in inter-industry gross ouput structure in the 1970s
(based on gross output at constant 1975 prices)

Sector	Industry	Proportion of gross output[f] by sector-percentage			Growth index of gross output[f] (1970 = 100)	
		1970	1975	1980	1975	1980
Primary	Agriculture	3.6	2.9	2.3	102	99
	Forestry & fishery	1.3	1.0	1.0	93	117
Secondary (Basic Material)	Mining	0.7	0.5	0.6	82	137
	Textile	3.5	2.8	2.4	102	109
	Lumber & wood products	1.9	1.6	1.4	106	111
	Pulp & paper products	1.0	0.9	0.9	110	134
	Chemicals	3.5	3.2	3.6	116	158
	Petroleum & coal products	2.7	2.9	2.4	133	138
	Non-metalic mineral products	1.8	1.5	1.6	101	137
	Basic metals	7.3	6.5	6.5	111	138
	Metal products	2.2	1.9	2.0	109	143
	(Subtotal) [g]	29.5	25.8	24.7	109	130
Secondary Processing and Assembly	Food	5.7	5.7	5.2	126	141
	Leather & rubber goods	0.6	0.5	0.5	104	136
	General machinery	3.8	3.9	4.3	127	175
	Electric machinery (except for [b])	1.8	1.4	1.9	96	162
	Transport equipment	4.5	4.5	5.1	127	179
	Other manufacturing products	1.5	1.3	1.4	112	152
	Constrction	10.3	10.3	9.5	125	143
	(Subtotal) [g]	28.2	27.6			

Secondary (Information)					
Information goods [a]	1.7	1.2	1.8	86	165
Information equipment [b]	2.3	2.3	3.9	123	256
Tertiary (Information)					
Information media [c]	3.5	3.0	2.8	108	123
Information services [d]	4.3	4.1	4.7	120	172
Social services [e]	4.1	5.3	4.8	162	183
(Subtotal) [g]	15.9	15.9	18.1	125	175
Tertiary (Service)					
Public utilities	1.9	2.0	2.1	133	170
Wholesale & retail	8.8	9.0	9.0	128	159
Real estates	3.3	4.8	4.2	181	196
Transportation	4.1	5.9	5.8	182	222
Other services	5.9	6.8	6.4	145	167
Miscellaneous	2.3	2.2	1.6	118	108
(Subtotal) [g]	26.3	30.7	29.1	146	172
All					
Total	100.0	100.0	100.0	125	155

Notes: [a] Includes electronic tubes, intregrated circuits, wires & cables, printing ink, paper, and office supplies.
[b] Includes telecommunication equipment, electronic computers and accessories, other electronic equipment, TV, radio & sound appliances, precision machinery, and printing & book-making machinery.
[c] Includes printing and publishing (including newspapers), telecommunications, postal service, broadcasting, and amusement services.
[d] Includes data processing, data base service, advertising, services to establishments, computer rentals, and finance & insurance.
[e] Includes education, research, health & social insurance, and other public services.
[f] Based on gross output at constant 1975 prices.
[g] Totals do not always sum exactly due to rounding.

Sources: Administrative Management Agency, *1955-60-65 Link Input-Output Table* (1980) and *1980 Input-Output Table* (1984).

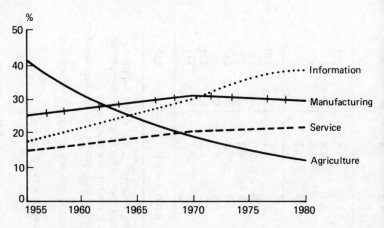

Source: Research Institution of Telecommunications and Economics (1984).

Figure 7.1 Trend in employee distribution among the four industrial sectors

of various softwares for information network systems, as shown in Figure 7.2.

Inter-industry convergence has been occurring, not only between telecommunications and its related industries, but also among the other primary information industries. For instance, there has been a rapid spread of convergence between financial institutions, wholesalers, and retailers and commodity freight transporters, because they all undertake financial settlements by using information network systems. Inter-industry convergence will continue to occur throughout all of the primary information industries because of the enormous potentialities of information technology.[5]

2.3 Deregulation

The progress of inter-industry convergence and the rapid growth of the information sector created pressure for the liberalisation of the telecommunication industry, where the domestic and international markets had been monopolised by the Nippon Telegraph and Telephone (NTT) Public Corporation and the Kokusai Densin Denwa Co. (KDD), respectively. The Telecommunications Industry Law (TIL) and the Privatisation Law of NTT were enacted in 1985 in order to open the telecommunications market to the entry of new firms, to effect the transformation of NTT from a public corporation into a joint

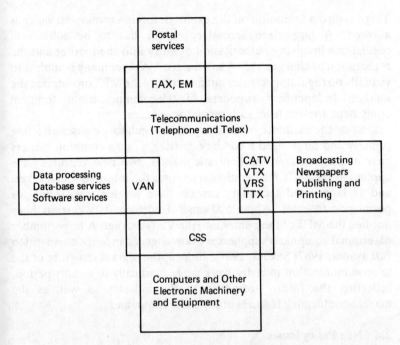

Notes: FAX: Facsimiles; EM: Electronic Mails; VAN: Value-added Network Services; CATV: Cable Television; VTX: Videotex; VRS: Video Response System; TTX: Teletext; CSS: Computer System Software.

Figure 7.2   Inter-industry convergence in the information industry

stock company under partial public ownership, and in order to improve allocative efficiency in the industry and managerial efficiency in NTT and KDD.

The TIL does not completely remove direct regulation, but contains many regulative clauses. Classifying telecommunications carriers into 'primary common carriers' (which own telecommunications lines and can supply basic services as well as enhanced ones), 'large-sized secondary carriers' (which lease lines and supply enhanced ones to the national or international market), and 'small-sized secondary ones' (which are small-sized VAN services suppliers), the law prescribes that a primary carrier has to be subject to the regulation of the MPT (Ministry of Posts and Telecommunications) in obtaining permission to enter the market, approval of the prices which it charges, and approval of equipment-interface agreements among carriers, etc.

There is also a limitation on the extent of foreign ownership which is allowed. A large-sized secondary carrier has to be subject to regulations involving authorisation of entry into the market and the registration of charges, etc. A small-sized VAN company is subject to virtually no regulatory clauses but most notify the MPT on entering the market. Independent suppliers of telecommunications terminal equipment are free from such regulatory clauses.

Despite the existence of the many strict regulatory clauses affecting primary and large-sized secondary carriers, 17 new common carriers have already entered the domestic market, two new ventures have applied to the MPT for permission to enter the international market, and 11 large-sized secondary carriers have finished registering for permission to enter. About 500 small-sized secondary carriers have notified the MPT of their entry into the VAN market. A large number of terminal equipment suppliers are now engaged in fierce competition (Okuyama, 1987; Sakata, 1987). Indeed, the market structure of the telecommunication industry has changed radically in a short period, reflecting the future prosperity of the industry as well as the market-conforming features of Japanese companies.

2.4   New Policy Issues

The structural changes in the telecommunications industry have given rise to many policy issues, but the most important one, as mentioned earlier, seems to be the question of how to form a new telephone rate structure. It has been a common feature in almost all nations that higher toll (long-distance) rates have long subsidised the lower local charges. In Japan, 70 per cent of all NTT telephone revenues has come from the long-distance calls, although in volume the latter have accounted for only 20 per cent of all telephone calls. As a result, most of the new common carriers (NCC) have entered the long-distance market (especially in the Tokyo-Osaka area with its high density of demand). They started providing private line services in the autumn of 1986, and are scheduled to supply switched telephone services in September 1987, with rates 20 and 25 per cent lower respectively than those charged by NTT. NTT applied to the MPT for permission to discount rates for long-distance private line services, and was allowed to introduce only a 10 per cent reduction, in order to protect NCCs. In the near future NTT is going to apply for further reductions in the rates for long-distance private lines and for reductions in long-distance telephone rates. If these applications are approved by the MPT, NTT will take action to raise local telephone rates in order to remove the deficits in local telephone services. If both long-distance and local rates reach a 'competitive equilibrium level' through the process of competition, a newly-balanced rate structure will have been formed.

But the rate rebalancing process is not easy. First, there is strong consumer pressure against rises in local telephone rates, and so the MPT has been expressing disapproval of any upward shift in local NTT rates. Secondly, some of the NCCs are going to supply telephone services in Tokyo and other big cities, at rates which are higher than the present NTT level, but lower than the new level proposed by NTT. Thirdly, the recent wave of technological innovations is bringing forth various types of 'bypass companies', which can provide telephone services at far lower charges. Finally, although it is at present against the Telecommunications Industry Law for resalers of private lines to supply public telephone services, a forthcoming revision will liberalise resales. Therefore it will not be easy for NTT to raise its local rates.

On the other hand, competition over rate reductions in long-distance services is also putting NTT into difficulties. Even if NTT lowers its toll rates to the present level of the NCCs, some of the NCCS, will be able to reduce their rates to a far lower level, because they are subsidiaries of big companies in the fields of electric utilities, railroads and highways which own telecommunications trunks and equipments, and so can set their telecommunications rates on the basis of incremental costs. Let us explain this theoretically because the statistical material is too complex for a short discussion.

First of all, let us limit our analysis to the long-distance private lines, where NTT and four NCCs (Daini Denden Inc., Nippon Telecom Co., Teleway Japan Co., and Tokyo Telecommunications Network (TTNet) are at present in competition. For simplicity, let us compare NTT with TTNet, which is a subsidiary of the Tokyo Electric Power Co. and entered the telecommunications industry by using its telecommunications facilities to administer the electric distribution network.

Let us denote the stand-alone costs incurred in constructing the telecommunications facilities for which the electric company administers the networks as $S(X1.0)$. If the company were to enter the telecommunications industry without any established facilities and had to establish its own from scratch, the stand-alone costs of entry would be $S(O, X2)$. If the company were to enter the industry and have such facilities provided, it would have to pay $S(X1, 0) + S(O, X2)$. But in fact the company is able to enter into the industry on the basis of its own existing facilities and with a relatively small amount of new investment, namely with the joint costs $J(X1, X2)$, enjoying 'economy of scope' to a fairly large extent. Hence,

$$J(X1, X2) - [S(X1, 0) + S(0, X2)] < 0 \tag{1}$$

$$\frac{J(X1, X2) - S(X1, 0)}{X2} \left\langle \frac{S(0, X2)}{X2} \right. \tag{2}$$

As shown by equation (2), the TTNet is able to supply its toll services with the incremental costs below new entry stand-alone costs. The MPT does not approve of such incremental pricing but takes the line that the rate for each service should be set on the basis of the 'fully-distributed costs' (FDC). But the MPT does not have the facilities and competence to screen fully the extent of cross-subsidy between TTNet and its parent company, which is subject to regulation by MITI. Thus, incremental pricing is adopted *de facto*.

It will be apparent from equation (2) that TTNet has a stronger degree of competitivenenss than companies which have entered the telecommunications industry with no existing facilities. It is claimed that TTNet has a superior position in competition with NTT. But we cannot claim the relation from equation (2). First, as NTT has nationwide transmission networks for long-distance services, it has enjoyed network externality. Secondly, it has the lion's share of the long-distance market, and has also benefited from economy of scope in the joint supply of long-distance and local services. Therefore, NTT does not necessarily have to pay the hypothetical amounts denoted above by $S(0, X2)$. In other words, NTT's supplies of $(X2)$ are far larger than TTNet's, and NTT enjoys economy of joint supply $J(0, X2, X3)$, where $X3$ denotes supplies of local services. If the stand-alone costs of the construction of telecomm facilities for local networks in many cities is $S(0, 0, X3)$, NTT's average costs for $X2$ are:

$$[J(0, X2, X3) - S(0, 0, X3)]/X2 \tag{3}$$

Despite NTT's dominant position in the toll market, and the vertically integrated power between the toll and local markets, it is reported that the NTT's average costs (shown in equation (3)) are higher than those of TTNet and some of the other NCCs (shown in the left-hand side clause in equation (2)), mainly because the NCCs use the newest facilities and do not need to pay access charges to

NTT.[6] Thus, some NCCs are able to reduce their rates more than NTT has (See Uekusa (1986) for more details).

Therefore, rate rebalancing is not easy. The methods taken by the MPT are as follows:

1. to limit the entry of NCCs into local areas and approve monopolistic pricing by NTT (namely the rise in local rates);
2. to approve the payment of access charge to NTT by NCCs;
3. to suppress sharp decreases in toll rate and approve the NTT toll-to-local subsidy to some extent, in order to maintain the latter's supply of universal services;
4. to entrust the resolution of all the rate rebalancing problems to the workings of the competitive process.

It is difficult to enforce the first method because several NCCs have already been allowed to enter local markets. The second method also causes difficulties because NTT has so far failed to take access charges from NCCs and the MPT has not supported such a policy up till now. The fourth will also be difficult because Japanese government ministries (like ministries in any country) do not like to relinquish any of their regulatory powers. Perhaps the third method, or a combination of the second and third methods, will be enforced in the near future, though this would not necessarily be in harmony with the primary purpose of deregulation.[7] In this case, NTT would have to achieve drastic improvements in its managerial efficiency and succeed in getting access charges from NCCs. In addition, the MPT and the Fair Trade Commission (FTC) would have to keep a close watch out for collusive behaviour among NTT and NCCs in setting toll rates.

As analogised from this conclusion, deregulation in Japan's telecommunications industry does not aim at eliminating past regulatory failures (symbolised in the large amount of the toll-to-local subsidy) through the dynamics of the competitive process, but at forming 'competition under regulation' (or, ironically, enlarging the number of the firms subject to regulation). There are always some problems inherent in competition under regulation: 'asymmetric or discriminatory regulation' such as stronger regulation of a dominant firm (or of foreign companies) and weaker regulation of NCCs (or domestic companies); conflicts between regulatory and competition-policy agencies, etc.[8] But deregulation has had some good effects. First, the privatisation of NTT and the transformation of the telecommunications industry into a competitive structure, taken in combination, have led to a remarkable improvement in the managerial efficiency of NTT. Secondly, the large number of new entrants into the VAN, data processing, data base and computer software fields have made a wide variety of information services available. Thirdly, deregulation in the telecommunications industry has caused a relaxation of public regulation, not only in the other communications industries, but also in the banking, transportation and public utilities industries, where competition has gradually been activated.

3   THE DEVELOPMENT OF INFORMATION

Another important effect of innovations in information technology has been seen in the rapid development of information networks. There are many definitions of an information network, but it is here defined as a system in which a variety of information transmitting and processing equipment (i.e., host computers, office computers, personal computers, time division multilisers, switching boards, facsimiles, telephones, and other terminals) is connected systematically by private and/or public lines within a firm or among firms, in order to accumulate, process and transmit promptly the data required by the firm or firms involved. The classic and most typical information network is the telephone network, in which each telephone subscriber's terminal is connected with the terminals of the other subscribers, by local loops joining subscribers to switching offices and by trunk lines between switching offices. The most recent rapid development of new elecronic machinery and equipment has led to a spread of information networks into many industries other than the telecommunications one, because of the large reductions in corporate management costs which it is possible to achieve thereby.

We can summarise the development of information networks as follows. In the first stage, intrafirm networks based on batch processing and off-line systems prevailed. In the second stage, batch and off-line systems gave way to on-line systems in which data-processing equipment and transmitting equipment were connected by private and/or public lines. At the present, third, stage, interfirm networks based on on-line systems prevail. The development of these on-line systems mainly depends on increases in secondary carriers to supply VAN services.[9] Let us examine the intrafirm and interfirm network systems in more detail.

3.1 Intrafirm and Interfirm Networks

Intrafirm networks include not only networks connecting various divisions within an office (the most developed form of which is the 'intelligent building'), a plant, a laboratory or a campus, which are generally called LAN,[10] but also networks connecting a central office, where the host computer is located, with its branches (i.e., factories, sales shops and inventory centres), in order to accumulate, process and transmit the data pertaining to production, sales, inventory, R&D, accounting, financial affairs, personnel affairs, etc. Information networks of this type have been developing in almost all larger firms (86 per cent of larger Japanese firms, with 1,000 employees or more, possess their own network, or participate in some kind of network – JISA, 1987). There has been particular diffusion of the following systems: 'on-line management and administration systems' in all industries; 'order entry systems' which aim at systematic control of a series of awarded orders, production, delivery and accounting in manufacturing industry; 'point-of-sales data control' (POS) systems in restaurants, drugstores, liquor shops and supermarkets; and 'commodity delivery control systems' in the motor freight transportation industry.

Interfirm information networks can be divided into three forms: horizontal, vertical and complex.

(A)   The horizontal interfirm information network:
Multiple firms within an industry establish and own collectively a computer centre. Members are connected to the centre by means of access lines and the centre accumulates and processes all business data concerning their awarded orders, purchases, production, sales (sometimes including prices), delivery, accounting of receipts and payments, customers' needs and other information in order to reduce management costs and help them to cope with business and financial risks. Representative examples are the Inter-Bank Cash Management Service, the Insurance Network, the Iron and Steel Data Bank System, the Fresh Concrete Transaction Management System, etc.

(B)   The vertical interfirm information network:
It is well known that in Japan there are various types of groupings of firms – groups formed by big businesses ('Kigyo Shudan'), groups clustering around major banks ('bank groups'), groups formed by a

manufacturer and its subcontractors ('subcontracting organisations'), and groups formed by a manufacturer and its distributors ('distribution organisations'). The members of these groups are linked as buyers and sellers of goods, shareholders and issuers of equity, borrowers and lenders of capital and technology, and/or as interlocking directorates. The close relationships mean that it should be easy to set up information networks within such groups. In practice, however, networks have not yet reached Kigyo Shudan and bank groups, but have been set up in subcontracting and distribution organisations, perhaps because of their greater need of data processing. The information networks in these organisations are typical of vertical interfirm information networks. A number of vertical interfirm networks have also been set up outside such group organisations, mainly among firms with a long buying-selling relationship. Most prevalent are networks between a particular maker and its wholesalers, and between a particular wholesaler and its retailers. Typical are the networks in the pharmaceutical industry – the PHARMA system.

(C)   The complex form combining (A) and (B):
This is a network in which a group of firms in industry X and a group of firms in industry Y, which have a vertical relationship, and thus a buying-selling relationship, collectively own a computer centre, and process and exchange the data of the types mentioned above. In this network we find two horizontal networks connected to each other. For a reason which will be pointed out later, such networks have yet to proliferate, but the National Banking Data Processing System and the Pulp and Paper Industry Network are typical examples (MITI, 1985).

There are no comprehensive data on intrafirm and interfirm networks. A Fair Trade Commission survey of VAN companies (which had completed their notification to the MPT) show that at the end of the fiscal year 1986 they were providing some 392 kinds of VAN services. Intrafirm network systems accounted for 25 per cent; horizontal interfirm systems 12 per cent; vertical interfirm systems 54 per cent (those associated with group organisations 23 per cent, and others 31 per cent); and complex systems 9 per cent (FTC, 1987). Although this data shows vertical interfirm network systems as occupying the largest share, if we take account of network systems established by individual firms as well as those provided by VAN companies, intrafirm network systems account for the largest share.

3.2 Economies to be Gained from Information Networks

The recent rapid development of information networks at both the intrafirm and interfirm levels has occurred for several reasons.

The first reason is, as pointed out earlier, that such networks have a potential contribution to make in reducing costs all down the line, from orders received, purchasing of raw materials and parts, production, sales and deliveries, to accounting and other management and administration expenses. Reductions depend not only on the fast data-processing abilities of computers, but also on the collective ownership of the computer centre or the specialised services of VAN companies.

The second reason involves economies inherent in networks as such, including (a) the 'externality of a network', which means that the larger a network the greater the access of each individual member to other members; (b) the 'economy of collected goods', which means that the larger a network the greater the amount of information collected from members and available for the use of each individual member; and (c) the 'economy of scope', which means that, in vertical interfirm networks especially, the member of a network can utilise the information and other management resources of the partner industry to which it is vertically connected (Noguchi, 1974; FTC, 1987).

The third reason is that, as also mentioned earlier, the members of a network will be better able to cope with business and financial risks by virtue of the large amount and variety of information accumulated in the network.

3.3 Barriers to the Development of Information Networks

Is full advantage being taken of the economies to be gained from these networks? It is impossible for the economies to be completely absorbed, because standardisation of network architecture is proceeding only slowly. In order to enlarge intrafirm and interfirm networks and benefit from the resultant economies, it is essential to connect individually different networks to each other. The interconnectability between different networks can not be fully achieved until the protocal in the following layers of network architecture have been standardised: the application of computers and terminal equipment; the presentation of language and format; the session of communications; the transportation of data; networks to transport data with homogeneous services; links between different networks; and the interfaces of terminal equipment. The definition of these layers and the formation of standard protocol have been intensively investigated by the ISO (International Standards Organisation) and the CCITT (Consultative Committee for Telegraph and Telecommunications) internationally, and by several organisations within the various developed nations. In Japan, the Agency of Industrial Science and Technology of MITI, the POSI (Promotion Conference for Open Systems Interconnection) and the INTAP (Interoperability Technology Association for Information Processing) have made efforts to construct open systems for interconnection (OSI).[11]

But the standardisation of network architecture has so far progressed only at a snail's pace, particularly in Japan. The first reason is that there are a larger number of manufacturers of computers, microprocessors, and other electronic machinery and equipment in Japan than in the United States and European countries, and they compete so fiercely in price setting, and in developing new products and new models, that they cannot afford to standardise. The second reason is that it is difficult to construct new network architecture which is not contrary to the SNA (Standard Network Architecture) of which IBM holds the intellectual property rights. Moreover, there are more concrete barriers to constructing OSI in addition to the above-mentioned general reasons. For instance, in the case of constructing horizontal interfirm networks, it is necessary to standardise the individually different business formats of each company, but this is extremely difficult because they have individually different corporate organisations and methods of management. This task is far more difficult in the case of the complex type of interfirm network, because organisation and business practices are also different. The most, and perhaps the only, successful case for constructing OSI may be the National Banking Data Processing System.

There is no denying that recent developments in information technology have provided a variety of useful information equipment and services. But such new developments have gone ahead leaving behind developments in the interoperability of equipment and the interconnectability of networks which would make standardisation of equipment and networks possible. Generally speaking, the primary information section has recently taken on the features of a 'contestable market', where new entry is easy as the result of technological innovations. Thus, today's environment reveals an increasing multiplicity of new products and services, a shortening of product economic life cycles, a prevalence of leaning curve pricing, the blurring of product boundary lines, and a continual proliferation of product substitutes (Irwin, 1981). Particularly contestable is the Japanese computer system software sector, where the individual industry line has been blurred among telecommunications, VAN, data proecessing, computer softwares and computer manufacturing industries. It is fierce competition in this sector that has generated a serious failure in the market – the slow progress in the standardisation of network architecture. It is essential to establish OSI as soon as possible.

3.4 Another Policy Issue affecting Information Networks

It was pointed out earlier that information networks contribute to reducing the business and financial risks faced by network members through making possible the exchange of information and the utilisation of the data base built up in the computer centre. Information exchange and the other functions of information networks can lead to collusive behaviour and other unfair business practices. Information networks should therefore be examined from the point of view of competition policy. Let us look at some candidates for examination.

Some of the horizontal interfirm networks are likely to file orders received from customers in the computer centre, which will give instructions regarding volumes of delivery (determined under a method of production and sales rationing) to members through the network and settle their financial accounting according to their price agreements. The impersonal functioning of the computer system seems to contribute to the settlement of the interfirm conflicts inherent in cartels, though it cannot resolve all conflicts. Such 'network cartels' seem to be effective in industries where collective behaviour is permitted under the laws for exemption from the Anti-monopoly Law – the Medium and Small Enterprise Organisation Law and the Co-operative Association Law. But, as the exemption clauses of the Anti-monopoly Law do not permit output rationing and price agreements even in those organisations,[12] the FTC should screen this type of network cartel.

Although the lack of standardised network architecture has so far prevented the spread of the complex type of interfirm network, if this type of network does start to proliferate and the members of such networks undertake collusive behaviour, such unfair trade practices as resale price maintenance, reciprocal dealing and exclusive dealing may appear.

4 CONCLUSION

Reviewing past studies of information technology and its impact on information-related industries, the author selected three policy issues (the rebalancing of the telephone rate structure, the slow progress in the standardisation of network architecture, and the appearance of 'network cartels') and suggested some policy solutions. It will take a fairly long time to resolve the first and second issues, but not the third one. The agency of competition policy will have little difficulty in restricting collusive behaviour by surveying the detailed contents of cartels and other unfair business practices which are made possible by information network systems. In addition, it is to be hoped that the agency will publish guidelines to clarify what functions of networks and what kinds of computer processing are illegal according to the Anti-monopoly Law, and what kinds of network systems promote competition. As information network systems have the facility to accumulate and process large amounts of information and to transmit such information to network members, if information is utilised effectively and fairly by the members, any type of interfirm network ought to contribute to reducing the uncertainty and risks caused by insufficiency of information and thus make market mechanisms more workable. For instance, if all the firms in an industry participate in a horizontal network with a common network architecture (so that they can all use the data base), and if they make it possible for their customers also to have access to information useful to them (either free of charge or at a reasonable rate), the network should contribute to the health of the market economy. Although there will be much debate as to what kinds of information should be utilisable, it is essential for developing information networks to come to clear decisions on this issue.

Notes

1. New industrial materials include titanium, gallium arsenide, carbon fibres, optical fibres, fine ceramics, superconductive materials, new composite materials, etc. Biochemicals are new foods and drugs produced

by such technology as gene recombination, bioreactor, cell fusion etc. New energy means new power generation systems and new energy utilisation systems such as solar generation, co-generation, fuel-cell generation, fast breeder reactors, nuclear fusion, etc.

2. For a comprehensive analysis of the impact of information technology on the entire economy and society, see Detouzos and Moses (1980).

3. It seems that the primary and secondary information sectors defined by Porat (1977) are overestimated because they include old types of information industries other than the new ones which have been formed or evolved by electronic and digitalised technology.

4. For the long-term trends in the information sectors in the United States and Japan, see RITE (1983) and RITE (1984).

5. For a more detailed examination of inter-industry convergence in the Japanese communications industries, see Komatsuzaki (1980) and Hayashi (1984).

6. The TTNet and other NCCs pay a kind of access charge to NTT which is not an access charge in US terms, but a payment for the use of NTT equipment in connecting their lines to NTT.

7. Wenders (1987) comes to similar conclusions with regard to rate rebalancing in the United States.

8. For asymmetric regulation and other economic issues concerning competition-under-regulation, see Owen and Braeutigam (1978), Sharkey (1982), Evans (1983) and Wenders (1987).

9. See MPT (1984) for more detail.

10. The term LAN is not fixed. It is used to refer, not only to networks within one establishment, but sometimes also to networks connecting several establishments. Recently the following terminologies have been used: LAN (Local Area Network), CAN (City Area Network = a network among several establishments in one city), MAN (Metropolitan Area Network = a network among several establishments in a metropolitan area) and WAN (Wide Area Network = a network among several establishments in more than one city).

11. For more detailed analysis of the interconnectability of networks, see the Japan Data Processing Development Association (1987).

12. For the Japanese Anti-monopoly Law and its enforcement, see Caves and Uekusa (1976), and Uekusa (1987).

References

Caves, R. E. and Uekusa, M. (1976) *Industrial Organization in Japan* (the Brookings Institution).

Detouzos, M. L. and Moses, J. (eds) (1980) *The Computer Age: A Twenty-Year View* (Cambridge, Mass.: Massachusetts Institute of Technology).

Evans, D. S. (ed.) (1983) *Breaking Up Bell* (New York: North Holland).

Fair Trade Commission (FTC) (1987) *Keizai Kozo no Henka to Sangyo Sosiki* (Changes in Economic Structure and Industrial Organization) (FTC, July 1987).

Hayashi, K. (1984) *Informmunication no Jidai* (The Age of 'Informmunication') (Chuokoronsha).

Imai, K. (1983) *Nihon no Sangyo Shakai* (Japan's Industrial Society) (Chikuma Shobo).

Imai, K. (1984) *Joho Network Shakai* (The Information Network Society) (Iwanami Shoten).

Irwin, M. (1981) *Technology and Telecommunications: A Policy Perspective for the 80s* (Ottawa: Economic Council of Canada) Working Paper no. 22 (March 1981).

Japan Data Processing Development Association (1987) *Network Sogo Setsuzoku no Genjo to Kadai* (Issues in the Interconnectability of Networks) (Japan Data Processing Development Association).

Japan Information Service Industry Association (JISA) (1987) *Joho Service Sangyo Hakusho* (White Paper on the Information Service Industry) (JISA).

Japan Telecommunications Promotion Association (1984) *New Media Hakusho* (White Paper on the New Media) (Nihon Keizai Shinbunsha).

Jonscher, C. (1983) 'Information Resources and Economic Productivity', *Information Economics and Policy*, vol 1(1), pp. 13–35.

Komatsuzaki, S. (1980) *Joho Sangyo* (The Information Industry) (Toyo Keizai Shinposha).

Machlup, F. (1962) *The Production and Distribution of Knowledge in the United States* (New Jersey: Princeton University Press).

Mclean, M. (ed.) (1985) *The Information Explosion* (London: Frances Pinter).

Ministry of International Trade and Industry (MITI) (1985) *Kigyo Joho Network* (Corporate Information Networks) (Computer Age Sha).

Ministry of Posts and Telecommunications (MPT), the Committee of Promotion of Telecommunication Networks (1984) *Network Shakai o Mezashite* (Towards a Network Society) (Computer Age Sha).

Noguchi, Y. (1974) *Joho no Keizai Riron* (The Economic Theory of Information) (Toyo Keizai Shinposha).

Okuyama, Y. (1987) 'Development of Telecommunication Competition and its Prospects in Japan', *New Era of Telecommunications in Japan*, newsletter, no. 31 (1 January 1987).

Owen, B. M. and Braeutigam, R. (eds) (1978) *The Regulation Game* (Cambridge, Mass.: Ballinger Publishing Company).

Porat, M. U. (1977) *The Information Economy* (Washington, DC: Department of Commerce, Office of Telecommunications).

Research Institution of Telecommunications and Economics (RITE) (1983) *80 Nendai ni okeru Joho Sangyo no Hatten Doko* (The Development of the Information Industry in the 1980s).

RITE (1984) *Wagakuni Joho Sangyo no Genjo to Hatten Doko ni kansuru Kenkyu* (Studies in the Present State and Future Development of the Information Industry in Japan).

Sakata, S. (1987) 'Denkitsushin Jigyo no Genjo to Tenbo' (The Present State and Future Prospects of the Telecommunications Industry), *Journal of Information & Communication Research*, vol. 15 (May 1987).

Sharkey, W. W. (1982) *The Theory of Natural Monopoly* (Cambridge:

Cambridge University Press).

Uekusa, M. (1986) 'Denki Tsushin Ryokin Seisaku o Minaose' (The Direction of Telecommunications Rate Policy), *Ekonomisuto* 1 May 1986.

Uekusa, M. (1987) 'Industrial Organization: The 1970s to the Present', in Yamamura, K. and Yasuba, Y. (eds) *The Political Economy of Japan*, vol. 1, *The Domestic Transformation* (Stanford, California: Stanford University Press).

Wenders, J. T. (1987) *The Economics of Telecommunications – Theory and Policy* (Cambridge, Mass.: Ballinger Publishing Company).

Comment

Tadao Kagono
KOBE UNIVERSITY

I shall comment on the two major issues discussed in this paper. The first is the issue of 'inter-industry convergence' and the deregulations that have been brought forth therefrom. The second is the economic and managerial implications of the interfirm information networks.

The major innovations have sometimes changed, not only the competitive structure of the focal industries, but also the boundaries of the industries or the inter-industry structure. The author calls the latter 'the inter-industry convergence'. The innovation in information technology is the typical case of changing the boundaries of the industries and fusing several industries into a new industry. The author gives two examples of convergence. The first is the convergence in the primary information industries, which is the fusion of the telecommunication, postal service, broadcasting, newspaper and publishing, printing, data-processing, data-base services, software services and computer industry. Second is the convergence of financial institutions, wholesalers, retailers and commodity transportation. The author argues that the fusions facilitate the deregulations in the telecommunication industry and he analyses the rate structure of the telecommunication industry as a policy issue of the deregulated industry.

I agree with the author's argument that the innovations in information technology do facilitate the convergence of industries. The concept of 'convergence' or 'fusion', however, needs to be clarified and the implications of the convergence should be discussed from a more dynamic perspective.

The two specific examples of fusions discussed in the paper differ from each other in nature. The fusion of the communication industry is the fusion of industries that provide substitutive services. It has the same nature as the fusion of the natural fibre and synthetic fibre industries, because both are the fusions of substitutive industries. This fusion might be called a horizontal fusion. The second example, the fusion of financial institutions, wholesalers, retailers, and commodity transportation is the fusion of industries that are vertically linked as the transaction partners in a value-added chain. It is the vertical fusion or the inter-penetration of industries. This fusion facilitates the recombination of various functions performed by the traditional industries and is coupled with the reorganisation of the inter-industry relations.

184

Assuming that the innovations in information techology bring forth different fusions, we have to analyse what are the kinds of fusion. The policy question may differ depending on the nature of the fusion. We also have to analyse how the various fusions are interrelated to each other. To make these analyses productive we need a theoretical classification scheme. The vertical-horizontal dimension mentioned above is tentative but may be one of the possible dimensions of classification.

The major implication of the fusion discussed in the paper is deregulation. I agree with the author's view that a certain kind of fusion, especially a horizontal fusion, makes the deregulation a necessity. The author assumes that the determination of new telephone rate structure is 'the most important' policy question concerning the deregulation that follows the fusion of industries. The most important question, in my opinion, is not to find out the optimal rate structure but to seek the means to manage the dynamic process of the industrial evolution. As the conditions of the optimal rate structure are changed by technological innovation, the actual competitive process would be a continuous, never-ending rebalancing process. It implies that the traditional famework of the theory of industrial organisation does not work because of its static nature. It assumes that the structure of industry is an independent variable of the competitive system and constrains the conduct of individual firms. However, fusion and deregulation are dynamic processes. They bring forth a dynamic game among regulators, competitors, and customers. The innovations change the structure of industry. In some situations it may not be an optimal policy to seek to achieve a competitive equilibrium of the industry, because a certain disequilibrium of the industry facilitates innovation, which in turn creates new disequilibria, and facilitates interactive dynamics of competition and innovation. It is the game to change the rules of games. The important policy question is to find out the rules of the game of changing the rules of competition.

Another important effect of the innovation in information technology is the development of information networks. The author argues that the information network was first developed as an intrafirm batch and off-line system, then an intrafirm on-line network emerged and eventually an interfirm network was formed. The author classifies the interfirm networks into three types. The first is the intra-industry network and called a horizontal interfirm network. Inter-bank networks and insurance networks are the examples of the first network. The second is the information networks of the firms in the different industries, such as Kigyo Shudan and bank groups, and the networks of transaction partners. The last is the compound networks of the first and second.

The author argues that various economies are gained by the interfirm networks and the lack of standardisation of network architecture makes it difficult to capitalise on the economies. Standardisation is a policy recommendation put forward by the author.

My comments concerning the discussion of interfirm networks are as follows:

First, the development of information technology is a necessary condition of network formation but not a sufficient condition. We have to ask why the firms seek to form information networks with other firms including competitors. The various economies are the reason why they do so. To gain the economies, however, firms have to pay costs which include not only the visible costs to form, maintain and use the information network, but also the invisible costs of cheating. For instance, a firm may send negative information concerning its good customers to protect them from the competitors. To form a useful information network firms have to agree on the sharing rules of visible costs and find out a suitable means to decrease the invisible costs of cheating. It implies that a certain innovation in the social system is required to form a useful interfirm information network. Franchising, or the formation of a coherent group of firms with shared values, are the examples of such social innovations.

Secondly, the standardisation of network architecture, which is recommended by the author, may have negative consequences as well as positive benefits. First, it constrains technological development. It inhibits one from developing an alternative architecture that is more efficient and effective than the standardised one. Secondly, standardised architecture may become inflexible when the market conditions change. Thirdly, as an information network is a part of a wider interfirm network, the optimal architecture of the network differs depending on the nature of the wider network. It seems to me that the coexistence of information networks with different architectures will be a rule rather than evidence of market failure. The competition between the different architectures is more beneficial to the individual firms than a forced standardisation, because a firm can use multiple networks at the same time. When a larger network is required for some reason, what is demanded is not the standardisation of the architecture, but the development of the architecture to interconnect different architectures.

Thirdly, the interfirm information networks will change the modes of competition and co-operation among the member firms and between members and the non-members. As the final comment I will touch on a few important effects of the interfirm network which will become possible topics of the future research:

A The network will change the key success factor of competition. When more information is shared among the competitors, the value of information itself decreases as a means to build a competitive advantage. Instead, the intelligence to draw out a new meaning from the information, another kind of information or meta-information, becomes more important. The boom of the establishments of the cultural research institute in consumer product firms, and of consulting divisions in the banking industry, is a reflection of this tendency.

B The network will give small firms a new opportunity to compete with large firms. The typical case is PHARMA. The network of small drugstores makes it possible to reduce costs and improve assortments to compete more effectively with the large chain stores. The network makes the economies of scale of individual firms less important.

C The network will change the bargaining power of transaction partners because information is an important power base. The network of small drugstores enlarges their bargaining power *vis-à-vis* wholesalers.

D As the network brings forth the opportunities for both co-operation and competition at the same time, individual firms face a complex game situation. For instance, a firm has to decide which information is shared with the other members, which should be kept secret, and which information should be reported correctly. It is very difficult to control the decisions by formal systems. Informal norms should be formed and shared among the members to regulate the working of network. We have to investigate the control mechanisms of the complex game.

Discussion

Rapporteur: Jenny Corbett
UNIVERSITY OF OXFORD

Professor Hurwicz noted that Kagono's point on truthfulness as an interesting case of the general work on revelation games (Green and Laffont) in which optimality is generally impossible. The need for central mechanisms of control, also pointed out by Kagono, is a nice illustration of institutional change which is is not endogenous and evolutionary but where there is scope for deliberate choice. Hurwicz posed two questions. First, why did Kagono argue that regulators should not seek optimal policies but merely attempt to manage? Secondly, have any comparisons with US experience been made, and if so how does Uekusa evaluate the prospects for survival of new Japanese firms and, further, how important is compatibility between electronic information systems?

Professor Noguchi asked for Uekusa's view of the TRON project which was under dispute between Matsushita and IBM.

Professor Malinvaud asked whether Japan could avoid the deterioration in quality of telephone service which, according to some American economists, resulted from deregulation in the USA.

Professor Uekusa accepted Kagono's comment that he should redefine his use of the term vertical integration. He had not thought of Kagono's distinction between vertical and horizontal integration. He remarked that the problem of the management of a dynamic process was central to the conference but it is not yet possible to see the outcome of deregulation. For example, the appropriate pricing policy for telephones might depend on aspects of the technology which have not yet been settled. The problems of management of telecommunications systems are also, as suggested in discussion, very difficult. Whether all information in a network should be shared by all participants, for example, raises questions of corporate strategy between competitors. Many of these problems have not yet been fully analysed. On the question of whether standardisation would inhibit growth, he wanted to stress the need for a standardised architecture for interconnection of systems. Once that had been achieved then a proliferation of different systems could be encouraged. Japan should follow the US pattern where market leaders establish industry standards. In summary, Uekusa agreed strongly with the first three of the four points made by Kagono.

In response to other participants' points Uekusa was optimistic about Japan's chance of maintaining the quality of services after deregulation. He cautioned that it was necessary for the developers of the TRON project to recognise any property rights which might belong to IBM.

Kagono replied to Hurwicz that policy-makers would be unable to make optimal decisions in a continuously changing situation, and that they should therefore be satisfied with managing the process.

Part IV
Incentives for Changing Society and Institutional Development: Significance of Privatisation

8 Changing Boundaries of State Activity: From Nationalisation to Privatisation

John A. Kay
LONDON BUSINESS SCHOOL

1 MARKET FAILURE AND REGULATORY FAILURE

For most of the twentieth century we have seen a steady increase in both the scope and the scale of government economic intervention. The last ten years have seen the first major reversal of that trend. That reversal may be seen in at least three primary areas. One is privatisation, by which I mean the sale of publicly-owned assets, particularly industrial assets, to the private sector. Secondly, there is deregulation – the removal of statutory restrictions on competition either with public enterprises or between private enterprises. Thirdly, there is tax reform where we have seen a move towards fiscal neutrality as the guiding principle in the design of tax structures. In all these areas we have seen a reduction in the extent of government intervention and a reduction in the belief of the capacity of governments to engage in useful intervention at the microeconomic level.

Why has this happened? There is a tendency for commentators to politicise these issues. In Britain, much is attributed to Mrs Thatcher. That kind of personalisation of economic issues is both trivialising and erroneous. It is wrong because politicians reflect rather than create changes in economic thinking, and it is wrong also because the incidence of these changes in economic policy is largely independent of political structures and political systems. For example, it has been the Labour governments of Australia and New Zealand which have been very much in the forefront of deregulation and tax reform, whereas the Conservative governments of Western Germany have done very little. We have seen similar moves to greater reliance on market forces within Eastern European economies. These changes in the political

193

climate which we observe everywhere are a reflection of more fundamental changes in economic thinking, and in particular a shift from emphasis on market failure to concern for regulatory failure. My purpose in this paper is to illuminate this evolution of economic policy by elaborating these concepts and the changing judgement of their significance and to illustrate that evolution by particular reference to the behaviour of the UK nationalised industries, culminating in the resort to widespread privatisation.

All economists are familiar with the concept of market failures, and these can be conventionally characterised under three principal headings – those of monopoly, of externalities, and of information. It is tautological to say that competitive markets fail in the presence of monopoly. These monopolies may be natural monopolies in industries where it is inefficient or improbable that an activity will be conducted by more than one firm, or they may be artificial monopolies created by private action or by statutory restriction. A second source of market failure arises from the existence of externalities and public goods. A third source of market failure, which has received an increasing amount of attention in the economic thinking of the last decade, is associated with some aspect of the production and distribution of information. Income distribution also provides a rationale for economic intervention. This rationale is not conventionally described as a market failure, but may nevertheless provide a reason for believing that governments may usefully intervene to modify the outcomes which would arise from market processes.

In the evolution of British economic policy we might identify 1950 as the high point of faith in the capacity of governments to intervene usefully in the microeconomy. It is easy to see how this faith was generated. In 1950 it was natural to contrast the very obvious failures of market capitalism during the 1930s with the successes of economic planning in the Second World War and its aftermath. Keynesian macroeconomics had created new opportunities for stabilisation policy. Microeconomics had developed the theory of welfare economics as a basis for scientifically-designed intervention. Subsequent economic thought habrought us to see regulatory failure as an issue of equivalent importance to market failure. Regulatory failure is best examined in a principal-agent[1] framework in which the principal (such as the government) operates through the mechanism of an agent (such as a nationalised industry). Any principal-agent problem is characterised by the twin problems of economic information and economic incentives. The essential features of a market as an economic institution are its economy in the use of information and its ability to harness individual incentives to a collective purpose. When we suppress the operation of the market through one means or another, we are obliged to confront these twin issues of information and incentives directly. That is the problem of controlling nationalised industries. The agent – the manager of the industry concerned – holds the information which is required to operate in that industry, but his objective differs from those of the government, his principal.

Now it should be apparent that the problems of information and of incentives are essentially interacting. If principal and agent had identical objectives then no difficulties would arise from the asymmetry of the information which they hold. If, on the other hand, the information which the agent possesses was readily available to the principal, then no difficulties would arise from any divergences in the objectives of principal and agent. Moreover, the principal-agent problem is actually one with multiple levels. There are analogous issues as between voters and politicians, ministers and officials, nationalised industry managers and their employees. Thus there is a principal-agent problem, not only involving the management of public industries, but also one involving the operations of the government itself. It follows that any government intervention which is undertaken in order to remedy market failure has itself to confront the possibility of regulatory failure.

2 NATIONALISATION AND PRIVATISATION[2]

It was the period around 1950 which saw the major extension of nationalisation in the UK. Under the Labour government which held power from 1945 to 1951 several major industries were nationalised – coal, gas, electricity, railways – and the British public sector took on the shape which it retained until very recently. The word used to describe the changes which were then made was nationalisation, not public ownership, and this demonstrates an important characteristic of the policy. Most gas and electricity utilities were already municipally owned, and the legislation was deliberately concerned to *nationalise* them. The centralisation of these activities was as significant as the change in ownership structure, and the rhetoric surrounding the legislation makes frequent reference to planning and co-ordination, although rarely with specific illustration of what such planning and co-ordination was to mean in practice. The most tangible example, both of co-ordination and of its potential economic advantages, the construction of the national transmission network for electricity, had in fact been undertaken with fragmented ownership during the 1930s. Similar developments were not to occur in the gas industry until the discovery of natural gas in the southern North Sea changed production technology completely.

The industries concerned were either ones in which free markets had never really worked at all – gas, electricity, railways – or where it was obvious to all that they had worked extremely badly – as with coal. The controversial areas were those in which markets were evidently a viable alternative. Steel and road haulage were nationalised by Labour and rapidly returned to the private sector by the incoming Conservative government. Sugar and construction were targets for nationalisation but escaped when the government lost its effective majority in 1950.

The structure of the nationalised concerns was based on the model which Herbert Morrison – the principal responsible minister – had developed for London Transport before the Second World War. In this model, as in theoretical welfare economics, it was sufficient to prescribe welfare maximisation rules. It was taken for granted that governments, and managers of public firms, would then be willing and able to implement appropriate policies. Thus Herbert Morrison had stressed that:

> the public corporation must not be a capitalist business ... it must have a different atmosphere at its board table from that of a shareholders meeting; the board and its officers must regard themselves as the high custodians of the public interest. (Morrison, 1933, pp. 156–7)

The boards which resulted were predominantly (in some cases exclusively) non-executive. The members were generally non-political, or at least not actively political, but the majority lacked business experience. Ministerial or departmental control of their activities was intended to be minimal. The intention was that the board members would interpret the public interest in the light of the somewhat vague injunctions of the implementing legislation.

The preference for platitude rather than specific injunction was characteristic, not only of the political discussion surrounding nationalisation, but also of the legislative framework itself. The industries were required to provide 'adequate' and 'economical' supplies. They were expected to break even, 'taking one year with another'. From a modern perspective it seems very obvious that organisations established with such an ill-defined sense of corporate purpose would encounter difficulties.

The failures of this approach were most quickly apparent in the area of financial control, or rather in its absence. The industries enjoyed, in the main, considerable market power in relation to their customers, and access to the capital market with the benefit of an assumed government guarantee. At the same time, their budgeting and control systems were rudimentary and, reflecting more general public sector norms, were principally concerned to ensure that expenditure was properly authorised rather than to secure its efficient allocation. Indeed, given the ill-defined nature of the industries' objectives, it is difficult to see how criteria for efficient allocation could have been established. Certainly they were not. The managerial culture which emerged was predominantly engineering-driven, stressing and achieving high technical standards; financial and marketing capabilities were relatively weak. This characteristic is self-reinforcing, and remains substantially true of the nationalised and formerly nationalised industries to the present day.

The most serious case of lost financial control was in the railway system. The industry embarked on an expensive scheme of modernisation, without any serious financial appraisal of the proposed investments. At the same time, demand for rail transport was crumbling rapidly as both road haulage and private motoring grew in importance. The industry began to incur large and increasing deficits. A Parliamentary Select Committee complained of laxity of financial control; this was hardly surprising when the Permanent Secretary at the Ministry of Transport had come before it to bemoan the fact that 'one of the most difficult things in the Ministry is to discover where money is being lost!' (Select Committee on Nationalised Industries, 1960, p. 270).

However, it is likely that the performance of the railways – where demand was falling – was only more visible, rather than intrinsically more serious, than those afflicting other industries where problems were concealed by the buoyancy of revenues. In retrospect poor project management within the electricity industry may have imposed far more economic damage than the widely-publicised failings of the railways.

By the early 1960s it was apparent that the Morrisonian framework of the autonomous public corporation with a distinguished board of arbiters of the public good was not an effective model with which to conduct industrial activities. A new approach was required. The period from 1960 to 1980 saw an attempt to develop a new structure whose main features were as follows: first the government was to prescribe a broad framework of financial control, supplemented by pricing and investment criteria and some specific directions (to provide universal service or to perform identified uneconomic activities, for example); secondly, within that framework and subject to these constraints, the management was to behave commercially, thirdly, the industries were no longer free to raise their own capital. A White Paper published in 1961 (Treasury, 1961) defined a series of financial targets, and later papers laid down rates of return to be used in investment appraisal and enjoined pricing at long-run marginal cost.

The weakness of this approach – which remains the stated basis of policy for those businesses which remain nationalised – is that the objectives of the industries concerned are, in reality, no better defined than before. The injunction to behave commercially has some negative force. It prevents managers justifying loss-making activities by reference to general public interest goals, but has little positive content. It is patently the case that commercial behaviour for electricity, or railways, does not mean maximising profits. For the first industry this would mean fully exploiting a highly inelastic demand for many of its services, protected by a *de facto* monopoly; for the second it means closing down. In the absence of more specific direction, the managers of the nationalised concerns have, in the main, pursued the objectives of managers everywhere, left to their own devices – the expansion of their business, or at least the defence of its existing structure, and a quiet life troubled as little as possible by customer complaint or industrial relations problems. The immediate outcome of the new framework was considerable over-investment in nationalised industries – accompanied, in electricity and telecommunications, by unsuccessful attempts to jump quickly to much more advanced technology – and a relative increase in public sector wages.

The primary government response to these developments was to tighten financial control and to increase detailed scrutiny of particular activities, especially investment programmes and pay policies. The number of different financial controls increased until the system was grossly over determined – a problem which existed only in theory because many of the controls existed only in theory. A National Economic Development Office report (NEDO, 1976) established, for example, that the rules requiring industries to relate prices to long-run marginal costs and to measure investment against a test discount rate made almost no impact on what nationalised industries had actually done. The pricing rules had been inoperative because the ambiguity and ignorance surrounding cost measures were sufficient to enable any price to be appropriately rationalised. The investment rules were ineffective because almost all investment had been defined as necessary to the integrity of the system and hence automatically met the appraisal criteria.

This ineffectiveness of broad direction reinforced the tendency to specific intervention, and hence undermined the arms-length concept of day-to-day commercial freedom, and eroded managerial responsibility. There were, in any event, strong political pressures for particular interventions; and however often politicians subscribed to the principle of avoiding such actions, practice could not correspond to principle. Such problems were evident from the very beginning. In 1963 the government issued a directive to BOAC stressing that 'the Corporation must operate as a commercial concern' (Ministry of Aviation, 1963) and 'the choice of aircraft is a matter for the Corporation's judgement' (BOAC, 1963), but when a year later the Corporation exercised its judgement to cancel an order for British aircraft and buy Boeings instead, the government intervened to overturn it. As inflation accelerated in the 1970s, the government increasingly sought to use the wage and prices policies of the nationalised industries as weapons of macroeconomic control. Pricing policies were also used for distributional objectives – the level of standing charges for utilities such as gas, electricity and telecommunications was a common subject of concern and discussion. The efficiency of the industries showed some improvement in the 1960s but deteriorated thereafter (Pryke, 1981).

The frustration which these events generated inevitably affected the morale and quality of management in nationalised concerns. The salaries of directors were a focus of political attention, and it was frequently expedient to delay increases or to trim them back. Pay levels for the top levels of management fell far below those in comparable private sector jobs, and this inevitably constrained what would be paid to intermediate level managers. This problem provoked the exasperated resignations of the senior executives of Cable and Wireless, and had clear effects on the quality of management across the nationalised sector as a whole. In particular, there were repeated difficulties in filling Finance Director and equivalent posts in several industries.

The history of British nationalisation comprises two main phases of policy failure. In the first – which lasted until 1961 – the substitution of markets by boards of the public-spirited failed in the face of inadequate definition of organisational objectives and a loss of financial control. In the second – from 1961 to around 1981 – the attempt to find a framework which reconciled broad public objectives with managerial autonomy failed to reconcile the conflicting aims of the government and the executive managers of the industry. The result was a proliferation of control instruments and a steady increase in day-to-day intervention, accompanied by repeated declarations of intent to reduce such control and intervention.

3 THE DEVELOPMENT OF PRIVATISATION[3]

The first industries to be privatised were ones whose activities were essentially peripheral to the public sector. Cable and Wireless was an international telecommunications company, operating mainly outside the UK (although it was to participate in, and ultimately to become, the 100 per cent owner of Mercury, the principal licensed competitor to British Telecom (BT) in the domestic market). Amersham International was a medical isotopes company which had been formed as a commercial spin-off from the Atomic Energy Authority. National Freight consisted of a variety of road haulage operations which had been associated with railway operations or left over from denationalisation in the 1950s.

Attention turned, thereafter, to industries in which there was more reason to anticipate market failure – industries which were characterised by extensive government intervention in all countries, which were nationalised in most of them, and whose continuation in public ownership had been until very recently regarded as relatively uncontroversial. Telecommunications fitted all these criteria.

The telephone industry itself had been part of the Post Office ever since the Courts had ruled in the late nineteenth century that the statutory monopoly of the Royal Mail extended to the newly-invented telephone. Until 1969 the Post Office had been a government department. At that time it became a public corporation, in line with the evolving Morrisonian model, and acquired an independent board and a chief executive rather than a political head. The Post Office was subsequently split into separate operations for posts and telecommunications. While telecommunications probably attracted a disproportionate share of the more imaginative managers within the old Post Office combined activity, the characteristics of its history as a government department died hard – including accounting systems with standards well below those required by the auditors of a limited company, a point to emerge when it became one.

The legislation which provided for the privatisation of BT also established a regulatory authority – the Office of Telecommunications, or OFTEL. OFTEL has two principal duties – the promotion of competition and the regulation of prices. The first of these is circumscribed by a variety of assurances given both to BT and to new entrants; further into mainstream telecommunications business (beyond BT and Mercury) is excluded till the end of the decade, and duopolies are established for most value-added network services. The most important issue has been the terms of Mercury access to the BT local network; discussions on heads of agreement on which some progress had been made before privatisation broke down, and, after some legal argument, OFTEL resolved the dispute on terms broadly favourable to Mercury.

The most common form of regulation in the United States is one which limits the utility concerned to a 'fair' rate of return on capital employed. This is known to encourage over-capitalisation and, more importantly, it incorporates a cost-plus element which severely reduces incentives to cost minimisation. This led to the creation of the (RPI-x) formula (Littlechild, 1983) for BT, in which the price of a basket of non-competitive services was to be increased by no more than x per cent less than the rate of inflation. After protracted negotiation, x was fixed at 3 per cent for a period of 5 years, with the opportunity for subsequent redetermination through OFTEL and the Monopolies and Mergers Commission.

The most efficient form of regulation is competition but, where this is impossible, other measures may be required. The weakness of the (RPI-x) approach is that it is not clear how x is to be determined. If, as appears to be the case, it is closely related to the industry's costs and its own expectations of movements in these costs – and it is hard to see what else it could be based on – then in practice it differs little from rate of return regulation.

The implicit problem is that there is no independent measure of the level of performance to which the industry ought to aspire. Two mechanisms which partially resolve this problem are yardstick competition and franchising. Yardstick competition requires the regionalisation of utilities, and then regulates the prices of each by reference to the average performance of all. This means that individual firms retain the benefit of their own superior performance, or suffer accordingly if they do worse than average. Franchising offers a management contract for a period of years, at the end of which new entrants may offer to provide a better service or a lower price than the incumbent. The job of the regulatory authority is then to select the strongest candidate and to monitor performance in relation to the prospectus. None of these more imaginative regulatory regimes has yet been tried and they are strongly disliked by the management of the industries concerned.

The major industries to be privatised subsequently have been the Trustee Savings Bank, British Gas and British Airways. The Trustee Savings Bank is somewhat different from other privatised industries. It had its origins in nineteenth century institutions established by public-spirited local citizens for the promotion of thrift, and by the mid-twentieth century there was a co-operating network of autonomous regional bodies. The centralisation of the whole organisation, and the public sale of its shares, was essentially a means of establishing a role and constitutional status of what was seen as an anomalously structured body with management of uneven quality. The date of public flotation was delayed several times by litigation – which yielded no decisive result – over who, if anyone, owned the assets of the bank. The TSB story deserves attention because it reveals an (implicit) aspect of the approach to privatisation – a belief that the public limited company, with a board, a stock exchange quotation, and a diffusion of shareholding, is much the most appropriate form of organisation for commercial activities.

The British Gas flotation followed broadly the Telecom model. British Gas had, until recent liberalisation, particularly in 1982, a statutory monopoly of the right to purchase, sell and distribute gas produced or discovered in the UK. It still enjoys a *de facto* monopoly of these functions. It owns a number of long-term gas supply contracts, negotiated before the 1973–4 oil crisis, which are now highly profitable. It has developed a national transmission network, a distribution system to households, and owns a chain of showrooms retailing gas appliances; after protracted dispute, it had been required to divest its oil and gas exploration activities.

After the success of the Telecom issue, the government felt able to dispose of the whole of its shareholding in gas (rather than a controlling 51 per cent), which made it an even larger issue than Telecom. The system of staging payment over three years was retained. A similar regulatory body – OFGAS (office of Gas) – was instituted. It operates a more complex version of the (RPI-x) formula, which allows the industry to pass on to its domestic consumers variations in the cost to it of purchasing gas (which should be distinguished from variations in energy prices). The provision to require OFGAS to promote competition in the industry was omitted from the original bill but inserted during its passage through Parliament as a result of back bench pressure.

4 THE INDUSTRIAL FUNCTIONS OF THE STATE

The history described above is one of parallel developments in economic thought and economic policy. Public economics shift from a principal concern with prescriptive welfare economics to an essentially descriptive analysis of public choice.[4] The change in policy thinking may be caricatured – but it is only a mild caricature – as a move from exclusive concern with market failure and neglect of regulatory failure, to exclusive concern with regulatory failure, to the neglect of market failure.

It is apparent that this extreme swing of the pendulum is equally unsatisfactory. In addressing the appropriate role of government intervention in the economy industry, it must be acknowledged that such intervention did not, in the main, result from sheer vexatiousness. If removing the intervention fails either to remove or to tackle in some different way, the problems which prompted it, then the removal is unlikely to prove permanent. The objective is to relieve market failure in ways which escape or minimise regulatory failure.

The first area for privatisation is therefore that in which markets are already working perfectly well, or would do so if they were allowed to – where the state enterprise is directly competitive with unregulated private business, or where this structure could easily be created. The state has no advantage in running hotels, or ferries, or trucks, or laundries, and these activities suffer only disadvantages in being subject to constraints of their financing and organisation structures, which are appropriate or necessary only where there is no commercial output or where there is political accountability for the results.

Attention should then turn to those areas where markets do not work perfectly, but where the market failure is a relatively trivial one. A good example is the demand for universal service. There are arguments for extending the provision of basic utilities beyond the areas where that might be strictly economically justified, but there are means of ensuring this which fall a long way short of nationalisation. Indeed it is likely that private firms will see public relations advantages, or social obligations, in such behaviour in any event. Where there are minor non-commercial aspects to what is fundamentally a commercial business – as with emergency and rural services in telecommunications – market solutions should in practice work perfectly well.

The more difficult areas arise where the market failure is by no means trivial. I identified three main issues – monopoly, public goods, and information. In each of these cases there is a conflict between an underlying market failure and the inevitable weaknesses of any regulatory intervention designed to tackle it. The answer, whenever possible, is to find mechanisms for making markets work – to lean with market forces rather than against them.

Where monopoly is the result of statutory restriction, the obvious response is to repeal the statute. But experience has shown that this is by no means enough. The endowment which incumbent firms have built up during a period of statutory monopoly – an endowment of marketing presence, and financial and technical advantages – is not easily challenged. UK experience in such varied industries as coaches and telecommunications has demonstrated that these advantages severely inhibit new competitors, and the need to give artificial support to emergent competition has eventually been recognised. In gas and electricity, measures to *permit* new competition unaccompanied by any other stimulus have had negligible practical effects. For similar reasons, it is desirable to split areas of the business which inevitably involve monopoly from those which do not. If this does not happen, the technical and financial advantages enjoyed by the monopoly operator will inevitably be used to support activities in the competitive business. This implies vertical disintegration of gas, electricity, and telecommunications.

Where monopoly is unavoidable, competition for the monopoly may be a possibility. An exclusive franchise for a period of years gives some of the incentives of a competitive solution while retaining the technical advantages of monopoly. Such solutions have been used in new industries such as broadcasting and cable and seem worth pursuing in the closely analogous local distribution networks for telecommunications, gas, electricity and water. To make competition for franchise, there have to be credible alternative suppliers, and this can be most effectively accomplished by creating a number of regional operators.

The theme of this paper has been the tension between the failure of markets and the failures of regulation, and the need to find structures which minimise the extent of either. The real objective of policy should be to reconstruct, as far as possible, the organisation of public sector activities to create the conditions that make private sector operations effective and efficient – the relative specificity of objectives, the greater clarity of the framework of constraints, and the pressures of competition. The possibilities for so doing extend far beyond public sector industrial activities. Nor can they be given full scope within those industrial activities unless the organisation of the industries concerned is given careful consideration before privatisation occurs.

Notes

1. See Hart (1983) for an introduction to problems of this kind.
2. Histories of the development of nationalised industry policy in the UK can be found, for example, in Tivey (1966), Kelf-Cohen (1969) and Pryke (1981).
3. For more extensive accounts of UK privatisation see Kay, Mayer and Thompson (1986) and Kay (1987).
4. Seminally in Buchanan and Tullock (1969).

References

BOAC (1963) Annual Report, 1962–1963.
Buchanan, J. M. and Tullock, G. (1969) *The Calculus of Consent* (Ann Arbor: University of Michigan Press).
Hart, O. (1983) 'Optimal labour contracts under asymmetric information', *Review of Economic Studies*, vol. 50, January. pp. 3–35.
Kay, J. A. (1987) 'The State and the Market: the UK Experience of Privatisation', Group of 30 Occasional Paper no. 23. (London and New York).
Kay, J. A., Mayer, C. P. and Thompson, D. A. (eds) (1986) *Privatisation and Regulation–the UK Experience* (Oxford: Oxford University Press).
Kelf-Cohen, R. (1969) *Twenty Years of Nationalisation* (London: Macmillan Press).
Littlechild, S. (1983) 'Regulation of British Telecommunications' Profitability' (London: Department of Industry).
Ministry of Aviation (1963) *The Financial Problems of the British Overseas Airways Corporation* (London: HMSO).
Morrison, H. (1933) *Socialisation and Transport*, (London: Constable).
NEDO (1976) 'A Study of UK Nationalised Industries' (London: NEDO).
Pryke, R. (1981) *The Nationalised Industries: Policies and Performance since 1968* (Oxford: Martin Roberson).

Select Committee on Nationalised Industries (1960) *British Railways* (London: HMSO).
Tivey, L. (1966) *Nationalisation in British Industry* (London: Cape).
Treasury (1961) *The Financial and Economic Objectives of the Nationalised Industries*, Cmnd B37 (London: HMSO).

Comment

Jun Ikegami
KYOTO UNIVERSITY

The paper presented by Professor Kay suggests that the process of privatisation in industrialised countries shows tension between the failure of markets and the failures of regulation.

I would like to raise a question on the significance of privatisation, deregulation, and so on. If the government had to choose between policies designed to redress market failure or to correct regulation failure, which do we think it should choose? Contemporary situations in our economy put us into a dilemma.

Generally speaking, major doctrines of public administration suggest that we have to be interested in non-profit-making organisations (or the third sector in Japan) to resolve such a problem. Of course, with non-profit-making organisations it is expected that regulations in the public interest will be compatible with market efficiency.

But some leaders of organisations in the third sector may be bureaucratic administrators of government and powerful business led by self-interested traders. In that case, we shall face the problem that inefficiency from bureaucratisation of government is compatible with speculative activities resulting from the self-seeking traders. These situations will promote stagflation and short supply.

If we want to find a better way with a more decentralised, efficient and democratic organisation, then co-oerative ownership and a network connected with grass-roots' democracy or consumers' movements in local communities may be the answer.

In 1982, Jessica Lipnack and Jeffrey Stamps published an excellent work named *Networking*. Following Y. Masuda (translator, Japanese edition), there is 'Another America' different from President Reagan's strong or powerful America in this valuable contribution.

In 'Another America' independent citizens communicate with each other and voluntarily form autonomous groups for common public purposes, such as environmental conservation, social security, education, human development, energy, health and new production systems, and autonomous groups work together and participate at all levels of the process of public decision-making. That is, an 'invisible hand' for the rational allocation of resources in our society compatible with a free market.

These networks can often collect money from supporters or establish co-operatives for the growth of their movement and the wider spread of their networking. In the 1980s we experienced rapid growth of co-operatives and workers' collectives in many countries.

We can call it revitalising co-operative ownership in the information society. In the 1960s co-operatives, supported by the labour unions in Western European countries, faced a kind of crisis resulting from the challenge of big business. However, in the 1980s we find a new type of co-operative originating with local citizens, which we can call a 'grass roots' type of co-operative.

When the co-operative was born at the beginning of the era of industrialisation, it was often regarded as Utopia; and since the Second World War it has been considered a kind of competitive element in the market supported by the labour union.

Now information technology gives co-operatives the base for decentralised, democratic, and united free organisations through the new transport system, telecommunication system, computers and news media. If such networking can connect with, and participate in, the system of public decision-making, we may be able to correct failures of privatisation and regulation.

Today, in the information society, it is necessary for us to co-ordinate useful information for decision-making. For this purpose we need all kinds of experts or professionals who can co-ordinate and lead different private interests and advice on social and equitable decision-making in the public interest.

If, on the contrary, these persons use their abilities for the benefit of companies that speculate or take concessions for profit, then the increase of power of the companies may create a crisis in human life resulting from the destruction of the environment, a poor standard of living and inflation through real estate exchange and stock speculation, etc. This is because these same people do not have access to scientific data and are not able to use their equitable judgement in decision-making, and thus do not have a chance to prevent such a company from destroying the environment.

Consequently we have to try to establish a kind of system in which experts and professionals can be independent from bureaucratic organisation and the companies that like speculation or concessions.

For this purpose, government must encourage the growth of funds for networking, co-operatives, etc., by means of a new tax or financial system.

If we succeed in establishing such a system of networking or co-operatives supported by professionals independent of a bureaucratic state and speculative traders seeking concessions, we can talk of networking supported by professionals.

Such a system will be the 'common stock' of our society.

Adam Smith in 1776 wrote as follows:

> The effects of those different geniuses and talents, for want of the power or disposition to barter and exchange, cannot be brought into a common stock, and do not in the least contribute to the better accommodation and conveniency of the species. Each animal is still obliged to support and defend itself, separately and independently, and derives no sort of advantage from that variety of talents with which nature has distinguished its fellows. Among men, on the contrary, the most dissimilar geniuses are of use to one another; the different produces of their respective talents, by the general disposition to truck, barter and exchange, being brought, as it were, into a common stock, where every man may purchase whatever part of the produce of other men's talents he has occasion for. (Smith, 1776, p. 15)

Since the days of Adam Smith, the power or disposition to exchange based on the division of labour and commodity production has brought a kind of 'invisible hand' to our human society. Today, networkings behind the division of labour and participation in the process of public decision-making, supported by professionals who work as co-ordinators of useful information, could bring us a contemporary 'invisible hand'.

Privatisation may not be able to succeed without these two kinds of invisible hands, that is, the disposition for free market and networking.

References

Lipnack, J. and Stamps, J. (1982) *Networking* (New York) (translated by Masamura, K. into Japanese; Tokyo: President Publishers).

Smith, A. (1776) *An Inquiry into the Nature and Causes of the Wealth of Nations*, 1960 edition, (London: Dent, Everyman Library), Vol. 1.

Comment

Yataro Fujii
KEIO UNIVERSITY

Professor Kay gives us several effective suggestions: privatisation and deregulation should be distinguished; privatisation should be individually assessed country by country, though the intellectual climate has changed world-wide; the objective is to relieve market failures in ways which avoid or minimise regulatory failures. I basically agree with him on all of these points.

I would like to make two comments. The first concerns the relationship of privatisation to fairness or equity. In this chapter, privatisation, market failures and regulatory failures are approached mainly in terms of efficiency. However, has public ownership been effected only for the reason of efficiency? If public ownership was selected, or at least partly selected, by objectives other than efficiency, then it is necessary to take into account the effect of privatisation on the attainment of such objectives.

Of course, this does not imply neglecting efficiency. The attainment of efficiency is the necessary condition for any objective. But it may not be sufficient. The demand upon public utilities from society these days is characterised by the fact that many of the requirements are founded on the perception of fairness or equity.

In the case of Japan, for example, the Expressway Network which is operated by the Japan Highway Public Corporation, is still at a low level compared with western countries. And the expansion of the network is in progress through a pooling system of toll revenues; in other words, through cross-subsidisation. The whole plan of the network is basically designed for access to the network from any point in the country within one hour. Apparently this is based on the concept of equality.

The second comment is related to efficiency. In the last part of the paper Professor Kay points out the increased productivity in some nationalised industries which have no plans for privatisation.[1] From this fact it is suggested that it is possible to attain the same increase of productivity in public enterprise as the private sector by the improvement of organisation and the appointment of enterprising management. The effect of privatisation on efficiency is concluded as a loose one.

This point is particularly interesting for people of this country

210

because similar arguments were raised when privatisation of the Japanese National Railways (JNR) was proposed. On that occasion there were assertions that the inefficiency of public enterprise largely resulted from the excess intervention from politics, and that if the freedom of management from politics were firmly established, then even in public enterprise it would be possible to attain efficient management. From this viewpoint, it was argued that JNR should not be privatised.

However, the public enterprise was originally selected as a tool of policy and therefore intervention from politics is more or less unavoidable. In that respect, Herbert Morrison's model of public enterprise, developed as minister responsible in the UK after the Second World War, reflects exactly its expected role. The separation of management from politics in public enterprise could not be sufficiently attained. Thus, when we evaluate whether or not the continuation of public enterprise will be preferable to privatisation, we should take into account the relationship between the changing role of public enterprise in the economy and the inherent constraints of public ownership.

Now I should like to deal with some aspects of privatisation in Japan. In this country many public utilities, for example, electricity, gas and many urban railways, have been operated by private companies under regulation. All three large-scale nationalised enterprises, railways, telecommunications and tobacco, are under the process of privatisation.

Privatisation may remove some regulations imposed on public enterprise, but it may be necessary to prevent the privatised enterprise from exploitative use of its monopolistic power which it obtained under public ownership.

In the case of air transport in Japan, recently a deregulation policy was adopted. While it encouraged existing airlines to compete against each other, it did not reduce the regulation of new entrants to reinforce the existing competitors against the semi-public enterprise, Japan Airlines. JAL is going to be entirely privatised by the sale of the remaining 30 per cent of stock held by the government. So this may be an example of the distinction between privatisation and deregulation to which Professor Kay referred.

As for Japanese National Railways, the first stage of privatisation was carried out this April by the formation from a public enterprise of companies which are virtually private ones, and all its stocks now held by the Settlement Corporation are going to be sold.

Privatisation of railways may be Japan's specific feature. In addition, privatisation of JNR was combined with the dismemberment of the network. JNR was divided into six regional passenger companies and a freight company. It was argued that the division into regions would offer the optimal size of management to meet demand in a competitive market, to constitute an efficient structure of administration, and to maintain cross-subsidisation. Regarding the Shinkansen network, in order to form an organisation of cross-subsidisation for the reimbursement of capital costs, and to maintain the consistency of nationwide planning, a public independent body was established holding the capital of the whole Shinkansen network, and has leased each line to the passenger company concerned locally.

Another aspect of privatisation is the rise of the so-called third sector, that is, hybrid, companies. The companies, financed and staffed from both the public and private sectors, are not new, but recently they have increasingly expanded their sphere of operation, including, for example, the construction and running of an international airport to small rural bus services. However, much more time is needed before any conclusions can be drawn about privatisation and the third sector in Japan.

Note

1. This point has been omitted in the revised version of the paper.

Discussion

Rapporteur: Jenny Corbett
UNIVERSITY OF OXFORD

Professor Lombardini pointed out that the standard definition of market failure in economic theory was limited. The definition worked well for the problem of externalities. It was necessary, however, to have a broader definition than one which captured only the static concept of monopoly power. A definition which encompassed the more fruitful dynamic concept of economic power was required. This would allow us to consider the problems of innovation and of the creation of those social and cultural conditions which are more favourable to growth.

In considering regulatory failure it was a mistake to evaluate the goals of the state in terms purely of the short run (as, for example, with stabilisation performance). The objectives of the state are more appropriately long run and there may be long-run benefits from short-run inefficiencies. Further, there are no theoretical reasons why certain activities not undertaken by the private sector should not be carried out by the state. There are efficient and inefficient public firms just as there are efficient and inefficient private ones. To understand why some state enterprises are inefficient we need to consider the relationship between the economic and political systems. For that exercise we need an appropriate definition of economic power.

Mr Crough noted that there have been two types of privatisation. There have been those, the 'Thatcher model', where the proceeds from privatisation go to the consolidated revenue of the government and those, the 'Australian-New Zealand model', where proceeds go to improving the capital structure of the privatised industry itself. He asked what had happened in the newly-privatised industries in the UK and how they had been able to improve their poor financial condition (high debt-equity ratios) after privatisation?

Professor Wheelright was concerned that, although Professor Kay discussed politics and public ownership, he had little to say about politics and private ownership. The links between big private corporations, political parties and governments are well-documented. Should this not be brought into the discussion? He also asked whether Kay had any observations on the fact that privatisation expanded the private sector and that the existing private sector had a

213

strong tendency towards increasing concentration and monopoly or oligopoly power?

Professor Hurwicz thought Kay's distinction between market and regulatory failure was very useful. This suggests it is desirable to distinguish between failures due to inherent (non-institutional) features of the economy (such as increasing returns technologies) and those specific to a particular institutional arrangement. Among the true market failures it is desirable to distinguish those where competition is possible but would have inefficient or undesirable outcomes (as in the presence of externalities) and those where competition is impossible (or very unlikely) – as in the presence of major economies of scale. Hurwicz asked why Kay favoured exclusive franchising in situations where monopoly is inevitable. Would it involve payment to a public authority and supervision of quality? In what way do unregulated franchises avoid the problems of ordinary monopolies?

Professor Schotter argued that Kay implied the major reason for privatisation was to deal with regulatory failures. The 'failure', however, seemed to be that nationalised firms did not behave like private firms. The difference in behaviour might in fact stem from a difference in objective function. Schotter quoted the example of airlines which, when privatised, no longer served small towns in the country. Schotter suspected that current calls for privatisation arose from a change in attitude to these different objectives. People were no longer willing to tolerate the degree of subsidy that was required to support the different objectives.

Professor Pajestka observed that our discussion implied that the only solution to regulatory failure was privatisation, while the only solution to market failure was public ownership. In fact a variety of solutions to regulatory failure are available, as is demonstrated by the experience of the USSR.

Professor Iwata pointed out that historical perspective was missing from the discussion. The pros and cons of markets versus government control were debated as early as 81 BC in China, in relation to the iron and salt industries.

Professor Tsuru agreed with Wheelwright in stressing the importance of relating politics to privatisation. The privatisation of the Japan National Railways, to paraphrase Kay, had 'its roots in Conservative planning while in power, to reduce the power of public sector trade unions'. Taking up Crough's point, in the NTT case the major portion of equity is held by the Treasury as a source of government revenue.

Professor Kay opened with a response to Crough, commenting that in UK privatisations there has typically been large outstanding debt and the decision on treatment of debt to the government has been important. Although the privatised industries have not retained any of the funds, the adjustment of outstanding debt to the government means that the debt/equity ratios of the new firms have been improved. Whether or not one motive for privatisation was to defeat the unions, experience has shown that the government has been more effective in defeating the unions by tackling them within the remaining public industries. Coal in the UK is an example. Kay also noted Ikegami's interesting suggestion that co-operatives could be an alternative to either public or private ownerships. It is puzzling why co-operatives have been so unsuccessful recently. They appear to have many characteristics of the weakest public industries. It appears that labour-managed industry has been resistant to change. Taking up Wheelwright's challenge, Kay agreed that the discussion of government industry relations was important. The term 'crony capitalism' implied close and comfortable relations between government and private firms. In the UK, on the contrary, the relationship between government and the nationalised industries had been abrasive. This contrasted with the experience in France, as note by Malinvaud. Kay acknowledged Hurwicz's doubts about franchising, saying that it should be the subject of a separate paper. He believed, however, that the outcome depended on how franchising contrasts were designed; good contracts give good results while bad ones give bad results. There are examples of both kinds in UK franchising experience.

To conclude, Kay stressed that privatisation is merely a different form or regulatory arrangement between the state and capital. Nationalisation does not imply the equality of state and management but is rather another type of relationship. The dichotomy should not be exaggerated. He disagreed with Schotter's argument that performance reflected different objective functions for nationalised industries. In particular, equity was not a major objective function for many industries. Arguments about fairness have been used after the fact by interest groups so that nationalised industries have become a means of using the political process to extract rents for those groups. Therefore, the real issue of the debate about privatisation and nationalisation is that it opens up the question of whether we need new patterns for the future.

Part V
Reviews and Conclusions

Closing Remarks on Part I

Phyllis Deane
UNIVERSITY OF CAMBRIDGE

The two papers scheduled for this session were Siro Lombardini's 'Market and Institutions' focused mainly on conceptual and theoretical issues, and Ted Wheelwright and Greg Crough's 'The Changing Pacific Rim Economy with Special Reference to Japanese Transnational Corporations: A View from Australia' which was an exercise in up-to-the-minute economic history. It should be said, however, that the flavour of the discussion of these two papers (and even of the authors' brief introductory remarks) was influenced by Professor Shigeto Tsuru's keynote address 'Economic Institutions or Institutional Economics' delivered at the opening session and thus fresh in the minds of participants in Session I that afternoon. Three messages from the keynote address recurred in the Session I debate! They were those stressing the need for modern economists – (1) to lay down a stronger and broader basis of empirical work; (2) to recognise and take full analytical account of the normative issues implicit in most economic problems; and (3) to focus on the real-world mixed economy rather than on some abstract or socialist economic system. Moreover, the main thrust of Professor Tsuru's argument for a conscious revival of the more broadly conceived discipline of political economy (in place of a purely positive economic science) synchronised with the underlying theme running through the Lombardini paper, was implicit in the analytical perspective of Wheelwright and Crough and informed much of the open discussion of Session I.

Professor Lombardini's paper opened up a rich vein of ideas at three levels; at ground level he examined the concept of the market – identifying five possible definitions and selecting two that were evidently relevant to existing economic theories of the market; at the second level he explored the interplay between the market economy and the political system on which it operates; at the third, he further developed what could be interpreted as his main theme by examining connections between sociopolitical and economic systems more generally, and, with special relevance to recent economic theorising, focused on the dynamic interactions between structural changes in the economic system and associated developments in social institutions. Finally he faced up bravely to some of the difficult normative issues inherent in the problems of designing a rational political system in conjunction with an efficient and just economic system.

Pressure of time means that I can do no more than refer selectively to what seem to me to be the most striking issues raised by the wide-ranging discussion on the Lombardini paper. A good deal of the debate revolved around the conceptual issues which needed to be ventilated at an early stage in the conference. Here the official discussant, Professor Schotter, set the ball rolling fast and effectively by defining both institution (which term Professor Lombardini had failed to define) and market, and to do so on a consistent basis. Schotter's preferred definition of an institution can be summarised as a regularity in the behaviour of economic agents which allows them to solve a set of recurrent problems that they face in a dynamic (i.e., a developed) economic system. He distinguished it from an alternative definition used by game theorists, by whom an economic institution has been defined as a set of rules which constrains the behaviour of economic agents and determines outcomes on the basis of the choices they make. Clearly choices between definitions ought to be made by reference to the analytical use that the concept is intended to serve, and other contributors to the debate suggested new variants of, or new perspectives on, the definition of an institution. The interesting thing about Schotter's preferred definition, however, was that it enabled him to define the market as an institution, and he then went on to a libertarian definition of markets, i.e., markets are what people who believe in free markets think they are. Such a definition is consistent with the classical invisible hand doctrine that optimal outcomes will result if no constraints are imposed on voluntary exchange: and it fits nicely both with Professor Lombardini's 'market culture' notion associated with self-interested behaviour, and with his central definition of the market as a set of procedures by which information is provided by sellers to purchasers (and vice versa), and in which individual agents interact to reach a general equilibrium.

Another area which attracted a number of contributions to the open debate was a listing of the weaknesses of traditional, formalist, economic theorising, though it must be said that not all those who spoke on this matter were persuaded of the total irrelevance of vigorous economic theorising. There was, however, a strong consensus (by no means new in the annals of economic thought) to the effect that economists are unlikely to make much progress in explaining or prescribing for the problems facing a developing economic system if they persist in insulating their applied analyses from all consideration of the non-economic determinants of economic development. Professor Malinvaud, for example, pointed to a need for more research at the interface between the study of economic and political institutions.

The Wheelwright and Crough paper brought some of the theoretical problems considered in the first part of Session I into a real-world arena by throwing a spotlight on a specific area in which the winds of change generated by market forces are currently transforming both the institutional framework and the economic structure of the world economy at a dramatic rate. They depicted an ongoing process of internationalisation of capitalism in the Pacific Rim economy, which has had the effect of eroding the role of the national states of that region by limiting their ability either to control markets or to influence the rules of the game under which transnational corporations have been able to expand their operations and the range of their influence over political institutions. What Wheelwright and Crough have illustrated above all, in their extraordinarily instructive and thought-provoking paper, is the urgent need for more empirical investigation in this research programme. Like all good research, their results raise more questions than can yet be answered. The research frontier is a moving one, and accordingly, the subsequent debate ranged over too wide an area to be encapsulated in a brief summary review. What is evident is that the long-term significance of the internationalisation process – its significance, that is to say, for the distribution and growth of world incomes, for the stability of the international economic order, for the relationships between national governments, transnational corporations, trade unions and other institutions, and for the power of small (and large) nations to control their own economic destinies – is still tantalisingly obscure.

In conclusion, let me say what has seemed to me the most remarkable feature of the debates unleashed at this conference. Schumpeter once wrote – I think it was in his *Theory of Economic Development* – that it is the task of 'we economists ... to pursue our exploratory efforts until we ground upon a non-economic bottom'. What we are now witnessing, I think, is the spectacle of more and more economists radically revising their charts showing the position of that non-economic bottom and displaying an almost reckless willingness to sail their frail analytical crafts into deeper and deeper waters. Some of these daring souls will no doubt sink without trace. But we may reasonably hope that some will be able to deliver the advances in economic knowledge that may assist in the creation and marriage of a rational political system and an efficient and just economic system.

Closing Remarks on Part II

Hirofumi Uzawa
UNIVERSITY OF TOKYO

The session reported in Part II of this volume was devoted to the problems of institutions, mechanisms and the evolution of economic systems. The first paper was presented by Professor Hurwicz, entitled 'Mechanisms and Institutions'. The second paper, 'Institutional Change for the Future: Socialist Experience and New Horizons', was presented by Professor Pajestka.

Hurwicz's paper is concerned with the nature and role of institutions in the processes of resource allocation and income distribution. The main analytical framework adopted by Professor Hurwicz to solve this problem is that of the theory of mechanisms which he and his associates have developed extensively in the last decade or so. The concept of mechanism he employs is broad enough to cover both market and command economies. A mechanism encompasses the pattern of response which each economic agent adopts under given environments, rules and information available to him, and the outcome in terms of the allocation of resources and the distribution of products. It also specifies the rules each agent is obliged to follow and the incentives which govern his behaviour. The outcome of the resource allocation under a given mechanism is compared in terms of various criteria or performance functions which relate the outcomes to economic environments. Hurwicz asks the following question: Given a performance function, is it possible to design a mechanism which realises it? The existence of such a mechanism is provided by direct revelation, but the relevant question is how to design a mechanism which realises the given performance function with minimum message space or other informational requirements.

The problem is then taken up from the game-theoretic framework in which it is possible to extend the criteria from those of Pareto optimality and individual rationality.

Hurwicz then goes on to discuss the conditions under which a given performance function may be implemented by institutional arrangements familiar to us, such as markets. In order to do this, it becomes necessary to extend the normal-form-game-theoretic approach to the model involving games in extensive form. In this respect he argues that the ownership problem is not as crucial as most authors tend to assume. Following the works of Williamson, he emphasises the extent to which residual control is vested in particular agents as the important feature of institutional arrangements.

Hurwicz's approach in his paper is similar to that of Schotter's standards of behaviour, that of the von Neumann-Morgenstern concept of solution in a co-operative game. There is an important difference. While Schotter's definition of a social institution regards it as a regularity in social behaviour, Hurwicz's definition regards such behaviour as a feature of a solution determined in part by individual characteristics and in part by the outcome functions which embody institutional arrangements.

Hurwicz emphasises that his concept does not exclude or minimise the importance of the endogenous evolution of institutions. The apparent contradiction between his approach and that of the more traditional one may be resolved if we think of the prevailing outcome function, embodying an enforcement system and various social conventions, as the result of a 'higher order' game with a higher order outcome function. Thus, as Ruttan has suggested, it is possible to explain the institutional evolution induced by technological innovation.

Professor Otsuki commented on Hurwicz's paper from three points of view. His first point was concerned with the cost-benefit analysis of mechanisms, which, however, was pointed out by Professor Hurwicz as being appropriately handled within his framework. Otsuki's second point was related to that of distributive justice and ownership. He argued that distributive justice might be a criterion much more important than Pareto efficiency, and also that the problem of ownership has to have a direct relevance to implement pre-assigned social goals, both of which have been pointed out by Professor Hurwicz as being within the framework of his approach.

Otsuki's third point was concerned with the game-theoretic approach for institutional evolution as outlined by Professor Hurwicz. Otsuki extended Hurwicz's suggestion to sketch an interesting formulation of the process of institutional evolution in terms of an extended form game.

While Hurwicz's paper was primarily concerned with formal and logical aspects of the theory of institutions, Professor Pajestka's paper addresses itself to the process of institutional evolution, societal, political and cultural, in a socialist country. He first points out that the problems of institutional evolution, property right economics and constitutional choice, are all familiar and basic concepts in the standard Marxian economics. The focus of the basic analysis presented in his paper is that of institutionalised socialism, based upon theoretical analysis of the scheme of institutional changes which take place in actual socialist countries. The actual changes in institutional set-up in Eastern Europe may be summarised as:

1. The abandonment of market institutions.
2. A planning apparatus from the top to the bottom.
3. Long-, medium- and short-term national planning.
4. Making the firm an element in the hierarchical management structure.
5. Strict control of prices and income distribution.
6. Freedom of consumer choice.
7. Limitation on the scope of the labour market.

Closing Remarks on Part III

Ken'ichi Imai
HITOTSUBASHI UNIVERSITY, TOKYO

Session III discussed Technological Change and Institutions: Development of Information Technologies. Two papers were presented.

The joint paper by Professors Aoki and Rosenberg entitled 'The Japanese Firm as an Innovative Institution', made an excellent analysis of economic institutions promoting technological innovation, putting special emphasis on the Japanese firm. The major messages of their paper may be summarised as follows:

First, in order to develop an improved understanding of the impressive performance of Japanese manufacturing innovation, it is necessary to modify drastically a widespread concept concerning the sources of new technology. Valuable new technological knowledge, comes from many sources. The useful linear model, i.e., from basic research to applied research, and further to development, production and marketing, should be criticised. Instead, a 'chain-linked model', to use their term, should be employed.

Secondly, in the chain-linked model, new technological knowledge is the outcome of an iterative and feedback process between upstream activities of the firm. Scientific research capability exists alongside a number of sources of technological improvement, including existing knowledge.

Thirdly, the Japanese firm has made highly effective use of short feedback loops, such as from marketing to production to redesign, from product design to analytic design, leading to new products and innovation. On the other hand, the Japanese firm has been comparatively weaker in utilising the long market feedback loop for the perception and implementation of radically new products.

Fourthly, one of the interesting organisational innovations emerging in Japanese private industry is the growth of research co-operative and projects organised by multiple independent firms from different industries. It is still too early to evaluate this. However, it clearly relates to the problem of institutional forms that are conducive to effective interaction among different scientific disciplines and different fields of technology.

There was much discussion centring on the long-run viability of the Japanese system. The institution which is well suited to a process of

225

technological catching-up will be different from the institution propelling innovation as a technological leader. An optimal combination between organisational arrangement, incentive structures, and learning procedures should be sought.

There was no definite conclusion to the discussions. However, it became clear that an understanding of the process through which institutions and technological learning interact is crucial for the comparative institutional analysis.

In the next paper by Professor Uekusa, the impact of information technology on Japanese industrial system was discussed.

There are two major issues. The first is how information technologies change the boundaries of firms and industries, as well as inter-organisational relationships, and how they create new institutional forms of corporate network. The second concerns the policy issues associated with such a tendency; How is it possible to cope with a deregulation process, a new price structure and the standardisation of network architecture.

The crucially important factor which became clear from the discussion, is the interdependence of different networks. How might an international standard be set up for such a purpose? Surely this may be the most important problem for international competition policy in the coming age. Because if the network architecture of the leading firm, IBM, became the *de facto* standard of the world, clearly a serious monopoly problem will arise in related industries. On the other hand, however, if some governments or governmental agencies such as ISO strongly force such a standard, flexibility required for our dynamic society will be lost. Therefore, a more flexible policy approach, or a new kind of adaptable institution, is needed. Not strict standardisation but possibilities of interconnects or inter-operations between different networks should be sought, including a development of new technological interfaces. If and I quote from the opening address by Professor Tsuru) 'What is required of us is to accommodate the modern technological progress into our evolvirs institutional setting', then I believe this problem is a new frontier for the study of institutions in a new dynamic society.

Closing Remarks on Part IV

Edmond Malinvaud
ECOLE PRATIQUE DES HAUTES ETUDES, PARIS

I shall concentrate my comments on the essential distinction between institutional economics and the economics of institutions, to which Professor Tsuru quite suitably drew our attention at the beginning of his stimulating keynote address. The distinction is essential, but should not be seen as an opposition. On the contrary I should like to see institutional economics and the economics of institutions complementing each other.

One may first observe that there are cases which may be difficult to classify as belonging to one rather than the other. I am thinking, for instance, of the work of Robert Triffin on the international monetary system, both in the years following the Second World War when he played the central role in setting up the European Payments Union and in the 1960s when he announced the collapse of the Bretton Woods system.

But I want mainly to argue that both approaches would greatly benefit from mutual cross-fertilisation. In order to suggest to you that the point is concerning me deeply, I may be permitted to report briefly on what happened to me last spring in Paris, at a conference where institutional economists had asked me come to play the role of the nasty opponent, before an audience of some 200 faithful people. Professor Michael Piore, the American institutional labour economist, was sitting beside me on the platform. While speaking, he said something rather like the following: 'I do not understand how Professor Malinvaud, who is well known as a neoclassical economist, can tolerate that so much work on institutional economics is being done in the institute he is heading'. My tolerance would have perhaps appeared less puzzling to him if he had realised that a good deal of work in econometrics and mathematical economics is also being done in my institute.

I must recognise that more generally there is often complete misunderstanding between what we may call, for short, institutional economics on one side and, on the other, mainstream economic theory, which has recently turned its attention to the economics of institutions. The misunderstanding is not new, as we were reminded by Professor Hurwicz with the quotation in the first paragraph of his paper. Indeed, it may be permanently regenerated by the fact that there are indeed irrelevant, or even misleading, contributions coming from both sides.

My point is that there is also good relevant work coming from both sides. The most dogmatic economists refuse to see it. For instance, some neoclassical economists refuse to see that a lot of work by institutionalists makes the hypothesis of full and permanent market clearing untenable for the analysis of a number of cases, for instance, for any analysis in which the change that occurred in the Western European labour market plays a significant role. Similarly some institutionalists postulating the instability of our economic system refuse to see that mainstream economics has studied various aspects of this hypothesis, both theoretically and econometrically: the results often are ambiguous, but significant nevertheless.

There is a long tradition in institutional economics for looking directly at the main questions that socioeconomic evolution raises. This tradition is very much alive in France now among economists, often of Marxist origin, who coined the expression 'école de la régulation', that I may translate as 'the regulation school'.[1] Listening to Professor Tsuru I found the same familiar flavour as in the writings of this school. When I am confronted with the research programme announced by this school, I agree that it concerns real and important issues of which I would be particularly pleased to know the objective laws. But I have no hope that these objective laws will be found before long. Indeed, when I read the writings of the regulation school, I realise that they hardly ever prove anything about these big issues. A too ambitious objective would make them sterile if there was not some interesting, although modest, by-products of this research effort.

Actually, institutional economics is at its best when it deals with questions that are neither too narrow nor too broad. If the subject is too narrow, then one is bound to limit oneself to the description of the details of a particular case that permits no generalisation. But if the subject is too broad, one is bound to specify conjectures that cannot be tested and that have very little chance to be as true as specified. But there is a medium range in which it is possible to go beyond detailed description and to obtain useful and suggestive synthesis, or even limited, but valid, generalisations that are close to deserving the name of objective laws.

There is a much better scope for this medium range now than was the case 50 years ago, and this for two reasons. On the one hand, the tremendous progress of statistical information gives a rich factual basis which still remains underutilised. This basis permits a serious scrutiny of the hypotheses that intuition or the non-systematic awareness of the facts may suggest. On the other hand, the recent trend of economic theory has brought it closer to many aspects of the realities that institutional economics studies. The economics of institutions is only one among several fields that are now the object of serious theoretical scrutiny and deviate from the traditional mainstream theory equilibrium and growth (theories of contracts, of industrial structures, of organisations, and the like). These new theoretical developments sharpen our conceptual approach to institutional economics; they even occasionally provide us with prototype models that permit approximate tests of some of the hypotheses that institutional economics discovers.

My own conclusion at the end of this stimulating round table conference is that it indeed shows that good prospects exist for the cross-fertilisation between mainstream economic theory and that part of institutional economics that deals with specific issues such as the development of transnational corporations, the innovative capabilities of various economies or the recent privatisation and deregulation movement. As for the bigger issues of global socioeconomic development, I have already called your attention during the discussion of Professor Lombardini's paper to the empirical analysis of economic growth, à la Kuznets, which makes a bridge between economic theory and institutional economics. Hence, misunderstanding, where it exists, is not founded.

Note

1. For a brief presentation of the approach followed by the regulation school, see, for instance, Boyer (1986).

Reference

Boyer, R. (1986) *La théorie de la régulation: une analyse critique* (Paris: Editions La Découverte).

The Problem of Dynamics of Modern Society

Tigran Khachaturov
ACADEMY OF SCIENCES OF THE USSR, MOSCOW

Among the big changes which have taken place in the economic and social structure of modern society in the twentieth century is the emergence of a new socialist system of economy which never existed before. At present it embraces 26 per cent of the world territory and 32 per cent of world population, produces 40 per cent of world industrial output, and accounts for one-third of world national income. The transition to the socialist system took place as a result of the October 1917 revolution in Russia and later as a result of revolutions in other countries after the Second World War.

Another change is that the post-war period witnessed the collapse of the world colonial system. Former colonies became sovereign states which account for 37 per cent of the territory of the world and 29 per cent of world population.

Substantial changes also occurred after the war in the economic level of developed countries – the emergence of the USA and USSR as superpowers, the rapid growth of production in Japan which moved into third place in the world in its economic development, and high growth rates in the Federal Republic of Germany. There was also considerable growth in some developing countries such as Brazil, Venezuela, South Korea and some others.

To these changes we should add global problems affecting the world as a whole: the demographic explosion, mainly in developing countries, the acceleration of scientific and technological progress, the problem of the pollution of natural resources and the environment, the growth of militarism and the mounting threat of thermonuclear war, with its possible catastrophic consequences for mankind. (This is mentioned in Professor Pajestka's paper as the institutional change for the future.)

All these shifts, big in themselves, led to important changes in the organisational and socioeconomic structure of modern society with its high dynamism.

Among the radical changes in the sphere of the economy are the shifts taking place in the framework of the socialist economic system. The basis for them was the establishment of socialist ownership giving rise to centralised economic management and planning. It is necessary to acknowledge that centralised planning demonstrated a number of advantages, making it possible to direct funds quickly in the desired direction to change the structure of production. This was of great importance to the USSR in helping to carry out the industrialisation of the country at a fast rate and in converting the economy to military production at the time of the fascist attack on the Soviet Union. During the Second World War some kind of planning was introduced even in capitalist countries. But with the passage of time many shortcomings appeared in the socialist economies, which became more and more negative when centralised planning was used, in particular as a means of solving by administrative methods many concrete questions of operational management, and when command methods of guidance were applied on a broad scale.

The defects of the system are connected with the attempts to fix from the top the entire multitude of the produced output, the universal drive for plan fulfilment at any price in terms of quantity, even to the detriment of quality, the inadequate incentives for improving the organisation and technical standards of production, the broad spread of bureaucratic practices, the fettering of initiative and autonomy, etc. The result of these was the decline of growth rates in the USSR.

Recently, on Mr Gorbachev's initiative, an important system of measures began to be implemented in the USSR with the aim of accelerating the development and restructuring of production and the entire socioeconomic sphere, and removing the existing deficiencies. Three principles, self-repaying, self-financing and self-management or self-planning, are the necessary substance for full self-support.

The administrative system of management shows that the main tendency of enterprises is to receive from the state and to give as little as possible. This tendency is the basis of the deficit, the obstacle to technological progress, and is in favour of the accumulation of stocks as much as possible in the fear of deficit and regardless of prices. In recent years it has become quite evident that to overcome these shortcomings with old methods is impossible. It is, however, possible to manage the enterprises with economic means, using economic norms, financial and credit sources, prices, state orders and other levers.

The main road leading to improvement is to ensure the initiative and autonomy of enterprises, to end interference from the top in their operational activity, to confine centralised planning to setting only general directions of development and effective shifts in the structure of the economy, to stimulate the growth of labour productivity through considerable intensification of social measures for good work, and improvement of the living standards of the people. Closely related to these new departures is the consolidation of democratic principles, the development of openness and other measures aimed at ensuring still deeper involvement of every collective, every enterprise in improving the management of production and in raising the well-being of society as a whole.

Increasing orientation on economic factors of development, coupled with the restriction of planned guidance to general directions, rates and proportions, is in evidence in other socialist countries. In China the reliance on commodity-money relations has led to considerable growth of production in recent years. Thus industrial output went up by 6.5 per cent in 1986 compared with the previous year and agricultural production was 14 per cent higher in 1985 than the year before. The economic mechanism based on the autonomy of enterprises plays a substantial role in Hungary. Lately, new ways of intensifying the operation of economic and democratic methods of development have been launched in Bulgaria. Economic methods of running the economy are applied in Poland and Czechoslovakia. In the German Democratic Republic the line is pursued for the maximum utilisation of material resources and recycling of primary and other materials.

In his paper on socialist experience and new horizons, Professor Pajestka showed the recent changes in the methods of economic management.

Many economic measures implemented in socialist countries are co-ordinated organisationally by the Council for Mutual Economic Assistance (CMEA). The identity of the political interests of socialist countries has one of its expressions in their defence policy co-ordinated by the Warsaw Treaty Organisation in the collectively elaborated principles of their general strategy.

A very important factor of the world economic growth in the whole of modern human society is technological progress. There was rapid development of technology after the Second World War, and in recent decades when the achievements of science were used more and more in the production sphere.

These achievements were very important for the rapid rise of the economy in the 1950s and 1960s. During the world depression at the end of the 1970s and beginning of the 1980s, technological progress did not stop. Atomic energy had a higher share in the total amount of energy production, in spite of some people's opposition. Every year there was growth in such new technology as electronics, microprocessors, automation, telecommunication and video technology. There was a very high rate of computerisation. In the USA in 1985 there were over 20 million personal computers. The number of computers in Japan, Western Germany and France is also rising.

With the extension of electronics, automation is growing in developed countries. In Japan there are now about 70 thousand robots in use – about five times more than in 1980, and very substantially greater than in the USA, FRG or the USSR where their use is also growing rapidly.

There are also such innovations as the introduction of new types of material – high-strength ceramics, composite materials, the use of metal powders, achievements of biotechnology etc.

Some of the newest kinds of technique are produced by multinational corporations, even in developing countries like South Korea, Hong Kong and Singapore, using their cheap labour. Through transnational corporations, the monopoly capital of a given country, the USA or Japan for example, operates on the markets of other countries, both developed and developing, building up its domination on these markets and its own might simultaneously. Professor Wheelwright and Mr Crough in their paper showed how the growing Japanese transnational corporations operate in the changing Pacific Rim economy. Another form of monopoly – multinational corporations – makes it possible to join the capital of different countries and thereby augment the possibilities for gaining control over the economy of the countries that are the target of their expansion. Monopoly associations, national and international, represent the biggest enterprises with an intricate system of management. Monopolisation does not eliminate competition, which is intensifying in many respects. At the same time, the process of monopolisation continues to advance.

In some European countries, enterprises and even whole industries become the property of the state through purchase or by state investments. The role of the capitalist state in the development of the contemporary economy is discussed in Professor Lombardini's paper on markets and institutions.

New forms of international organisation are appearing in capitalist countries. The process of monopolisation is continuing. The measures taken in some countries, the USA in particular, to limit this process have not changed the general trend. The monopolies have begun to sprawl beyond national boundaries and assume international proportions. This process has particularly intensified in the last few decades with the general economic and strategic tasks of the state. And railways themselves, with their centralised control and well-ordered operation by graphs and timetables, were more than other branches prepared for the transfer to state ownership.

In France and the UK the state began to buy other enterprises, such as power and fuel, and the motor industry, especially when governments of the left were in office. In time these state-controlled enterprises were pronounced to be inefficient and working at a loss. Yet it seems that in the case of state-controlled enterprises it is possible to achieve high efficiency, flexibility and manoeuvrability in their development and the accomplishment of the tasks set before them. For this it is necessary to get rid of the frequent instances of formalism and bureaucratic practices and to give more room for enterprise and initiative.

In recent years in Britain and France the tendency towards privatisation appeared with the coming of conservative governments. The usual motive is their unprofitable operation and the hope that they will become more efficient after transfer to private owners. Professor Kay analyses the different motives for privatisation, and among them are much formalism and bureaucracy in state enterprises and lack of initiative and entrepreneurship. This refers to various enterprises – the motor industry, television etc.

Recently the tendency to establish small enterprises in new science-intensive branches of industry has appeared in some countries, among them the USA. The emergence of such enterprises, known as venture, risk-running, is connected with the achievements of modern scientific and technological progress, advances in the field of electronics, information science, automation, development of new materials, bioengineering, and so on. In a number of cases such enterprises form the basis for establishing modern forms of dynamic progress in the economy.

It is interesting that, as many experts admit, some big corporations are losing, or have already lost, interest in innovations. Big firms are not always initiators of technical shifts in production, and if this happens, it is only at a time when they can operate as small enterprises with regard to new types of product.

It is necessary to mention an important socioeconomic problem in connection with the development of technological progress. In several developed countries there exists a fear of technological progress from the point of view of possible unemployment increase. But is it really an irresistible danger? We heard Professor Uekusa's very interesting report about the success of information technology in Japan, and we know that in this country unemployment is less than in many other developed countries. I have no time to analyse this case, but this example shows that it is possible to avoid a rise in unemployment in the case of automation and other achievements of technological progress.

In some developed capitalist countries, Japan and France for instance, some forms of centralised planning were used, but in a particularly mild form. In Japan, use was made of so-called indicative plans which do not contain directive assignments but indicate advisable volumes of economic growth in a given period for the economy as a whole and for individual branches, which give some general orientation of desirable development. Five-year plans for socioeconomic development were drawn up in France.

In contemporary capitalist society there is a tendency towards integration in the form of international economic organisations, like the EEC and similar institutions in other continents. They are all designed to introduce elements of order in relations between countries. Of course, it is still a long way to the establishment of international organisations with functions similar to government functions. Sovereign rights of states are not infringed in any of these organisations.

Environmental protection is an example of the pressing problems on which agreements are concluded. It is acquiring increasing international importance. With the growth of production and technological advance some types of natural resources (oil, wood, fresh water) are being depleted and environmental pollution grows. This pollution has become trans-boundary. In Europe, the Scandinavian countries, and first and foremost Norway, suffer from the atmospheric pollution from the industrial exhausts of the UK and West Germany. In the south of the FRG the Schwarzwald is going to ruin from acid rain and other pollutants. There are many more similar examples. Questions of nature conservation are important, not only internationally, but also for the economy of each developed country. This is a major task facing the new dynamic society.

In this new society, shifts are taking place in the structure of the working masses. Technological progress requires skilled personnel. So a characteristic feature of the modern world is the spread of education in developed and some developing countries. In the developed countries the composition of the working class is changing, for ever-higher demands are presented to workers' skills and their ability to operate up-to-date sophisticated machines and instruments, while the demand for unskilled labour is declining steadily.

Among other features of the modern dynamic world, mention should be made of international debt and militarism. The debts owed by countries, especially developing nations, are very big. Latin American countries owe about 400 billion dollars to the World Bank and governments, chiefly the USA. A considerable part of this vast sum was, evidently, invested in the national economy of the debtor countries – Brazil (ranking eighth in the world in the level of industrial development), Argentina, Mexico, Venezuela. But still more was spent on administration and military needs. The debts of African countries run at 200 billion dollars. Asian countries are also deeply in debt. This high indebtedness impedes the economic development of the respective countries. Suffice it to say only that interest payments constitute a rather significant part of foreign trade deficits of debtor countries which find themselves in a rather difficult economic position in consequence.

As for military expenditures, their burden is very heavy. At present, world military expenditures, chiefly those of the superpowers, amount to more than one trillion dollars a year, or about three billion a day. This extremely large burden cannot but tell on the level of economic development of various countries, has negative influence on many countries, depressing the rates of growth. Hence the struggle of all mankind for peace, for the prevention of a new universal war threatening the survival of mankind. But this is the theme of a special discussion lying outside the framework of the present conference.

The Conference in Perspective

Michael Kaser
ST ANTONY'S COLLEGE, OXFORD

From prehistoric times until a couple of centuries ago the institutions, conventions and arrangements that governed economic activity were static over long periods. The overwhelming prevalence of subsistence farming and crafts, the weak diffusion of information and slow technical progress (occasionally negative) promoted neither productive growth nor institutional adjustment to it. Social and political change was by contrast relatively rapid, whether one looks through Marx's perspective of the supersession of one form of productive relations by another, or considers the spread of world religions – Buddhism, Christianity and Islam – or of empires – the Persian, Roman, Mongol, Iberian or British.

In what we term the Industrial Revolution institutional and productive dynamism went hand in hand, accompanying monetisation, the creation of a world-wide network of communications and rapid technical progress. So powerful was the invisible hand characterised by Adam Smith in analysing market capitalism that substantial state intervention was brought largely by war and revolution. A century ago the Russian thinker Alexander Herzen could claim that the economic power of the state would be 'Ghengis Khan with railways and telegraphs'.

The papers invited for this conference cumulate on an already extensive literature (as their numerous references testify) in pointing to a further and far-reaching institutional revolution. As our conference title implies, 'Economic Institutions in a Dynamic Society: Search for a New Frontier', we tried to assess its effect on society and on the dynamics of the world economy.

Tsuru in his keynote speech found the constraint on markets, profits and wages, the growth of transnational corporations and the extension of the welfare state, so pervasive as to justify classification of the 'mixed economy' as a new Marxian mode of production. Professor Wheelwright and Mr Crough had 'little doubt that the world economy has been undergoing a fundamental process of structural change in recent decades' and were pessimistic in warning of 'some of the most far-reaching, and potentially destabilising, forces seen this century' (p. 61). The interlinked expansion of communications and information has, to abbreviate their argument, enabled transnational corporations 'to undertake activities on a scale unprecedented in modern history' (p. 62) and to embrace those 'that were once thought to be the domain only of governments'. The IEA has just run a Round Table on international policy co-ordination under the title 'Global Macroeconomics: Policy Conflict and Co-operation' and those proceedings complement these. In addition to two empirical case studies – of co-operation in the European Monetary System, and of conflicting interests in the North-South interface on debts and on supply shocks – that Round Table heard evidence that, while governmental policy co-ordination could yield net gains, risk-averse policy-makers may have little incentive to co-operate.

That conclusion reinforces Wheelwright and Crough in perceiving a 'new corporate world economic order ... less susceptible to tradi-tional market forces and to control by national governments' (p. 64). They thence identified a broad range of domestic relationships keenly sensitive to transnational corporate decisions – from balances of payments and domestic concentration to industrial relations and political sovereignty.

Tsuchiya was distinctly more optimistic in pointing out that corporations can be made subject to governmental authority and that they could be liquidated, whereas nations could not. There may indeed be a general governmental consensus on deregulation, but that in turn stimulated small and medium companies to compete with the large corporations. Deregulation and privatisation were the themes of Kay's analysis of the economic role of the state in the UK since the Second World War, and there were parallels to be found in Pajestka's reflections on the same issue for the same period in Eastern Europe. The similarity of post-war socialist intentions is by no means strained if one recalls a comment of 1947 by the Soviet economist, Eugene Varga, Head of the Institute of World Economy, who saw the UK of the day being run by 'a sort of Gosplan'. The British 'Gosplan' chief, Morrison, as Kay describes, saw the managers of a nationalised corporation as 'the high custodians of the public interest' (p. 196). He goes on to show how that expectation was eroded as it became apparent that the Morrisonian framework of the autonomous public corporation, with a distinguished board of arbiters of the public good, was not an effective model with which to conduct industrial activities (pp. 197–8).

The efficacy of the anti-trust laws in the USA was questioned by Lombardini, and Pajestka states that the development process 'cannot be achieved by bureaucratic methods previously applied widely by socialist planning' (p. 177). In commenting, Iwata noted Pajestka's book of 1986 where he warns against 'the bureaucratic *homo oeconomicus*'. Both Pajestka and Iwata saw the failure of the state under central planning to fulfil expectations raised in a welfare state as a factor in the present wave of decentralisation in the planned economies.

There was an even more devolved paradigm posed by Ikegami in the voluntary co-operation of citizens 'for common public purposes' (p. 207) in 'networking or co-operatives supported by professionals independent of a bureaucratic state' (pp. 208–9). Fujii, commenting on Kay's paper, was also concerned lest privatisation be postulated solely on grounds of efficiency when it should be judged 'on the perception of fairness or equity' (p. 210).

It was nevertheless the criterion of efficiency which dominated our discussion on the institution of the corporate enterprise. Pajestka made the autonomy of the state enterprise the touchstone of socialist economic reform, as Khachaturov has just done in terms of the present Soviet 'restructuring'. For the capitalist firm Dosi saw 'three basic functions ... procedures ... for coordination ... incentive ... [and] specific problem-solving capabilities' (p. 155). In the Japanese case the combination of these attributes within single firms led to 'an impressive technological and competitive success' (p. 157), whereas progress on each count was often effected in the United States 'by means of selection amongst a relatively high number of firms' (p. 158). That contention was a comment on Aoki and Rosenberg who drew a parallel contrast between Japan and the United States in institutions fostering innovation. The 'linear model', tracing innovation from basic research to application, development, production and marketing, might seem to endow 'America's generally acknowledged leadership in frontier science' (p. 138) with commercial advantage. But a 'chain-linked model' which characterised the Japanese firm drew on iterative technological improvement at all stages of the innovative process.

Whether certain institutions promote innovation remained in debate, but there was no doubt of reverse causality in Uekusa's paper: innovation brings institutional change. He took as cases of 'inter-industry convergence' the two sectors generating and distributing respectively information and financial services. So powerful has been the drive in the case of the information sector in Japan during the quarter century from 1955 that it had virtually exchanged places with agriculture in terms of work force shares. From occupying over 40 per cent in 1955, agriculture had dropped to little more than 10 per cent in 1980, while the reverse quantitative trend was shown for the information sector; manufacturing and other services than information exhibited comparatively stable shares (p. 168). Kagono accepted, in comments on this paper, that inter-industry convergence was fostered by deregulation but postulated that 'the important policy question is to find out the rules of the game of changing the rules of competition' (p. 185).

On this, fundamental issues were defined by Hurwicz in comparing 'various mechanisms with respect to the degree of informational decentralisation, the required amount of communication between agents ... and the complexity of calculations required of agents' (p. 89). The outcome functions which emerge from such a mechanism must be within an admissible set, but each set may have been determined at some higher level. As he put it, 'while the highest order game may be the battle over the basic system (the constitution, or, say, capitalism versus socialism), the lowest one may be just the process of bargaining over the particular wage' (p. 100).

Schotter, too, stated 'an intimate link between our economic and political system, is that while the market may be viewed as an allocative process which *provides* goods to people, it is also a device which *denies* people things, and this denial must be justified' (pp. 54). This was as a comment on Lombardini who examined the conditions under which the market culture could be consistent with a 'workable state (pp. 43). And it was Otsuki who included among his comments on Hurwicz a phrase that would stir many an institutional economist, 'Much more important [than Pareto efficiency] is distributive justice' (p. 106).

Index